Learn Perl®

Sunrise Midday Sunset

In a Weekend

Sunset Evening Sunrise

THOMAS NOWERS

Premier

Press

This book is dedicated to Small, whose timely lap-naps kept me hunched over the keyboard for hours after I was ready to give in. Without her intervention, I might have never finished this book.

ACKNOWLEDGMENTS

I owe thanks to many people for their work on this book—especially the team at Premier Press, including Amy Pettinella, Todd Jensen, Michelle Jones, and Cathleen Snyder. The text belongs to them as much as it belongs to me. I also want to express my gratitude to Brad Jones and Kieron Murphy for this opportunity, their helpful suggestions, and their support.

I would like to thank my family for their love over the years, and my work colleagues for having faith in my ability and aptitude. My friends deserve thanks as well; I've learned many lessons from them that are more valuable than I could ever hope to repay.

I especially want to thank my lovely wife, Susan, for her perseverance, patience, and editing prowess, and for making me the happiest man on the planet.

ABOUT THE AUTHOR

Thomas Nowers is a software engineer and freelance writer. He is a columnist for the INT Media group, and his articles have appeared on many sites, including Gamelan, Earthweb, and Developer.com. This is his first book. Thomas has worked for a number of software and technical companies in various capacities, including Northwest Link, Homegrocer, Webvan, and most recently Widevine Technologies.

Thomas lives in Washington with his lovely wife, Susan, and their four cats: Sidney, Jasmine, Hailey, and Small.

CONTENTS AT A GLANCE

CONTENTS

INTRODUCTION

Welcome to *Learn Perl In a Weekend*. Perl is one of the most widespread and popular programming languages. It has been called "The Duct Tape of the Internet," and chances are, if you have ever browsed the Web, you have used Perl.

The goal of this book is to teach you the basics of the Perl programming language. By Sunday evening, you will be able to write complete Perl programs and modules. You will also understand basic programming concepts and constructs, such as variables, loops, subroutines, and arrays.

At the same time, you will learn about the Perl programming community at large. I will also introduce advanced programming techniques and advanced Perl, and I will list resources for the advanced topics that are beyond the scope of this book so that you can take your skills to the next level.

Who Should Read This Book?

This book starts from the very beginning; I assume that you have never done any programming. That doesn't mean that this book is remedial; programming and Perl are both complex subjects. It simply means that the book explains each and every lesson in detail (sometimes painstakingly).

The tutorials assume that you have some computer experience and know your way around the Windows operating system. You should be comfortable with files and folders, using a browser, such as Internet Explorer (which I use for all examples where a browser is present), and maneuvering around your computer's file system. If you are uncomfortable on a Windows system,

I suggest that you pick up a copy of *Learn Windows XP In a Weekend* or *Windows XP Fast and Easy,* published by Premier Press.

Perl was actually born in UNIX, but most nonprogrammers today haven't had any experience with UNIX systems, so I chose to write this book with a Windows frame of mind. All of the code samples were written and tested on the Windows XP operating system. If you are a UNIX guru and you want to learn Perl on a UNIX-based system, much of this book still will be applicable, although you will want to pay particular attention to the Sunday Evening session, "Learning Advanced Perl Techniques," for an advanced section on Windows and UNIX compatibility.

What You Need to Begin

When you embark on *Learn Perl In a Weekend,* I assume that you have the following necessary components.

➤ **A computer.** Just about any computer will work; however, the examples and figures in this book are from the Windows XP operating system. I wrote the book with the assumption that you are running some version of the Windows platform.

➤ **Internet access.** All of the code snippets and examples are available for download at Premier Press's Web site. You will need to download and install a copy of ActivePerl 5.6.1 to take full advantage of the lessons in this book.

➤ **Text editor.** All of the examples in this book assume that you are writing scripts using Notepad, the default text editor that comes with Windows operating systems.

How This Book Is Organized

This book is written so that it can be finished in a weekend. The seven sections that make up the weekend are as follows:

➤ **Friday Evening, "Introducing Perl."** This session introduces Perl and walks you through installing ActivePerl on your home machine. It briefly covers maneuvering through DOS to run sample Perl programs. You will then create an HTML page from scratch that uses a simple Perl script to display text.

➤ **Saturday Morning, "Variables and Other Fun Stuff."** This session introduces basic building blocks, including variables, scalars, data types, names, strings, unary and binary, internal data types, and environment variables. You will then be shown how to organize these blocks by putting them together in lists, arrays, and hashes.

➤ **Saturday Afternoon, "Using Files and Perl Operations."** This session teaches you to manipulate files and directories using directory operations and file handlers. The session also covers basic and common Perl operators.

➤ **Saturday Evening, "Expressing and Stating."** This session explains the concepts surrounding statements and expressions, including if and unless program blocks and loops. The session also explores the ideas behind structured programming and provides extensive coverage of subroutines.

➤ **Sunday Morning, "Objects and Object-Oriented Programming."** This session covers object-oriented programming and how classes, objects, and inheritance are used in Perl.

➤ **Sunday Afternoon, "Putting It All Together."** This session links each earlier lesson and puts together concepts in the form of a completed Perl game program.

➤ **Sunday Evening, "Learning Advanced Perl Techniques."** The final session briefly covers several advanced Perl topics, including modules and packages, debugging programs, security, XML integration, and using Perl with CGI.

Special Features of This Book

This book has a few print conventions to make it easier to read.

NOTE Notes provide additional information that is usually interesting or helpful, but not necessarily required to complete a given lesson or tutorial.

CAUTION

◆ ◆
Cautions include information about common errors and problems you might face.
◆ ◆

When an important new term or new vocabulary word is introduced, the word is presented in *italics*. All of these italicized terms are also defined in the glossary for your convenience.

Finally, code samples and commands are presented in a monospaced font to make them stand out.

```
This is an example of one line of code.
```

This is an example of a `code command` in a sentence.

```
This is
an example
of several
lines
of code.
```

About the Companion Web Site

All the source code is available for download on Premier Press's Web site. Details about the Web site and where to find the code samples can be found in Appendix A, "Using the Companion Web Site."

Introducing Perl

- ➤ What is Perl?
- ➤ A brief look at programming
- ➤ Installing ActivePerl on your machine
- ➤ Running Perl with DOS
- ➤ Writing a Perl program with HTML
- ➤ Block One: Program Planning

Thank goodness it's Friday! Tonight you will take your first step into the world of Perl, and this versatile and popular language will be explained in depth. You will write and run your first Perl program, and you will also delve into the basics of DOS (*Disk Operating System*) and HTML (*Hypertext Markup Language*).

If you're familiar with DOS and HTML, and you have already successfully installed Perl onto your workstation, you might want to skip ahead to the later sections. Keep reading, however, to get a feeling for the basics of Perl and Perl programming.

What Is Perl?

Perl (*Practical Extraction and Report Language*) is used most often to create interactive Web pages. If you have used an interactive form or a Web page guest book, or if you have read a bulletin board online, then most likely you have used Perl. Perl was built originally as a simple language to scan text files, extract information from those files, and print reports based on that information (thus the terms *Practical*, *Extract*, and *Report* in the name).

Perl is a full programming language (as are Java and C++). Perl is often grouped with languages like C++ because it is object oriented (which I cover in the Sunday Morning session) and expandable using common supplemental libraries. Because Perl is also easy to learn and commonly found on the Web, you may see it associated with languages, such as JavaScript and HTML.

So what makes Perl the widespread and popular language that it is today? The main reason is probably the *P* (Practical) in its name. Perl was designed to be easy to use. Rather than making the language elegant, minimal, multi-platform, or robust, prime Perl architects decided to make it *expansive,* which means that it provides many different ways to solve problems or write programs. For example, in this chapter you will write two introductory scripts using Perl. The first script is designed to run as part of a Web page. The second script is written in Notepad and runs on Microsoft DOS. This kind of versatility and the ability to use different methods is one of the major selling points of the Perl language and platform.

Because of its versatility, Perl appeals to programmers who want to do something quickly, easily, and in their own way. Perl is commonly used to integrate different Internet-based technologies and manipulate databases that contain large numbers of text entries. Perl programmers have been known to boast (jokingly) that all programs can be converted into one line of Perl.

Because it was designed to work with text, Perl is an optimal language when combined with HTML, the basic building block of Web pages. Perl is often used as a gateway between HTML-based Web pages and Web server databases. It is also an excellent tool for building computer system management tools. Perl did not originate as a Web-based language, however; it grew into that role as it evolved from a simple tool into a full-grown programming language. Perl was one of the first computer languages distributed freely on the Internet, and because of this distribution, many different people have made contributions to turn Perl into the complex and wide-ranging language it is today.

Although it is optimal for scanning text, Perl also deals well with other types of data. Perl has a language syntax that is similar to the programming language C, which makes it easy for programmers who have studied C or similar structured languages to learn to use Perl quickly. C programmers often use Perl to build Web applications because it is easier to program than C. Some Perl proponents also claim that Perl is a more secure language than C.

Perl operates on a number of platforms and is Windows, UNIX, and Macintosh friendly. This platform independence has made Perl a popular scripting language; you can find Perl running on almost any server or platform on the planet.

Perl is probably most often used by Web system administrators who use it to develop forms and other interactive Web tools. However, Perl has gone beyond the Web, and there is an extremely large Perl community both online and offline. System administrators, programmers, students, computer hobbyists, teachers, and professors all use Perl. Soon, you will be a Perl programmer too.

Finally, Perl is free. It can be downloaded and used by anyone who has an Internet connection. It is also open source software, which means that anyone can download Perl in its basic form to see how it is put together.

To summarize, Perl is easy to use, works well with text, is widely supported, and runs on just about any platform.

Different Types of Perl

Perl comes in many shapes and sizes. It is designed to work on every platform from Solaris to Windows to Novell. Each platform generally has several different types of Perl. For example, LMOLNAR, Dosperl, and Dosperlp are all different versions of Perl that run on DOS. These different versions of Perl are called *distributions*, which have subtle but significant differences between them. The Perl distribution you will learn to use in this book is ActivePerl 5.6.1.

ActivePerl is possibly the most prevalent of all the Windows distributions of Perl, which is why I chose to use it for this book. Because anyone can create his or her own version of Perl, a number of other options are available. If you would like to use a different version of Perl, I have outlined a few resources (particularly www.cpan.org) in the Sunday Evening session, "Learning Advanced Perl Techniques," where you can go and download different Perl distributions.

A Whirlwind History of Perl

Perl was created in 1987 by Larry Wall, who was working for the National Security Agency on a project called *Blacker*. Perl was an attempt to take computer programming and mix it with common sense. Optimizing a programming language for common sense meant taking common applications for the language and making them easy and quick to implement. Even today, after Perl has been collaborated on, reworked, and redefined by the online community, there are still dozens of shortcuts and multiple ways of doing common programming tasks in different ways, and you will see many of these shortcuts in action in the chapters to follow.

Perl took concepts from several popular languages of the time, including C, UNIX Shell, SED, and AWK. Perl was used internally for almost a full year before Larry released it as open source software to the comp.sources.misc newsgroup near the end of 1987. Larry has been known to refer to this nine-month period in Perl's history as its gestation.

Perl was released again in 1989 under the GNU public license—an open source, free software distribution model. Versions of Perl for the Macintosh came out in the early 1990s. By then, Perl was popular enough that books about how to program with it in a UNIX environment began to show up on bookshelves across the United States. By the late 1990s Perl was everywhere, from trade journals to conferences, to book series. In 2000, the origin of the language was researched so the word *Perl* could be included in the next edition of the Oxford English Dictionary.

A Brief Look at Programming

Many people have the idea that programming is a glorified, complicated process that only highly educated and technical people can do without damaging their hard drives and operating systems. Often programmers propagate this idea, and technical books (perhaps Perl books in particular) help promulgate it as well, usually by assuming that readers already have prior technical, UNIX, or programming experience. The truth is that programming is fairly simple. All it entails is writing a few lines in a different language—a language that a computer can understand.

Anything that runs on a computer is a program of some sort. A *program* is a list of instructions that is carried out by your computer. Unfortunately, computers do not understand English (at least, not yet). Instead, they use binary, a language composed only of ones and zeroes. Because computers speak in binary, and humans do not, you need some sort of translator or intermediary to take human language and turn it into instructions a computer can understand. Programming languages, like Perl, function as translators by being intermediaries between human communication, or language, and the computer's binary language. This will be covered in more depth in the upcoming section, "Examining How the Perl Compile Process Works."

There isn't much difference between a program and a script. Normally, a program refers to a finished or completed piece of code, whereas a script is a collection of lines or code that is not necessarily a completed program but might be. For the purposes of this book, a Perl script will be a collection of lines of code that contain Perl instructions and are saved as a text document in Microsoft Notepad. Saving code in Notepad is a fairly simple process, as out lined in the following steps, and shown in Figure 1.1.

1. Locate and open Notepad. It is normally found in the Accessories submenu of the Programs menu, which you can access by clicking on the Start button.

2. Type in the code.

3. Select File, Save to save the code.

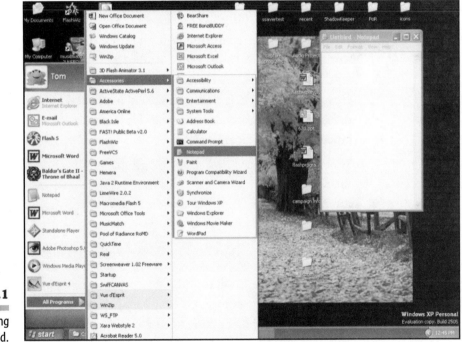

Figure 1.1

Opening and using Notepad.

Examining How the Perl Compile Process Works

Perl is a *compiled* language, which means that a Perl program compiles, or translates, itself into something that the computer can run. The compilation process involves writing a list of instructions in Perl, saving the instructions as a script, and then running the script through the Perl compiler. The Perl compiler acts as the translator that converts the Perl script into something similar to binary that the computer can understand, called *machine code*. Machine code is close enough to binary that the computer can translate and run the code as it reads along. Most modern programming languages, such as C, C++, Java, and C#, are compiled into a type of machine code in this manner.

Perl is also considered an *interpretive* language, because it is interpreted into machine code by the computer while the program is running. Not many common programming languages are interpretive; Perl's predecessor, AWK, is one of the few.

When the Perl compiler takes the program and converts it into data, that data is called an *executable* and is then prompted to run. When the Perl program is being compiled, the process is called *compile time*. When the Perl program is running, the process is called *run time*.

To go a little deeper, during compile time the Perl compiler actually runs through the script code several times to ensure everything is syntactically legal. When the compiler translates the script code into machine code, it creates several different files and then *interleaves* these files together to try to optimize them into an executable program that will run as quickly and efficiently as possible.

When you fire up a Perl script or program, Perl goes through two stages. First, the Perl compiler translates the Perl code into an optimized form that can be read by the Perl interpreter. If your script survives compilation, the optimized code is then read during run or execution time, which is the second stage. During this second stage, your computer, with the help of the Perl interpreter, follows the actions and instructions in the code and runs the script or program.

Using Perl with UNIX and CGI

UNIX is a common operating system, and it is also the operating system on which Perl first operated. Because Perl was born in UNIX, it is portable to almost all common UNIX distributions. (A Perl compiler is installed by default on most UNIX operating systems.) Perl also has access to all the common UNIX system calls. This is probably why most Perl reference and tutorial books have a UNIX flavor, unlike this book.

CGI (*Common Gateway Interface*) is a *protocol*—in other words, a way of doing something. In particular, CGI is the protocol that Web servers often use to talk to programs with which they interact. CGI is the gateway that enables a user to execute code on a Web server, and then returns the results to a Web browser. Perl is often used with CGI for Web-based applications. CGI applications can also be written in C, Visual Basic, Java, and a number of other languages, as long as the language can be run on a Web server.

The Perl Creed: TIMTOWTDI

The Perl creed is "There Is More Than One Way To Do It!" Perl is fairly robust compared to most programming languages. It has many functions and expressions that do the same or similar things. Also, the language syntax is very flexible, which means that you can code a specific program in more than one way. Writing in Perl is easier than writing in many other programming languages (especially those that use specific commands and syntax and have rules that need to be followed precisely), because there are many different commands that have similar functions in Perl, and these commands are flexible and forgiving and have many shortcuts. The downside is that Perl programs are often very difficult to read. This is because programs that do similar or identical things often look very different, and flexible commands with many shortcuts can soon become extremely difficult to decipher.

Using Open Source Software

Perl is considered open source software, and is distributable as long as the rules set forth within the Perl artistic license are followed. Both the artistic license and the details of the GNU public license can be found within the Perl readme documents, and more information can be found online at the following Web sites:

> **ActiveState's ActivePerl license:** http://www.activestate.com/ Products/ActivePerl/license_agreement.plex

> **ActiveState's posting of the GNU general public license:** http://aspn.activestate.com/ASPN/Legal/ GNU_License_Agreement_Text.txt

> ➤ **ActiveState's posting of Perl's artistic license:**
> http://aspn.activestate.com/ASPN/Legal/Artistic_License_Text.txt

> ➤ **CPAN's FAQ on the Perl license:** http://www.cpan.org/misc/
> cpan-faq.html#How_is_Perl_licensed

> ➤ **The Open Source Initiative:** http://www.opensource.org/licenses/
> index.html

Installing ActivePerl on Your Machine

The contributions of the many people in Perl's history contribute to the ease in which it can now be installed and run on almost any computer on the planet. In this section, I walk through getting your computer up and running with Perl. A copy of ActivePerl 5.6.1 is available on this book's companion Web site at http://www.premierpressbooks.com/downloads.asp. You can also download ActivePerl 5.6.1 from the ActiveState Web site, or from CPAN (the Comprehensive Perl Archive Network). ActivePerl is a free, open source Perl distribution that works with the Windows operating system. The URLs for these locations are:

> ➤ **ActiveState:** http://www.activestate.com/Products/Download/
> Get.plex?id=ActivePerl

> ➤ **The Comprehensive Perl Archive Network:**
> http://www.cpan.valueclick.com/src/

> ➤ **Premier Press Companion Web site:**
> http://www.premierpressbooks.com/downloads.asp

The Premier Press download section for this chapter contains a Web page with these links from ActiveState and CPAN (called getperl.html). When downloading ActivePerl from these sites, you will want to make sure that

> ➤ You are downloading a stable release as opposed to a release in development. Perl is still undergoing changes and alterations (more on this in the Sunday Evening session), and you need to download a release that has been adequately tested. This book utilizes ActivePerl version 5.6.1.

➤ You download a binary distribution as opposed to the Perl source code. The inner workings of Perl are available via source code, but in order to run the source code, you need a compiler. The binary distribution is Perl in a compiled form, which is capable of running like any executable program. The binary and source files should be labeled as such.

➤ You have the necessary software to unpack your download. Some of these sites store ActivePerl in a compressed form, and you may need Winzip (http://www.winzip.com) to uncompress the files and run them.

➤ You avoid downloading the tar archives. The Perl files you find on these sites that end in either .tar or .gz are compressed for Unix type platforms, and you will most likely experience trouble uncompressing these versions of Perl if you download them.

Installing ActivePerl is easy. Just follow these instructions:

1. Locate the ActivePerl 5.6.1 link on one of the above web sites and click it to start the download process.

2. Once ActivePerl has downloaded double-click on the Install ActivePerl icon to begin installation. The ActivePerl 5.6.1 Build 630 Setup Wizard appears, as shown in Figure 1.2.

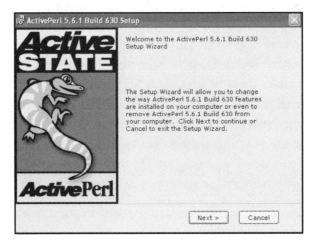

Figure 1.2

Installing ActivePerl on your machine.

3. If you choose the default menu options by simply clicking the Next and Finish buttons as they appear during the install, ActivePerl will be installed on your C drive in its own folder, conveniently named Perl.

For more specific installation instructions for Windows operating systems other than Windows XP, please refer to the sidebar "Troubleshooting ActivePerl Windows Installation."

NOTE Perl has several distributions for Windows, including IndigoPerl, SiePerl, and Prebuilt Perls. If you are interested in obtaining a different Perl distribution, the Comprehensive Perl Archive Network at http://www.cpan.org keeps copies of different distributions online. Just visit the Web site and take a look to see what's available.

ActivePerl is actually a merge of two previous and popular Windows versions of Perl—one that was built for Windows 95/98 and one that was built for Windows NT.

Using Perl with DOS

A sample program is installed with ActivePerl, so you can test to see whether Perl is installed correctly. To run this program, you need to navigate to the appropriate folder using the Windows DOS command line.

What Is DOS?

DOS is a simple, text-based operating system that is underneath, or in addition to, the normal Windows operating system. Windows XP uses Windows DOS, which enables users to navigate to different directories and change, delete, move, rename, and alter folders and files. In this and other versions of DOS, almost everything you can do in Windows is also possible via the command line, but no graphical symbols are available to help you navigate. Perl was born on this sort of operating system, and you will need to use the command line interface often to exercise your newfound Perl skills.

NOTE Earlier versions of Windows use an early version of Windows DOS called MS-DOS, or Microsoft DOS.

TROUBLESHOOTING ACTIVEPERL WINDOWS INSTALLATION

ActivePerl is designed to run on the Win32 platform, specifically these:

➤ Windows 95

➤ Windows 98

➤ Windows Me

➤ Windows NT

➤ Windows 2000

➤ Windows XP

However, the older your operating system is, the more likely it is that you will need supplemental patches or support to install the ActivePerl package. For Windows Me, 2000, and XP, you should have everything you need already installed. ActiveState recommends that you have the latest version of Microsoft Windows Installer if you are running an earlier operating system. (You can download the latest Microsoft Windows Installer from http://download.microsoft.com. Look for Windows Installer within the product listing.) A recent version of Internet Explorer is also helpful (version 5.0 or later). Other specifics for your platform are as follows:

➤ **Windows NT:** Service Pack 5 or higher should be installed.

➤ **Windows 98:** DCOM for Windows 98 should be installed (available at http://www.microsoft.com/com/resources/downloads.asp).

➤ **Windows 95:** Microsoft suspended support for Windows 95 in January of 2002, although you may still be able to receive updates or support. ActiveState suggests looking for Microsoft's DCOM for Windows 95 and Microsoft's MSVCRT, which may or may not be available through Windows Update or Microsoft's download sites.

Besides these operating system updates, you should also ensure that you have 35MB of free hard disk space for a typical ActivePerl installation.

ActivePerl 5.6.1 includes core Per Win32 files and also comes with the Perl Package Manager (PPM for short) which you will learn more about in the Sunday Morning session.

NOTE   You can uninstall Perl through the Windows Control Panel. Navigate to the Control Panel through the Windows Start Menu and open up Add/Remove Programs. ActivePerl is displayed here and can be removed just like any other program.

Accessing the Windows DOS Command Line

To access the Windows command line, click on the Start menu, and then click on Run. The Run dialog box opens, and contains an Open field.

To access the Microsoft Windows DOS command line, follow these steps:

1. Click on the Start menu.

2. Click on Run. The Run dialog box appears, containing an Open line.

3. Type **command** at the Open prompt, as shown in Figure 1.3. If you are using Windows NT or 2000, you can also type **CMD**.

Figure 1.3

Using Run to open a command line.

4. Click on OK. The DOS command line interface appears.

• •

NOTE   On many Windows operating systems, a shortcut to the DOS prompt in the Program menu can be found in the Start button menu.

• •

Using the Command Line Prompt

When you reach DOS, you will see a *command line prompt*, which is where you enter commands. For convenience, Windows DOS tells you in which directory you reside at the beginning of the command line prompt. In Figure 1.4, the command line prompt is C:\DOCUME~1\TOM>. Reading backwards, this tells you that you are in the TOM folder, which is in the DOCUME~1 folder, which is in the C drive. The ~1 after DOCUME means the folder name, Documents and Settings, is a long name that DOS has cut short so it can fit the name on this line. Notice also that the folders are listed in uppercase letters.

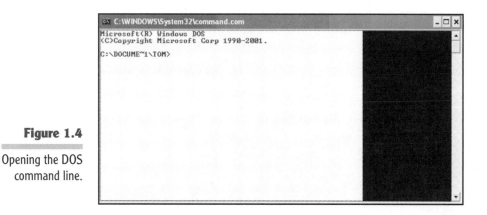

Figure 1.4

Opening the DOS
command line.

Navigating with DOS

To navigate the operating system, you will use two simple DOS commands: CD (Change Directory) and DIR (Directory). To see the contents of any folder you are in, just type in DIR and press Enter. DIR helps you determine where you are in the file structure. If I type DIR at the location shown in Figure 1.5, DOS will list the contents of everything that is in C:\DOCUMENTS AND FOLDERS\TOM, along with other miscellaneous information.

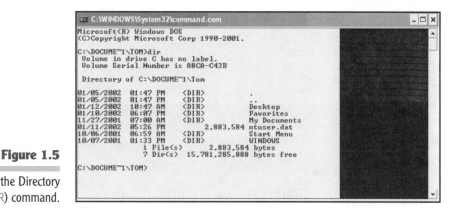

Figure 1.5

Using the Directory
(DIR) command.

Change Directory (CD) is another important command that allows you to navigate to different folders and directories. To navigate to the Perl folder, just type:

```
CD \Perl
```

You need to type this exactly as it is shown, including the space between the change directory CD command and the backslash (\). You will know you have succeeded when the command prompt displays C:\PERL>. When you are in this folder, type:

DIR

You will see that the Perl folder contains a number of other folders, including bin, Docs, eg, lib, site, and so on.

NOTE ActivePerl automatically installs itself on the primary drive, which is the C:\\ drive, although the C may vary in some cases. For Windows operating systems, C will be the default drive Perl will install on.

Running Your First Perl Program

You need to run an example Perl file that is in the eg folder, so use the DOS command you just learned to navigate into this folder and display its contents by typing the following line (see Figure 1.6).

CD \PERL\EG

Press Enter, and then type:

DIR

```
C:\WINDOWS\System32\command.com                                    _ □ ×

C:\PERL>cd\Perl\eg

C:\PERL\EG>dir
 Volume in drive C has no label.
 Volume Serial Number is A8CA-C43B

 Directory of C:\PERL\EG

01/12/2002  09:33 AM    <DIR>          .
01/12/2002  09:33 AM    <DIR>          ..
12/11/2001  07:17 PM    <DIR>          aspSamples
12/11/2001  07:17 PM    <DIR>          cgi
12/11/2001  07:17 PM    <DIR>          Core
08/20/2001  11:09 AM                33 example.pl
12/11/2001  07:17 PM    <DIR>          fork
12/11/2001  07:17 PM    <DIR>          IEExamples
08/20/2001  11:10 AM               836 Readme.txt
01/12/2002  10:22 AM    <DIR>          Weekend
12/11/2001  07:17 PM    <DIR>          Windows Script Components
12/11/2001  07:17 PM    <DIR>          Windows Script Host
               2 File(s)            869 bytes
              10 Dir(s)  15,786,479,616 bytes free

C:\PERL\EG>_
```

Figure 1.6

Sample contents of the eg folder.

The example program is called example.pl. To run it, simply type:

```
example.pl
```

You should receive the response, "Hello from ActivePerl!"

NOTE   If you did not receive the response "Hello from ActivePerl" a number of troubleshooting techniques are available. First, make sure you typed the example as indicated, including using all lowercase letters. Second, make sure you are in the appropriate directory, your DOS prompt should say C:\PERL\EG>. Another possibility is that Perl did not install properly on your machine. Do not panic. Instead, take a look at ActivePerl's documentation that should now be located in C:\Perl\Docs. If the help documentation did not install, you can go directly to ActivePerl's Web site at http://aspn.activestate.com/ASPN/Downloads/ActivePerl for documentation or help.

Congratulations! You have just run your first Perl program on your own machine! To exit DOS, simply type:

```
EXIT
```

This will close the DOS command prompt and return you to Windows.

Take a Break

You have been through quite a bit for a Friday evening. After a whirlwind overview of Perl and a sampling of DOS, you have managed to install Perl and run your first Perl program. Congratulate yourself on a job well done and take a short break. When you come back, you'll start coding and learning some basic HTML.

Writing Your First Perl Program with HTML

Now that you know how to run a Perl program, you can walk through a simple, short script written from scratch. This time, however, you will use HTML to build a sample Web page that uses Perl.

What Is HTML?

HTML is a programming language specifically designed to develop, encode, and display documents on the Web. In this section, you will use HTML to write Perl scripts that operate within a browser. (ActivePerl installs a default client-side version of Perl that allows you to run Perl scripts within Internet Explorer.) However, the Web page scripts that you write for this exercise might not work on a Web server. If you want to upload these pages to a Web site, make sure the Web server that hosts the site is using a compatible Perl distribution. (You'll learn more about this in the Sunday Evening session, "Learning Advanced Perl Techniques.") Because this is a book about Perl and not HTML, I will only cover commands in HTML that you need to write Perl scripts. For a good introduction to HTML, read *Learn HTML In A Weekend,* 3rd Edition (Premier Press, Inc., 2000).

Creating an HTML Document

You can create HTML documents in Windows in a number of ways. For example, in some versions of Windows, you can open a new text document, type the code, and save it as an HTML file. You can also purchase software packages, such as Dreamweaver, Director, GoLive, and Xara Webstyle, to help you create HTML documents. If you are already comfortable using another program to create HTML files, feel free to use it instead of the following method. If you aren't comfortable creating HTML files, the following method should work regardless of which version of Windows you are using.

1. Right-click on your desktop. A shortcut menu appears.

2. Select New, Text Document (see Figure 1.7). A new, blank text document is created.

Figure 1.7

Creating a new text document.

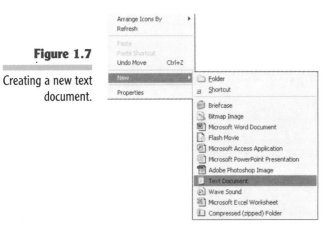

3. Next you must convert the new text document into an HTML document. Click the name of the file once to highlight it and change the .txt extension to .html. For this example, change the name of the file to test.html.

4. Windows might display a warning that you are changing the file's properties by converting it, as shown in Figure 1.8. Click on Yes. The icon on your desktop changes to an Internet Explorer Web Page icon.

NOTE Some of the Windows operating systems allow you the shortcut of simply right-clicking and choosing Create HTML to generate a new Web page, rather than following the steps to create a blank text document first and then changing to an HTML document. Feel free to use whatever method makes sense to you when creating these files.

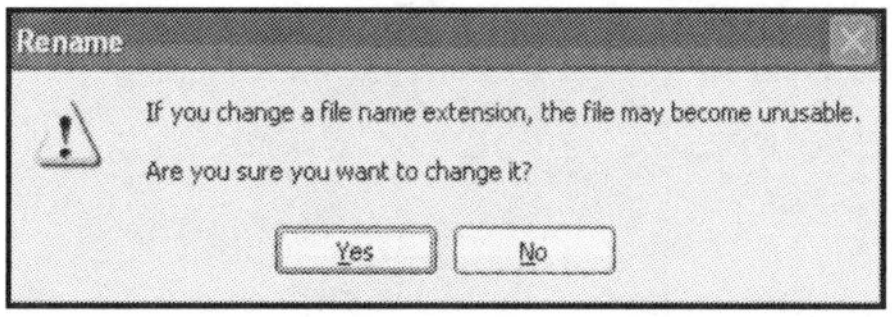

Figure 1.8

Windows issues a warning that you are changing extensions.

Altering HTML Files

To open your new test.html file in your default browser, double-click on the test.html icon on your desktop. This view of the file doesn't enable you to change any code, however. To alter the code, choose View, Source, as shown in Figure 1.10. The source code for the HTML page will open in the default Windows text editor, which is normally Notepad. Right now, of course, it will be blank.

NOTE It is also possible to access the source code with Notepad by right-clicking on the blank Web page itself and choosing View Source from the menu that appears.

FINDING YOUR WINDOWS EXTENSIONS

In some cases, file extensions (for example, .txt or .html) aren't visible in Windows. This is because there is a folder option that allows you to turn them off and on. If you cannot see the .txt extension when you create a new text document, you might have difficulty renaming the file as an HTML document.

To change your view settings so that you can see the file extensions, follow these steps:

1. Double-click on the My Computer icon. The My Computer window appears.

2. Choose Tools, Folder Options to open the Folder Options dialog box.

3. Click on the View tab, as shown in Figure 1.9. The View tab contains an option for viewing file extensions that you can toggle on or off. Make sure the check box is selected to enable viewing of file extensions.

4. Click on Apply to apply the option to all folders.

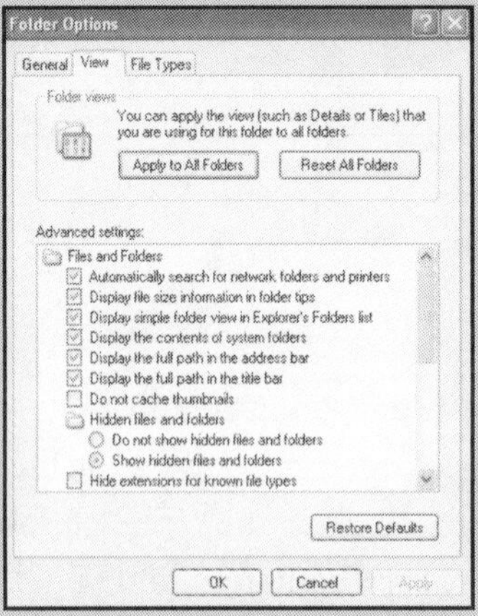

Figure 1.9

Setting your folder options.

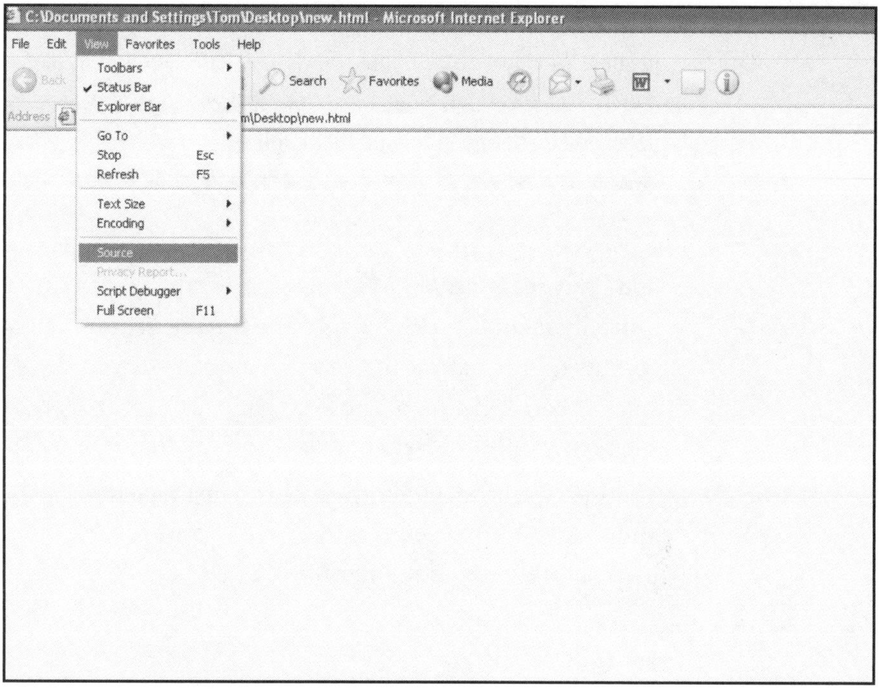

Figure 1.10

Altering your new
HTML test file.

Understanding HTML Tags

HTML and Perl often go hand in hand, and you need to learn a little HTML before you can move ahead. HTML uses *tags* (< >) to signify commands. When an Internet browser opens a Web page, it looks for these tag commands. Tagged commands usually look like this:

```
<TAG>command goes here</TAG>
```

The first <TAG> initiates the command. The second command contains a forward slash (/), which indicates that the command no longer applies.

The first tags a Web page needs are HTML tags. All HTML commands must be between these HTML tags to be recognized as HTML code. Simply type:

```
<HTML>
</HTML>
```

Any standard browser will now know that everything between the <HTML> and </HTML> tags is HTML code, and that these tags mark the beginning and the end of the Web page.

Now you need to add more code to the HTML page and insert the head and body sections. HTML pages are normally split into two sections, which typically include a *head section* and a *body section*. The head section usually contains information the browser needs, such as the page identifier, page title, or base location of the Web page. The body section generally contains the text, graphics, sounds, and so on for the Web page.

To insert the head and body sections, just type the <HEAD>, </HEAD>, <BODY>, and </BODY> tags between the <HTML> and </HTML> tags. The code for the page should now look like this:

```
<HTML>
<HEAD>
</HEAD>

<BODY>
</BODY>
</HTML>
```

Next, you need to tell the browser that you want to use Perl. To do so, enter the <SCRIPT> tags within the body of the page. Type the following code between <BODY> and </BODY>:

```
<SCRIPT LANGUAGE="PerlScript">
</SCRIPT>
```

This tells the browser that you are using the script language PerlScript within these tags.

Now you actually get to write some Perl. You will get into the actual details of these commands in the Saturday Morning session. In the meantime, just type the following line between the two <SCRIPT> tags:

```
$window->document->write('Hello and Welcome to Perl!');
```

The complete HTML script in Notepad should look like Figure 1.11:

```
<HTML>
<HEAD>
</HEAD>
<BODY>
<SCRIPT LANGUAGE="PerlScript">
$window->document->write('Hello and welcome to Perl!');
</SCRIPT>
</BODY>
</HTML>
```

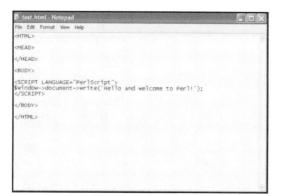

Figure 1.11

Editing an HTML page.

Now you should save the document by following these steps:

1. Click on File, Save.

2. Close Notepad, then go back to the browser and click on Refresh. (Alternatively, you can reopen the test.html page by double-clicking on its icon.) The browser opens, calls PerlScript, and runs the command listed. The message "Hello and Welcome to Perl!" prints within the browser window.

If you have trouble running this or other scripts in any of the chapters, all of the example files are included on the companion Web site. When run correctly, however, the script should display a Web page like the one shown in Figure 1.12.

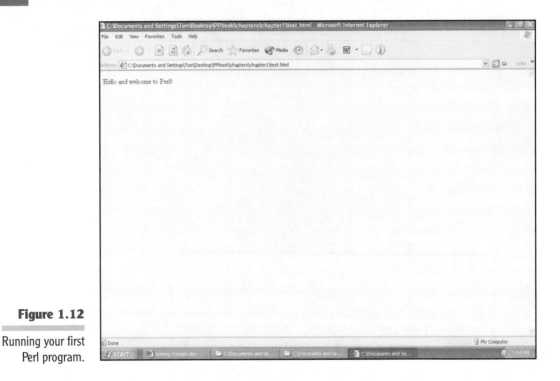

Figure 1.12

Running your first
Perl program.

Translating the Perl Code

So, what does that magic line of Perl in the HTML code do? Well, first the
easy part. Perl is often easier to read from right to left. This is because Perl
often runs commands or makes assignments from right to left. It may feel
counter-intuitive to read code backwards at first, but it becomes more natural
as time passes and you get used to the way Perl reads and understands scripts.

In Perl, a statement almost always ends on the right side with a semicolon.
The semicolon used at the end of every command tells Perl to execute
whatever script precedes the semicolon and then go on to the next line and
command. Before the semicolon is a *text string*, separated by parentheses
and single quotation marks, like this:

```
('Hello and welcome to Perl!');
```

Perl uses single quotation marks in many different ways. In this context,
the quotation marks tell Perl that you want the text string printed as quoted.

Parentheses are commonly used to hold input for a command. The parentheses here separate all of the input that needs to go to the command from the rest of the line of code. The command in question, `write`, is placed to the left of the text string.

The `write` command seems pretty straightforward, and for the most part, it is. The `write` command in Perl is used specifically to print text in a specified or implied format, and in this example it is used to print the words contained in quotes.

The `->` operator is an *arrow operator*. The arrow operator is a *dereferencing operator* that Perl uses to reference information or data. In this case, the arrows tell the window to reference the document and the document to reference the write command. Perl normally uses symbols as dereferencers.

```
window->document->
```

The `$` is an important and common command in Perl and is known in Perl as a *prefix dereferencer*. Each type of data within Perl has its own dereferencer; the `$` is the dereferencer that refers to a text string or variable. In Perl, this type of variable is called a *scalar*, which is any data that is composed of either a numerical value or a string of text. Basically, all data in Perl are scalars. Almost all values are either a piece of text or a number, and scalars are used to represent both of these.

So, whenever you see `$` in Perl code, you know that somewhere close by there is a variable or a text string that Perl needs to track. In this case, `$` warns Perl that the text string `Hello and welcome to Perl!` needs to be tracked. The rest of the code tells Perl where to place that variable and where to write it. Without the scalar dereferencer, Perl would assume that `Hello and Welcome to Perl!` was some sort of command it had to run, and the compiler would throw you an error when it looked for that command and couldn't find it. With the scalar dereferencer, Perl knows that `Hello and Welcome to Perl!` is a text string that the programmer wants to use somewhere in the program.

Block One: Program Planning

Throughout this book, you will be using Perl to put together actual programs. Most of the chapters contain small snippets of code and short scripts to illustrate certain Perl features, but at the end of each chapter you will spend some time putting these snippets together into the building blocks of a larger program. These building blocks are laid out in the first four chapters, so that by the end of the Saturday Evening session, you will have a fully functional, full-length Perl computer game. On Sunday, you will revisit the code and make modifications to optimize it using the more advanced techniques you will be learning.

Some programmers argue that the bulk of the work of writing a program should be conducted on planning and research. Others contend that the focus should be at the end of a project and focus on integration, bugs, kinks, and optimization. Some programmers believe in using only specific programming methodologies, and others programmers change methodologies depending upon the project.

I try to stay away from using any one specific method. I do spend some time covering structured programming in the Saturday Evening session, and object-oriented programming in the Sunday Morning session. I do this because Perl was born when structured programming was the dominant programming paradigm, and Perl has adopted object-oriented programming features as they have risen in popularity. Both of these methods are important for understanding how Perl works.

With that in mind, I want keep the planning for this computer game simple, so I will flesh out a basic game first, with plans for expanding upon it later. Some programmers like to start out a program with user scenarios or feature lists. For the purposes of getting something out and scripted quickly, I'll make a quick list of features:

➤ The game will be called "Trapped."

➤ Players will use the keyboard to navigate.

➤ Initially, the game will be text based.

➤ The game will consist of a lost player navigating a cave map trying to reach the surface.

➤ The map will be random each time for playability.

Based on my brainstorm, I can generate corresponding programming code I think I will need:

➤ Code that prints information to the screen.

➤ Code that takes information from the keyboard.

➤ Code that times the display of text/information.

➤ Code that generates a random map.

➤ Code that tracks the player's progress on the map.

Now, before I lose inertia, I want to begin programming. Because all I really have is a "to do" list of programming needs, I'll create a script that outlines, separates, and displays my to do list. I can do this in Perl by using a comment marker.

All modern programming languages allow programmers to insert comments in their code. Comments are extremely important, not only to the professional programmer who needs to write code that other people may need to change or maintain, but also to individuals or independent programmers who need to look at their code again to see how they did something or modify an existing program.

Perl recognizes the pound sign (#) as a comment marker, and any text that follows # on a line the Perl compiler will ignore. This makes it fairly easy to put notes or ideas down. To start creating the Trapped program, open up Notepad and write some notes that begin with the # sign:

```
##############################################
#Trapped
##############################################


##################################################
# block1- planning
# What I need:
# Code that prints information to the screen.
# Code that takes information from the keyboard.
# Code that generates a random map
# Code that tracks the player's progress on the map
```

Save this Notepad file as block1.pl. Although this code doesn't do anything yet, you will be coming back to it in the next chapter.

Summary

Your Friday evening lesson is over. Although you have written only a few lines of actual Perl code, you now have a much better base for understanding the language and you can run Perl programs on your own computer. You have also been introduced to CGI, HTML, and the DOS command prompt, and you have learned more about the Perl language. Most important, you have written your first program, using not one but two new programming languages!

Variables and Other Fun Stuff

- ➤ Using print and getting input
- ➤ Using scalars
- ➤ Exploring lists
- ➤ Arrays and hashes
- ➤ Retrieving user input

ood morning and welcome back to *Learn Perl in a Weekend*. I
hope you have your coffee and OJ in hand because you are about
to embark upon a voyage of intense discovery. If you have thumbed
through or scanned ahead in the text, you might have noticed that the
early morning chapters are a bit more lengthy than the evening ones. I
focus on the more important and complex Perl foundations in the morning
chapters, so you can wade through the difficult topics early. This morning,
you are going to tackle Perl data fundamentals, including scalars, printing,
arrays, and hashes.

Using Print and Getting Input

You are going to start off this morning by reviewing the Perl `print` function.
`Print` is an extremely simple and useful function that allows you to print
things to the screen. I probably use `print` in scripts more often than any
other command, so you need to become intimately familiar with it.

Using Print

Before you start your first official Perl program of the chapter, create a new
folder to store your test Perl scripts in. In the sections to follow, I will run
you through dozens of Perl scripts, and having a local place to store and
keep track of these scripts will help you when I refer back to the scripts
later. Follow these steps to create a new folder for your Perl projects in your
existing c:\Perl\eg file. (If you are familiar with creating folders in Windows
you can skip this series of steps.)

1. Right-click on the My Computer icon and select Explore from the shortcut menu, as shown in Figure 2.1. (Alternatively, you can choose Windows Explorer from the Start Menu.)

Figure 2.1

Using Windows Explorer to create a new Perl folder.

2. In your C drive, open the new Perl folder that you created last night.

3. Open the eg folder, which contains the example you used last night. This folder is where you will create and write most of your Perl scripts.

4. Right-click and select New Folder to create a new folder.

5. Name the folder Weekend, as shown in Figure 2.2.

6. Double-click on the Weekend folder to open it.

Now that you have a Weekend folder to store your projects, you can create a new Perl script for the print project, as described in the following steps:

1. Right-click in the Weekend folder.

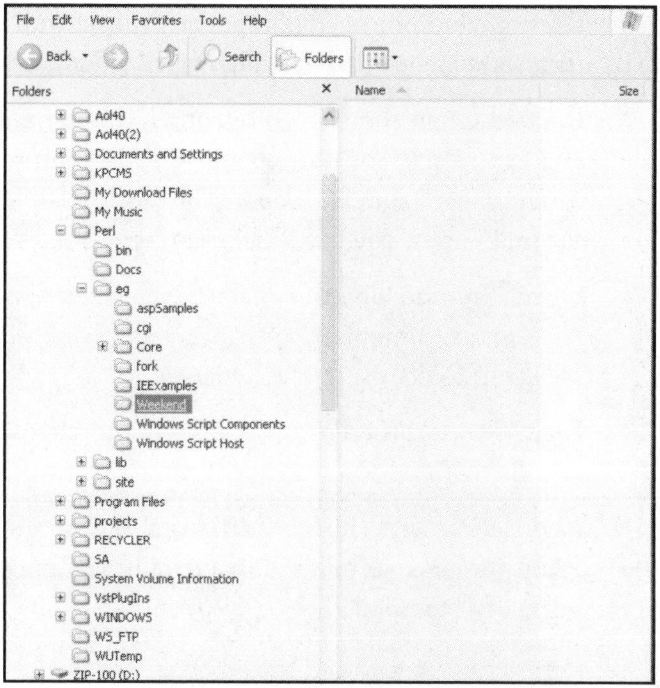

Figure 2.2

Creating the
Weekend folder.

2. Select New Text Document from the shortcut menu. A new text document appears.

3. Rename the new document Print.pl. Click OK if the Windows warning appears.

You now have a new Perl program named Print located in the Weekend folder. You should be able to determine that it is a Perl program because the icon will be a small, golden pearl.

NOTE Remember that all the program examples are stored on our companion Web site at http:// www.premierpressbooks.com/downloads.asp. If you have difficulty putting together the scripts or running them, you can always download them and take a look at the finished product.

In order to edit and program your new Print.pl script, you need to open the script in a text editor. Windows provides a built-in text editor called Notepad you can use to edit Print.pl. You can open Print.pl with Notepad a number of different ways (depending on which type of Windows you are running):

➤ Right-click on the Print program. There are a number of options you can select. You can choose Open With and select Notepad. Alternatively, you can choose Edit. Both methods will get you into the program so you can start scripting.

➤ Open Notepad on your Start menu (located at Start, Programs, Accessories, Notepad), and then have Notepad navigate to your Weekend folder using File, Open.

➤ Right-click on the Print.pl file itself and choose Open With. You can then choose Notepad as the program to open Print.pl.

➤ Right-click and choose Edit from the menu (see Figure 2.3). Print.pl opens with Window's default editing program, which is normally Notepad.

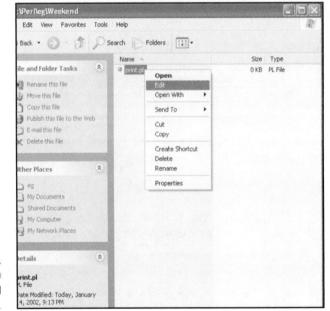

Figure 2.3

Using the editing option.

If you are accustomed to using a different editing program when programming, feel free to do so when writing these examples. Emacs is a popular editor that is also free, and Windows Visual Studio also provides mechanisms for editing Perl files.

CAUTION When editing Perl scripts (and other programming scripts) do not use word processor programs, such as Microsoft Word or Wordpad. Full text editors contain characters and formats that Perl will not understand, and scripts you write with these applications will not compile and run. On the same token, be wary of some of the advanced features of Notepad, which can also format text into a form that Perl cannot read.

You that have created the Print.pl file, Notepad is open and showing you a blank page. Now you need to fill that page with commands that Perl will understand. The first command you will learn this morning in Perl is the `print` command. To use the `print` command, type **print** followed by the file or text that you want printed in quotation marks. Type the following line of code in the Notepad Edit box that you just opened:

```
print "Hello";
```

Now close the Edit box by clicking on the X in the upper-right corner of the box. Choose Yes when Windows asks you if you want to keep the changes. Double-click on the new Print program to run it.

Not quite what you expected, right? If you did everything correctly, you didn't see `Hello`. Instead, you saw a flashing rectangle that appeared and then went away. Rest assured, your program is actually running correctly. The problem is that Perl is sending output into DOS, not to Windows. This means that when the Print program runs, a DOS box is opened, the program runs in the DOS box, and then the DOS box is automatically closed again, all within the blink of an eye.

In order to keep the DOS box from disappearing, you need to make it wait for a period of time or until someone tells it to close. This brings me to the next section—user input.

Getting User Input

Perl can take different kinds of input and use them in different ways. In your Print.pl program, you simply need Perl to halt and wait a moment before the program continues and exits. You accomplish this by using the <> operator. To make DOS wait for a user to catch up, you place these brackets at the end of the script.

```
print "Hello!";
<>
```

This isn't going to help someone else who runs the program, though. The script will simply run and then freeze, so it's a good idea to add a second print line to explain what exactly is happening.

```
print "Hello!";
print "Press <ENTER> to continue…";
<>
```

Run the edited Print.pl program, and your output appears, as shown in Figure 2.4.

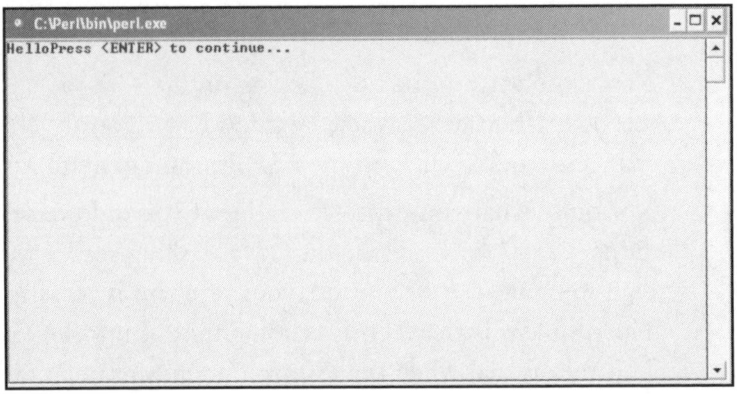

Figure 2.4

The Print.pl program waits for a user to press enter.

Now you are going to improve the program. First, the two text strings, Hello and Press <ENTER> to continue, fall on the same line. Perl formats text strings exactly the way you tell it. Unless you specify that you want spaces or a new line start, it will not add spaces or start a new line. To put the Press <ENTER> string on its own line, you need to add an *escape sequence*. Escape sequences are small bits of code that represent common typing commands, such as carriage returns, tabs, indents, and so on. You can add escape sequences to text strings and other places. The \ tells Perl that you want to use an escape sequence, and the n character specifies a carriage return or new line. Add \n to the Print.pl code where indicated.

```
print "Hello!\n";
print "Press <ENTER> to continue…";
<>
```

Perl will recognize the escape character and put a carriage return at the end of the first Hello line.

Escape sequences are also used to print special characters that Perl would normally consider part of a command (quotation marks, for instance). Table 2.1 shows the Perl escape sequences.

TIP The most commonly used escape characters are ones that replicate typewriter functions, such as \b for backspace, \f for form feed, \t for tab, and \n for a new line. If you want to use single or double quotation marks in a text string, you will need to include a slash in front of the symbol so that Perl does not think it is part of the command. If you wanted to quote someone, for instance, you would have to type: **print"And then George said \"hello\"!\n";**. Perl escape sequences are also referred to as *string literals*.

Another extremely important and frequently used Perl command is the *comment*. Perl uses the pound sign (#) to designate comments, which are normally simple explanations that programmers put into their code to remind them of what they were doing. Comments make code more readable when you come back to it after time, and they help other readers understand what you meant when you were writing it. Because there are so many different ways to do things in Perl, long pieces of code can be difficult to read, and commenting is very important. For the sake of practice, add some comments to the code you just wrote. Add a comment (#) before each line of code, explaining what the program does.

```
# a simple print string followed by a new-line escape
print "Hello!\n";
# another line explaining to the reader what to do next
print "Press <Enter> to continue…";
# Perl waits at these brackets for user input
<>
```

NOTE There is an exception to the # line being used as a comment. In UNIX Perl, you can specify where the Perl compiler resides by using the # character on the first line. If you are downloading Perl code from the Internet and you come across something like this

```
#!/usr/bin/perl
```

on the first line, the programmer is simply telling the program that Perl lies within the Perl directory, which is in the bin folder, which is in the usr folder. Unless you need to move Perl from the command path, don't worry about this. I just wanted to mention it in case you came across it in the future.

Character	Effect
\'	single quotation mark
\"	double quotation mark
\t	tab
\n	new line
\r	return
\f	form feed or return
\b	backspace
\a	alarm (bell)
\e	escape
\033	octal char

TABLE 2.1 PERL ESCAPE SEQUENCES

Using Scalars

When it comes right down to it, almost all computer programs handle data to produce output. Understanding how Perl stores and gets data is the foundation for programming in Perl. In this section, you'll learn to get values into Perl, and in the next chapter, you'll manipulate those values.

Perl excels at handling data. (It was originally designed to play with text, remember?) It can hold single items, such as a word (called a *string of characters*) or a number (called a *variable*), in a structure that Perl gurus like to call a *scalar variable*, or a *scalar* for short.

TABLE 2.1 (CONTINUED)	
Character	Effect
\x1b	hex char
\c[	control char
\l	lowercase next char
\u	uppercase next char
\L	lowercase till \E
\U	uppercase till \E
\E	end case modification
\N	insert named characters
\Q	add backslash to all following non-alphanumeric characters

Scalar values were introduced in last night's chapter. Now that you have a few more programming tricks up your sleeve, I am going to show you some of the scalar's advanced features.

Digging into Scalars

Unlike some other programming languages, in Perl you cannot force a scalar to be only text or a variable. Perl automatically handles operations with scalars and makes assumptions on how to use them based on their content. This means that if you put text in a scalar, Perl will assume that the scalar is a text string. If you put a number in a scalar, Perl will assume that it is a number and treat it accordingly. If you put both numbers and letters in a scalar, Perl will try to determine what you are attempting to do based on the command context, which might lead to some interesting results.

An important thing to keep in mind is that all scalars in Perl are case sensitive. This means that Perl treats x and X completely differently. If you assign the value 10 to the scalar Number, you will not get the value 10 using nUMBER because Perl treats Number and nUMBER differently.

NOTE You might have noticed that almost all Perl commands are lowercase. Only a handful of commands in Perl are uppercase. If you have trouble executing a script, and you receive an unrecognized error, you might have accidentally used an uppercase letter in place of a lowercase one. Because Perl has dominion over many of the common lowercase words, you might find that other Perl programmers use uppercase in their code for specific types of important values or scalars because uppercase terms are easy to find when scanning the script.

$ is the prefix dereferencer for scalars. It is like a warning sign that tells Perl how to react to whatever follows. In Perl, you normally use $ to create a scalar variable and = to assign something to that variable. If you wanted to create the variable CurrentChapter and assign it the value 2, you would input

```
$CurrentChapter = 2;
```

Going over this line piece by piece, from right to left, you have the semicolon at the end that tells Perl the command is over and can be executed. Before the semicolon is the number 2, which is assigned to the scalar in question

($CurrentChapter) by the equal sign. In English, the equal sign basically says, "Take whatever is on my right side and assign it to whatever is on my left."

Scalars can represent numbers and strings of text. You assign text and numbers in the exactly same way. For example, if you want to assign the word Variables instead of the number 2 to CurrentChapter, you can copy the command and just change the number 2 to the text string Variables.

```
$CurrentChapter = "Variables";
```

Notice that I need to include quotation marks to help Perl sort out exactly what is in the text string.

You can try this out yourself using the following script. First, create a new Perl file called Chapter.pl by right-clicking, choosing New Text Document, and changing the name to Chapter.pl. Then open the file to edit it by right-clicking and choosing Edit. Use = to assign two to a scalar called CurrentChapter on one line, then print CurrentChapter to the screen using the print command. Do not forget to add the <> section to the end so you can watch the code while it works.

```
# assign two to CurrentChapter
$CurrentChapter = "two";
# and print it out
print "$CurrentChapter\n";


# another print statement telling the reader what to do next
print "Press <ENTER> to continue...";


# Perl waits at these brackets for user input
<>
```

As you can see, you can insert a scalar almost anywhere, even within a text string, and Perl knows how to use it. When you run this program, you should see DOS print the word two followed by the Press <ENTER> to continue string.

Now, add these lines before the <ENTER> string:

```
# assign 2 to CurrentChapter
$CurrentChapter = "2";
```

```
# and print it out
print "$CurrentChapter\n";
```

When Perl runs through this code (see Figure 2.5), it first assigns the text string two to CurrentChapter, and then prints CurrentChapter, putting two on the screen. Perl then reassigns the variable 2 to current chapter and prints it again, placing the 2 onto the screen. The full source code should look something like this:

```
# assign two to CurrentChapter
$CurrentChapter = "two";
# and print it out
print "$CurrentChapter\n";

# assign 2 to CurrentChapter
$CurrentChapter = "2";
# and print it out
print "$CurrentChapter\n";

# another print statement telling the reader what to do next
print "Press <ENTER> to continue...";

# Perl waits at these brackets for user input
<>
```

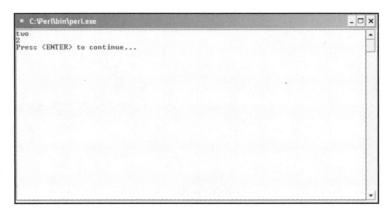

Figure 2.5

Running the Chapter.pl program.

If you want to see Chapter.pl in its complete form, you can find it on the companion Web site with the Chapter 2 scripts.

Perl Data Types

There are some limits to what can actually be placed within a scalar. Normally, scalars can hold letters, numbers, and underscores as variables. However, other characters (such as %, <, #, and $) aren't allowed, although there are special rules for dealing with these instances, namely the escape sequences outlined in Table 2.1.

Each scalar has a maximum character length, which is dependent on the operating system and hardware platform you possess. Perl is also capable of supporting different kinds of numbers, from regular integers to scientific notation, as outlined in Table 2.2. (Some of these types are discussed in more length in the upcoming section, "Counting Systems Used in Perl.")

Perl will make assumptions as to how to treat the data based on the data you assign to a scalar. When you assign a floating point number to a scalar, Perl will treat the variable as a floating point number. If you later assign a number in scientific notation to the scalar, Perl will treat operations against the scalar as operations against scientific notation and not against a floating point number. If you do not point out what type of data Perl will be utilizing when you assign a scalar, Perl will assume the number is a floating point number.

TABLE 2.2 NUMERIC DATA TYPES IN PERL	
Data Type	**Example**
Binary	01101
Floating Point	1.11
Hexadecimal	0x111
Integer	11
Octal	01101
Scientific	1.1E11

Perl has a number of different functions to alter data types. For instance, if you need to change a data type into a normal integer, Perl has an int function just for this purpose. In the following example named round.pl, I assign a floating point number to the $number scalar, print the scalar, and then print the scalar a second time after int has been applied to the number.

```
# Assign a floating point number to the scalar $number
$number = 1.1111;

# Print $number
print "$number\n";

# Use int and then print the number a second time
print int "$number\n";

# Add our ending changed to user input
# standard ending
print "\nPress any key to continue...";

<>
```

A more elegant way to get rid of a pesky decimal place is to use the built-in sprintf function. Perl's sprintf will round a floating point number to a specified length using the following format:

```
sprintf "argument", number;
```

The argument is the number of decimal places you want to keep preceded by a percentage sign % and followed by an f. If you wanted to cut $number to two decimal places in the above example, you could add a line of code that looks like this:

```
print sprintf "%.2f\n", $number;
```

The sprintf command is extremely versatile and is capable of altering the way Perl data types are displayed. The sprintf command is sometimes called the *format string command,* and it allows you to alter a string or list (more on lists in the upcoming section, "Exploring Lists") by changing the data type from one to the next, using the same format of:

```
sprintf "format", stringorlist;
```

To illustrate the power of `sprintf`, start a new Perl script called format.pl and create a scalar with a floating point number:

```
# Assign a floating point number to the scalar $number
$number = 1.1111;

# Print $number
print "$number\n";

# Add our ending changed to user input
# standard ending
print "\nPress any key to continue...";

<>
```

Now to add a number of `sprintf` lines that format `$number` in different ways. You have already seen decimal rounding in action:

```
print sprintf "%.2f\n", $number;
```

You can use `sprintf` to change the number to octal using %o as the argument:

```
print sprintf "%.2f\n", $number;
```

Or you can change the number to a percentage using %% as the argument:

```
print sprintf "%%f\n", $number;
```

You can also change the number to a character string using %c as the argument:

```
print sprintf "%cf\n", $number;
```

These examples are put together in the source code that follows and is a complete example that is downloadable from the Premier Press Web site as format.pl. Some of the more common arguments available for `sprintf` are shown in Table 2.3.

```
# Assign a floating point number to the scalar $number
$number = 1.1111;

# Print $number
print "$number\n";

# Cut the decimal place to two
```

```
print sprintf "%.2f\n", $number;

# Change to an octal number
print sprintf "%of\n", $number;

# Change to a percentage
print sprintf "%%f\n", $number;

# Change to a string
print sprintf "%sf\n", $number;

# Add our ending changed to user input
# standard ending
print "\nPress any key to continue...";

<>
```

Scope and Limits

Scalar variables are also *global* by default. In programming terms, a global variable is one that is available anywhere within the script or program. Global variables can be limited to specific areas in the program by other commands (such as my and local), which is something I will revisit when I discuss subroutines and separate program blocks in this evening's session, "Expressing and Stating." Programmers often refer to a variable's availability in a certain part of a script or program as its *scope*.

TIP Unlike other programming languages, such as Java or C, in Perl you do not need to declare variables before you use them. The first time you use a variable in a script, Perl automatically creates and assigns space for it. In many other programs, you need to list many of your variables initially, so the programming language can make sure to set aside space for them.

Realize, however, that many programmers consider it poor form to use variables before declaring them. Perl actually provides a special rule set called *Strict* that forces you to write code so that it is consistent with several standard program conventions, including declaring variables before using them. Strict is extremely useful, so I talk about it in Sunday evening's session (in the Perl Security section).

TABLE 2.3	**ARGUMENTS FOR THE SPRINTF FORMAT STRING COMMAND**
Argument	**Result**
%%	A percent sign
%c	A character
%d	A signed decimal integer
%e	A floating point number in scientific notation
%f	A floating point number
$o	An unsigned integer
%p	A pointer
%s	A string
%u	An unsigned integer
%x	An unsigned integer in hexadecimal

Using Operators

You can make more than one scalar assignment on a line of code. For instance, the following line takes the variable open and assigns it to shop4, which assigns it to shop3, which assigns it to shop2, and so on.

```
$shop1 = $shop2 = $shop3 = &shop4 = "open";
```

You can also use operators on scalars. I will go into more detail about operators in this afternoon's session, "Using Files and Perl Operations," but the following Perl script shows how you can use scalars to perform simple math for you.

Create a third Perl script in your Weekend folder and name it Math.pl.

Start editing and add the routine <> ending to the script. Then create two scalars and assign them numerical values.

```
$guitar = 10;
$piano = 20;
$dulcimer = 30;
$violin = 40;

# another print statement telling the reader what to do next
print "\nPress <ENTER> to continue...";

# Perl waits at these brackets for user input
<>
```

Now add some `print` statements so that Perl can print out these values for you. The complete code should look like this:

```
$guitar = 10;
$piano = 20;
$dulcimer = 30;
$violin = 40;

print "guitar is equal to $guitar\n";
print "piano is equal to $piano\n";
print "dulcimer is equal to $dulcimer\n";
print "violin is equal to $violin\n";

# another print statement telling the reader what to do next
print "Press <ENTER> to continue...";

# Perl waits at these brackets for user input
<>
```

Run this program, and you should see this output:

```
guitar is equal to 10
piano is equal to 20
dulcimer is equal to 30
```

```
violin is equal to 40
Press <ENTER> to continue
```

Now try some mathematical operators. Perl supports all sorts of mathematical symbols. The most common ones are the + sign for addition, – sign for subtraction, asterisk (*) for multiplication, and the backslash (/) for division. You can actually use these operators on your scalar assignment code line. Just add an operator to the last part of each scalar assignment and run the program again.

```
$guitar = 10 * 5;
$piano = 20 / 2;
$dulcimer = 30 + 5;
$violin = 40 - 15;
print "guitar is equal to $guitar\n";
print "piano is equal to $piano\n";
print "dulcimer is equal to $dulcimer\n";
print "violin is equal to $violin\n";

# another print statement telling the reader what to do next
print "Press <ENTER> to continue...";

# Perl waits at these brackets for user input
<>
```

When you run the program now, your output is very different:

```
guitar is equal to 50
piano is equal to 10
dulcimer is equal to 35
violin is equal to 25
Press <ENTER> to continue
```

Counting Systems Used in Perl

Perl has built-in support for all ranges of mathematics, including regular and ten base whole numbers (integers). I have mentioned that Perl also supports numbers with decimal places (*floating point*), scientific notation, and it also supports different counting systems including hexadecimal, octal, binary, and Boolean.

Different counting systems are simply mathematical systems that use a number other than ten as their base. This is an important concept for programming, so I will explore it a bit here.

For general purposes, mathematics uses a ten base counting system, consisting of digits 0 through 9. When you count upward, you start at one and go to nine. When you pass nine, you need to add another numerical place so that you can keep counting upward (9+1 becomes 10, 9+2 becomes 11, and so on).

Computers use a two base counting system (binary), consisting of only 1s and 0s that translate into actual physical switches that can be either on or off. When a computer counts upward, it starts at 0, hits 1, and then immediately needs to add another place so that it can continue to count. 1+1 becomes 00, 1+2 becomes 01, 1+3 becomes 000, 1+4 becomes 001, and so on.

Hexadecimal and octal counting systems are like the binary system, but they have different base numbers. Hexadecimal systems only go up through 16 (using the digits 0-9 and the letters A-F, and octal only goes up through 8 (using the digits 0-7). Boolean is a special case. In the Boolean system, a value is either true or false. In Perl, scalars are generally considered true in the Boolean sense if they hold a value. This means that a scalar is Boolean true unless it is empty (holds a blank space) or is assigned the number 0, in which case it is Boolean false. This all might seem obscure, but being able to use these different systems can make certain programming tricks much easier to implement. (For instance, the Boolean systems make it easy to perform loops, which you will see later in this chapter. You will start writing loops in this afternoon's session, "Using Files and Perl Operations.")

NOTE   Perl has a unique counting trick. If you place underscore characters (_) within number strings, Perl will ignore the underscores. For instance, the following two number values are identical to Perl:

```
$number = 1245000;
$number = 1_245_000;
```

This doesn't change the value of 1245000, but it does make the number much easier to read, particularly when trying to sort through dozens or hundreds of lines of numbers. I've included it here in case you happen to run into it, but also to show off some of Perl's flexibility. Remember, TMTOWTDI.

Exploring Lists

Lists are generally used as a programming convention to group things together. A list is simply a row of data elements. It can be composed of scalar variables or other constructs, such as arrays or hashes.

In Perl, lists are assigned just like scalar variables. You simply need to warn Perl that you are making a list instead of a scalar by adding parentheses around the different variables and their assignments. Writing a list is like assigning many variables at the same time.

Creating a List

To make a list, create a new Perl script and name it List.pl. You are going to set up a list of variables called `groceries`, where each item will have a number assignment attached to it. To create a list in Perl, you first include a list of scalars within a set of parentheses.

```
($apples $oranges, $grapes, $walnuts,)
```

Then, as if you were treating it like a scalar, you include the equal sign (=) so you can assign values to these scalars.

```
($apples $oranges, $grapes, $walnuts,) =
```

Finally, you assign values to these scalars, all within a second set of parentheses.

```
($apples $oranges, $grapes, $walnuts,) = (4.99, 3.99, 1.99, 12.99,);
```

You now possess a list of grocery items, each associated with a particular cost. The four numerical values will be assigned to the groceries in the same order.

You might have noticed the extra commas at the end of the assignments (after `walnuts` and `12.99`). This was done intentionally, but it isn't necessary. A common programming convention is to leave in the ending commas when setting up lists, so that you can save some typing time later when you're adding more items to the lists. The code would function just as well without the commas.

CAUTION

◆ ◆

One of the things that can be confusing about Perl is that it treats all data as either a scalar variable or a list based on the data's context. (This will become second nature to you as you become more familiar with Perl.) This means that if Perl is expecting a list, and you provide it with scalar values, it will treat those values like a list.

Some functions in Perl assume that you are always working with a list, and some assume that you are always working with a scalar. Learning how Perl treats a value, and whether Perl is assuming a scalar or list, is a skill that just takes time and practice with the language.

◆ ◆

You can print this list just as you would print a scalar. Add print lines to your new print code so the user can keep track of your values. Don't forget your standard ending <>.

```
($apples, $oranges, $grapes, $walnuts,) = (4.99, 3.99, 1.99,
    12.99,);

print "apples are worth $apples\n";
print "oranges are worth $oranges\n";
print "grapes are worth $grapes\n";
print "walnuts are worth $walnuts\n";



# another print statement telling the reader what to do next

print "Press <ENTER> to continue...";

# Perl waits at these brackets for user input
<>
```

Now run List.pl, and you will see that each scalar has been assigned its corresponding value, as shown in Figure 2.6

Assigning List Items

Instead of assigning multiple items to multiple scalars as in the previous example, you can assign a list of items to one scalar. In the following example, I take several verbs and assign them to the scalar action.

Figure 2.6

Perl displays the contents of a list.

```perl
$action = (run, throw, leap, jump,);
print $action;
# another print statement telling the reader what to do next

print "\nPress <ENTER> to continue...";

# Perl waits at these brackets for user input
<>
```

Code this example into a new file called Action.pl and run it. As you can see, the list does not seem to assign itself correctly, and the program only prints the last item (jump).

To print something other than the last entry in a list, you need to tell Perl to which entry you are referring. You can use brackets to change the reference Perl will use when it accesses the list. If you add brackets and the number 1 to the end of the first line, Perl will reference the value assigned to 1 instead of the last value in the list.

```perl
$action = (run, throw, leap, jump,)[1];
```

Run the program again and you should a DOS box, as shown in Figure 2.7.

But wait! Shouldn't the code be printing the first value (run) instead of the second value (throw)? Actually, the 1 value is correctly assigned to the text string throw. The text string run is referenced by the number 0. Remember that you are using a computer, which uses a different numbering system. Because the computer uses binary, it will almost always start counting with 0, then follow with 1. This is also true when dealing with lists, arrays, or hashes.

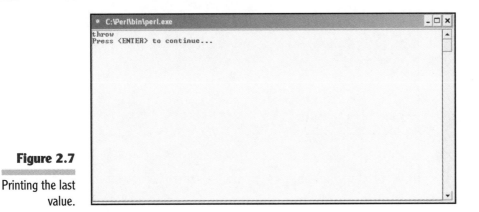

Figure 2.7

Printing the last
value.

Manipulating Lists

Now that you know how to create and print a list, you can focus on other
ways to use it. Lists are used most commonly to group items and then
manipulate those items as a whole. For instance, to sort the grocery list
from the smallest to the largest number, Perl uses the sort function.

Sort is often used in conjunction with the print function. The following
script prints several scalars, first without and then with the sort command,
and illustrate some of the power Perl can exercise on scalars and lists.

```perl
print (2,  4,  6, 9, 5, 8,);

print "\n";

print sort (2, 4, 6, 9, 5, 8,);

# another print statement telling the reader what to do next

print "Press <ENTER> to continue...";

# Perl waits at these brackets for user input
<>
```

Put these lines into a new Perl file called Sorter. Perl's sort command will
alphabetize automatically or put a list in numerical order, and in this
case, sort puts all of the numbers in the second print statement in
numerical order.

Because print can be unruly at times, lists are often a preferred way to work with text strings. Take this code example that prints a list of words:

```
# printing a list
print ("Why", "hello", "there",);
```

When run, the output isn't "Why hello there." Instead all of the words run together producing "Whyhellothere." Perl's built-in functions are capable of dealing with this. For a simple solution the command join can be used.

Perl's join surrounds each item in a list with a given expression, with the context:

```
join expression, list
```

In the preceding example, I want to join the three words together with spaces to make the print statement readable. I can use join to place the list items together with a space as the expression between them:

```
print join (" ", ("Why", "hello", "there",));
```

The join command will now print out the words joined by spaces, making the sentence readable. You can test this out by creating a new script called joinem.pl and compare the two print statements:

```
# printing a list
print ("Why", "hello", "there",);

# list printed and joined by spaces;
print join (" ", ("Why", "hello", "there",));

# Add our ending changed to user input
# standard ending
print "\nPress any key to continue...";
```

<>

You can actually put any character or group of characters in as an expression for the join command; for instance, you could join this list together with dashes:

```
print join ("--", ("Why", "hello", "there",));
```

Or you could join the list with phrases:

```
print join ("Go ahead and say:", ("Why", "hello", "there",));
```

The opposite of the join command is the split command. Whereas join takes a list and puts it into a string, split takes a string and converts it into a list. The common syntax for a split is:

```
split /pattern/, expression
```

Take the example from the preceding join command above:

```
print ("Why, hello, there,");
```

This line of code prints out Why, hello, there. The split command can be used to take out the commas and convert this string into a list:

```
print ((split " ", "Why, hello, there,"));
```

The backslashes / / section-off the three words into a list, and when printed you will see Why hello there on the screen without the commas. With split you can reference the string as a list and pull specific entries, like in this example where you print only the second word hello by using brackets and the number of the word in the list:

```
print ((split " ", "Why, hello, there,")[1]);
```

The entire source code for playing with split is also included as part of this chapter's downloads under the name splitting.pl:

```
# Before split
print ("Why, hello, there,");

# After split
print ((split /,/, "Why, hello, there,"));

# print only the second word
print ((split " ", "Why, hello, there,")[1]);

# Add our ending changed to user input
# standard ending
print "\nPress any key to continue...";

<>
```

Now, for a final example of list manipulation, look at Perl's `map` function. The `map` command enables you to make sweeping changes that affect every item in a list. The basic syntax for `map` is:

```
map {expression}, list
```

The expression is actually a block of code (more on blocks in this evening's session), but for the sake of illustration, I will keep things simple. Build a new Perl called mapping.pl, and create a list of numbers and then print them:

```
# create a list of numbers
print (1, 2, 3,);



# Add our ending changed to user input
# standard ending
print "\nPress any key to continue...";


<>
```

You could use `map` in this program to multiply each item in the list by 2 by making a small change to the print line:

```
print (map {2 * $_}1, 2, 3,);
```

This change asks Perl to take the input of each item in the list (represented by $_) and multiply the item by 2 (2 *). When you change the mapping.pl to:

```
# create a list of numbers
print (map {2 * $_}1, 2, 3,);



# Add our ending changed to user input
# standard ending
print "\nPress any key to continue...";


<>
```

Instead of seeing the output "123" you will see "246" instead.

Take a Break

You have waded through some extremely important and difficult topics, and you've really only just begun. Scalar values are used in almost every Perl program, so comprehension of this morning's material is extremely important. Go ahead a take a break; stand up, stretch, and meditate on your newfound knowledge. When you are ready, come back, and I will stray into Perl arrays and hashes.

Arrays and Hashes

All data in Perl are scalars of some sort. Scalars are marked by beginning with a dollar sign ($) and can contain numbers (called *variables*) or a sting of letters (called a *text string*). Scalars can also hold references. When a scalar is used as a reference, it usually points to an array or a hash.

In addition to the $, there are two other extremely important dereferencers in Perl. The first is the at sign (@), which tells Perl that whatever follows the sign is an array. The second important dereferencer is the percentage sign (%), which refers to a programming construct called a *hash*. Hashes and arrays are similar. They are both mechanisms for storing items or lists of items; they just keep track of the items in different ways.

What Are Arrays?

Arrays organize lists of items by a numeric index, which enables you to refer to an item by a number or numeric reference. Therefore, you might think arrays are very similar to lists in Perl. In many ways they are similar; however, there are subtle differences, such as in how they are initiated.

Initiating an Array

You assign an array just as you would make a list assignment. However, you begin the assignment with an @ instead of a $. If you wanted to build an array of numbers that are divisible by 10, you would initiate it this way:

```
@divisible = (10,20,30);
```

Perl reads this command and creates an entry called `divisible`, which now contains '102030'.

To use or reference one of the values in the divisible array, you need to use a dollar sign ($), brackets ([]), and a specific number. All entries within an array are considered to be scalars, which is why you need to use the $ to reference them. The brackets and the number tell Perl which entry you want to work with. Each entry in an array has a numeric reference that starts with 0 and counts upward. In the divisible array, the 10 is in slot 0, the 20 is in slot 1, and the 30 is in slot 2.

If you need to reference and print the number 30 in the divisible array, you could code it like this:

```
Print $divisible[2];
```

Translated into plain English, this line tells Perl to print the third scalar in the divisible data structure.

■ ■

You may have noticed that in the divisible array, Perl starts the array order at the number 0, just like when printing the list $action in the last section. This is typical for Perl and most programming languages. When counting, unless instructed to do differently, Perl starts counting with the number 0, then follows with the number 1, and then upwards depending on the counting system that has been specified. All of this counting starting with 0 might be difficult to keep in mind when you are first coding, but the switch will seem natural after you write a few lists or arrays.

Older distributions of Perl supported commands and switches that would always make Perl start counting with a 1 rather than a 0. These features have since been marked for removal from most distributions, although you may still run across the commands when dealing with legacy code. Although Perl strongly advocates TMTOWTDI, keep in mind that this particular way is no longer supported, so you might as well get used to coding arrays in which the count starts at 0.

■ ■

Arrays are considered to be extremely powerful for programmers. Because you can reference all items in an array with a number, arrays are great for handling loops (as you will see in this evening's session, "Expressing and Stating"). Perl also has numerous built-in commands used to manipulate, alter, change, and sort through data held within arrays. I look at some of these commands in upcoming sections, and you will use some of these commands to optimize code in the Sunday afternoon session.

Perl creates and allocates memory for arrays when you use them, just as it does for scalars, so you don't have to worry about setting aside memory yourself. Like scalars, arrays are also global in scope, and you can access them anywhere in the program unless they are localized. (I will cover localization in this evening's session.)

Writing Your First Array Script

Now that you have an overview of arrays, you can script one. Create a new Perl script and name it Profile.pl. Add the usual ending and initiate an array called `profile` with four text entries.

```
@profile = (Luca, second, upstairs,);
```

```
# another print statement telling the reader what to do next
print "\nPress <ENTER> to continue...";
```

```
# Perl waits at these brackets for user input
<>
```

Perl now has an array data structure that holds these three values. Now print those values and look at them. Add a `print` line following the `profile` array assignment and run the program.

```
# first print attempt
```

```
print @profile;
```

Not quite what you expected, right? Perl does print out the array, but it also strips out the white space between each letter, making it difficult to read. Perl strips the white space so that the arrays stay small and easy to reference. You will have to alter the code to get it to print in an orderly way, as shown in the following code.

```
# second print attempt
print "$profile[0]\n";
print "$profile[1]\n";
print "$profile[-1]\n";
```

You probably noticed that I used a -1 to reference upstairs in the last array. You can reference arrays using both positive and negative numbers. Negative numbers reference an array backwards. By using -1, you automatically reference the last item in the array, regardless of how long the array is. This is an extremely useful trick because you often will need to reference the last variable in an array.

Altogether the code should look like the following. (You can also grab the completed version, called luca array, from the companion Web site.):

```
@profile = (Luca, second, upstairs,);
# first print attempt
print @profile;

# second print attempt
print "$profile[0]\n";
print "$profile[1]\n";
print "$profile[-1]\n";



# another print statement telling the reader what to do next
print "\nPress <ENTER> to continue...";

# Perl waits at these brackets for user input
<>
```

Common Array Commands

Perl contains many supporting commands that help programmers manipulate their arrays. For instance, arrays enable programmers to add and remove entries easily. You can add to an array using the Perl command called push, which I use in the following script:

```
@gimmeanh = ( n, n, n,);

# Print out the gimmeanh array before the push
print "$gimmeanh[0]\n";
```

```
print "$gimmeanh[1]\n";
print "$gimmeanh[-1]\n\n";


# use the Push command to add an h


push (@gimmeanh, "h");


# Print out the array with the h included
print "$gimmeanh[0]\n";
print "$gimmeanh[1]\n";
print "$gimmeanh[-1]\n\n";



# another print statement telling the reader what to do next
print "\nPress <ENTER> to continue...";


# Perl waits at these brackets for user input
<>
```

Most of this script contains print lines, but pay attention to the line with push. You can see that push is given the name of an array, a comma, and then scalar value to add to the array, all contained in nice, neat parentheses.

Perl also has a command that removes the last item of an array called pop. The syntax that pop uses is similar to the push syntax; you simply need to give pop the array name in a pair of parentheses. By adding the following lines of code to the push example, you can remove the h after placing it in the array with push.

```
# use pop to remove the h
pop (@gimmeanh);
print "$gimmeanh[0]\n";
print "$gimmeanh[1]\n";
print "$gimmeanh[-1]\n\n";
```

When you use pop, you do not need to specify a scalar value; pop automatically removes the last entry in the array regardless of which value is there. If you have trouble running this script yourself, this example is also downloadable from the companion Web site. The entire source code for the script is as follows (for practice write it out and save it as pushpop.pl):

```
@gimmeanh = ( n, n, n,);


# Print out the gimmeanh array before the push
print "$gimmeanh[0]\n";
print "$gimmeanh[1]\n";
print "$gimmeanh[-1]\n\n";


# use the Push command to add an h

push (@gimmeanh, "h");

# Print out the array with the h included
print "$gimmeanh[0]\n";
print "$gimmeanh[1]\n";
print "$gimmeanh[-1]\n\n";


# use pop to remove the h
pop (@gimmeanh);
print "$gimmeanh[0]\n";
print "$gimmeanh[1]\n";
print "$gimmeanh[-1]\n\n";


# another print statement telling the reader what to do next
print "\nPress <ENTER> to continue...";

# Perl waits at these brackets for user input
<>
```

Corresponding commands are used to add and subtract from the beginning of an array. The `shift` command adds a new entry at the numeric reference 0, and the `unshift` command takes away the value at entry 0. The following code adds the text string `bestseller` to the array `weekend`, and then removes it. You can see this is exactly opposite of what `push` and `pop` do when they manipulate the end of an array.

```
shift (@weekend, "bestseller");
Unshift (@weekend);
```

You can find the length of an array by referencing the last index or item within the array. In any given @array the expression $#array holds the index to the last value. If you needed to print out the number of elements in the @array:

```
@array = (2, 4, 6, 8,);
```

You could use this code:

```
print "The array has ($#array) plus one elements";
```

Notice how you need to add one to $#array, simply because Perl always starts counting at 0.

Because the $#array expression holds the last element index of a given array, you can change the size of an array by manipulating the $#array expression directly. One example of this is that you can increment $#array instead of utilizing the pop command. The following line of code makes @array a ten-element array:

```
#Change the index of @array to ten
$#array = 10;
```

You can also completely clear the @array by setting $#array to -1:

```
# Wipe the array completely
$#array = -1;
```

Code that runs through using $#array is listed in its entirety as sizearray.pl and also follows:

```
# create an array
@array = (2, 4, 6, 8,);

# print the last index of the array
print "The array has ($#array) plus one elements\n";

#Change the index of @array to ten
$#array = 10;

# print the last index of the array
```

```
print "The array has ($#array) plus one elements\n";

# Wipe the array completely
$#array = -1;

# print the last index of the array
print "The array has ($#array) plus one elements\n";

# Add our ending changed to user input
# standard ending
print "\nPress any key to continue...";

<>
```

Merging arrays is another common programming endeavor, especially when combining two different lists or databases. Merging arrays is as easy as assigning them. Create a new Perl file called mergeme.pl and create two separate arrays:

```
# create an array
@array1 = (2, 4, 6, 8,);

# create a second array
@array2 = (1, 3, 5, 7, 9,);
```

Merging two arrays together is accomplished by creating a third array with the first two arrays assigned to it:

```
# Merge the first two arrays into @array3
@array3 = (@array1, @array2);
```

Perl automatically flattens out the two arrays into one long workable new array. All you need to finish mergeme.pl is a print statement proving that the array contains all the elements. (This code is also available on the Web site.)

```
 # create an array
@array1 = (2, 4, 6, 8,);

# create a second array
```

```
@array2 = (1, 3, 5, 7, 9,);

# Merge the first two arrays into @array3
@array3 = (@array1, @array2);

# print the array as proof it works
print @array3;

# Add our ending changed to user input
# standard ending
print "\nPress any key to continue...";


<>
```

How about splitting up an array into more than one piece? Perl has a few built-in commands to help you pull sections or parts of an array to work with. Say you have a large array initialized within a new Perl script called slicing.pl:

```
# create a array
@array1 = (a, e, i, o, u, b, c, d, e, f,);
```

If you want to work only with the first half of the array, you can slice out the vowels using brackets []. The following script slices the first four elements of @array1 and assigns then to @array2:

```
@array2 = @array1[0, 1, 2, 3,];
```

Add a few print lines to slicing.pl to show that the program is working, and you will have a full source code listing like the one that follows. (This source code is also available on the companion Web site.)

```
 # create an array
@array1 = (a, e, i, o, u, b, c, d, e, f,);

#print out the array
print "@array1\n";

# slice the first five elements of @array1 and assign them to
  @array2
```

```
@array2 = @array1[0, 1, 2, 3,];
```

```
#print out @array2
print "@array2\n";
```

```
# Add our ending changed to user input
# standard ending
print "\nPress any key to continue...";
```

The final Perl array command I want to review in this section is the splice command. The splice command may be the most widely used array command in Perl because it is capable of replacing elements within an array and adding elements to an array. The syntax for splice looks like this:

```
splice (array, element, length, list)
```

The splice command will add the elements within the list to the given array. (Splice begins adding these items at element for the given length.) To illustrate splice, create a new Perl file called splicing.pl. Create an array of letters like the slicing.pl example and have the script print out the array:

```
# create an array
@array = (a, e, i, o, u, b, c, d, e, f,);
```

```
#print out the array
print "@array\n";
```

Now you need to fill in the gaps for the splice syntax. You already know the name of the array:

```
splice (@array, element, length, list);
```

Start the splicing at the fifth element, which is the consonant b:

```
splice (@array, 5, length, list);
```

You will replace all the consonants with vowels, so the length has to reach the end of the array, or five elements:

```
splice (@array, 5, 5, list);
```

Finally, include a list of vowels within another set of parentheses, and your finished splice line is ready:

```
splice (@array, 5, 5, (a, e, I, o, u,));
```

Add a second print line and the waiting brackets at the end of the code, and you have a finished example exemplifying the splice command, listed as full source here and also available as part of this chapter's online downloads:

```
# create an array
@array = (a, e, i, o, u, b, c, d, e, f,);

#print out the array
print "@array\n";

# splice the consonant with more vowels
splice (@array, 5, 5, (a, e, i, o, u,));

#print out @array2
print "@array\n";

# Add our ending changed to user input
# standard ending
print "\nPress any key to continue...";

<>
```

Perl has many commands that work with arrays to enable you to sort, mix, match, append, splice, loop, grow, shrink, and merge them. I cover many of these terms as you progress through the book, but it would be impossible to address all of them in one weekend. I spend some time covering how to optimize Perl code in the Sunday afternoon session, and in the Sunday Evening session, I discuss many of the more advanced features of Perl and point you to some resources where you can learn more about utilizing Perl arrays. In this next section, I outline a few of the quick tricks you can employ to make array assigning and manipulation a snap in Perl.

Array Shortcuts

Because it can be troublesome to write-in every single entry for a large array, there are a number of nifty shortcuts in Perl for filling arrays. One such shortcut is the *multiplier*, which gets more coverage in the Saturday

Afternoon session where I talk about Perl operations. It is fairly simple to use, as you can see from the following code line.

```
@array = (10) x 100;
```

Perl reads the code and creates the `@array`. When Perl is finished, the `@array` will hold 100 separate entries, all of which are the number 10. Perl interprets the x 100 multiplier to mean that the programmer needs 100 different entries, all with 10 contained within.

You can also have use dashes (-) to determine a range in the alphabet or in a number sequence. The following line creates an array filled with numbers starting with 10 and going through the number 200.

```
@array = (10-200);
```

The next line creates an array filled with letters starting with the lowercase a and going through the lowercase f.

```
@array = (a-f);
```

Perl can also determine the range you are trying to imply by using the .. notation. For instance, in the following line of code, Perl will use pattern matching to fill in the ranges and count by twos. (Pretty smart, eh?)

```
@array = (2, 4, 6, .., 12);
```

Another quick trick is the reverse command, which enables you to reverse the contents of a given array:

```
# this array goes 123
@array1 = (1,2,3,);


# this array goes 321
@array2 = reverse @array1;
```

Finally, one more shortcut you will see often in written code is the `qw` shortcut, which defeats the need to include quotation marks in your array assignments.

```
@textarray = (
    "first", "second", "third", "fourth", "etc"
    );
```

If you include qw in the previous array assignment, you can skip typing all the quotation marks. Instead, your array assignment will look like this:

```
@textarray = qw(first second third fourth etc);
```

What Are Hashes?

Hashes work just like arrays, except that you use a name or text string to reference the items within them. Because of this, hashes are sometimes called *associative arrays*. This means that instead of referencing what is in an array by a numerical value like so:

```
print "$arrayvalue[1]";
```

You would use a text string to refer to the items in the array:

```
print "$arrayvalue{'valuenumberone'}";
```

At first, you may think that hashes look like more programming work because you need to include an actual name instead of a number, and you may be right. Hashes are mainly used to help bridge the understanding gap between human and machine. For example, instead of organizing a list of employee information by numbers in an array (employee[1], employee[2], employee[3], employee[4]), you can refer to them by name in a hash (employee[Tom], employee[Bob], employee[Roy], employee[Jason]).

Initiating a Hash

You initiate a hash the same way you initiate an array, except you also include a *key*, which is the word association. The general structure is

```
$hash{'key'} = 'values in the hash';
```

I used braces ({ }) instead of brackets ([ ]). I also used $ and single quotes instead of @ and parentheses.

To turn the profile array into a hash with the key name and the entry Luca, you would change the code around like this:

```
$profile{'name'} = 'Luca';
```

Referencing a hash is also similar to referencing an array. The following code prints Luca on the screen.

```
print "$profile{'name'}";
```

The entire Luca.pl file should look like this when finished (and is also available for download on the companion Web site):

```
$profile{'name'} = 'Luca';

print "$profile{'name'}";

# another print statement telling the reader what to do next
print "\nPress <ENTER> to continue...";

# Perl waits at these brackets for user input
<>
```

What if you want more than one value in your hash? Well, the normal prefix dereferencer is the percentage sign (%). Assigning a large group for references (for example, a record collection) to a hash works something like this:

```
%album = (
    'II'                ,       'Led Zeppelin',
    'Unforgettable'     ,       'Natalie Cole',
    'Fundamentals'      ,       'DTCFE',
    'White Ladder'      ,       'David Gray',
);
```

You now have several album names that each reference the artist. This is a simple example where hashes are used.

Hashes are considered more intuitive than arrays because using a text name or key is sometimes easier to conceptualize than using a number. For example, referencing $10 to weeklyallowance is easier than referencing it to some random number.

Unlike in arrays, Perl doesn't necessarily store the entries in a hash in order. For example, if you attempt to print out the album hash using the following code you might find that you do not get the entries in the order that you created them.

```
# assign hash
%album = (
        'II'        ,       'Led Zeppelin',
        'Unforgettable'         ,       'Natalie Cole',
```

```
        'Fundamentals'      ,      'DTCFE',
        'White Ladder'      ,      'David Gray',
        );
```

```
# print out hash
print %album;
```

```
# another print statement telling the reader what to do next
print "\nPress <ENTER> to continue...";
```

```
# Perl waits at these brackets for user input
<>
```

Perl automatically mixes and moves hash entries around to make it easier and quicker for both the computer and the program to store and reference them.

Hashes, like arrays, have many commands associated with them, only some of which I will cover this weekend. An important hash for Perl is the %ENV hash.

What the Heck Is the %ENV Hash?

You may not believe this but hashes already exist on your computer. The %ENV hash is used to store common computer environmental variables. Environmental variables answer questions, such as *"What operating system am I using?" "Which Disk Drive is the CD on?" "What is the Computer Network name?"* and *"Which user is currently using me?"* The information that is actually accessible varies greatly depending on the operating system and the computer, but in this section I will try to pull some information about Windows XP to personalize the script just a little bit.

First, use the print function and the %ENV hash to pull the computer user's account name. Create new Perl script and name it environment.pl. To get and print the user name, type this code:

```
print "Hello, $ENV{USERDOMAIN}.\n";
```

Notice that we are using $ENV to pull information from the %ENV hash. Although we are accessing the %ENV hash, this script only uses scalar $ dereferencers. You only need the percentage sign % when you are creating or pushing values into a hash. You need to use the $ dereferencers to pull the information.

The standard print line uses the scalar symbol to reference the hash value associated with USERDOMAIN within the %ENV hash. Add the standard ending to the code and run this example to make sure it works.

Now add another print line to the code to add the operating system call. The full source code follows, and the output when you run the command on my machine is shown in Figure 2.8.

```
print "Hello, $ENV{USERDOMAIN}.\n";

print "Your Operating System is $ENV{OS}\n";

# another print statement telling the reader what to do next
print "\nPress <ENTER> to continue...";

# Perl waits at these brackets for user input
<>
```

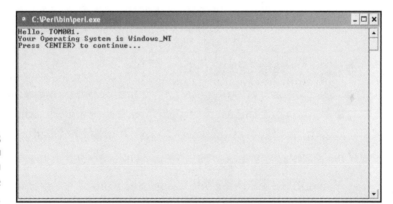

Figure 2.8

Getting information
from the
%ENV hash.

The %ENV hash is designed to hold basic information about your computer; you will use it in future code examples to get the information you need about the computing environment. This code sample is available on the Web site as Environment.pl.

Retrieving User Input

One thing you must do is learn to take input from the keyboard or a user. It is extremely difficult to create useful programs without some sort of interaction. The bases of this interaction in Perl are STDIN (*standard in*) and STDOUT (*standard out*).

Standard In and Standard Out

STDIN is the normal default pipe or channel to accept input, and STDOUT is the default pipe or channel that Perl uses to send information out. STDIN and STDOUT are typically used to pipe or send information from a keyboard to a command (STDIN) or from a command to a monitor screen (STOUT). STDIN is normally typed from the keyboard, and STDOUT is generally printed to the screen.

The chomp command is often used with STDIN and STDOUT. Chomp is used to gather user input because it removes, or "chomps off," the last character given by a user in STDIN. Perl is set to automatically recognize and feed carriage returns or new line escape sequences when reading STDIN, so if you don't cut off the last character, you end up with a \n at the end of each string you pick up.

Using Chomp with Standard In

To get a better grip on chomp, try a simple program that takes input from a user to record the user's name. Create a new Perl script and add a print statement that asks the user to type in his or her name.

```
Print "Please type in your name";
```

Now add the following line, using chomp and STDIN after the print statement.

```
chomp($name=<STDIN>);
```

And finally, add a line to print the input.

```
print "\nYour name is $name\n";
```

The scalar value $name will now hold the name entered by the person typing. Save the whole source code as Name1.pl. (You can check our Web site for the script if you encounter difficulties.)

```
# ask for user input
```

```
print "Please type in your name\n";

# chomp grabs stdin, places stdin into name
chomp($name=<STDIN>);

# print out the input
print "\nYour name is $name\n";

# another print statement telling the reader what to do next
print "\nPress <ENTER> to continue...";

# Perl waits at these brackets for user input
<>
```

You can also use STDIN and STDOUT to mimic a typewriter or word processor by retrieving any key press of the keyboard using STDIN and printing out all key presses to the monitor screen by using STDOUT.

```
print STDOUT "Print text here. Enter blank space to quit.\n";
while ($input = <STDIN>) {
print STDOUT "$input \n";
if ($input eq ' '){ print STDERR "Null Input\n"; }
print STDOUT "Continue typing or close to window to end\n";
```

This might be the most complex program you've written so far. It uses a while loop, which I don't even cover until this evening, so don't be worried if the code looks confusing at first.

The first line is a simple print statement; the second is the while loop. Basically, the while loop accepts STDIN and puts it into $input. While it does that, it executes whatever is in the curly brackets ({ }).

NOTE You might have noticed that STDIN and STDOUT are different than the other commands so far. They are the first commands I have covered that are uppercase. As I mentioned earlier, almost all Perl commands are in lowercase letters.

The code in the braces takes $input (what is entered) and prints it to the screen using print, unless nothing is entered. The possibility of nothing being entered is represented by the if statement, which I will discuss in more detail in this afternoon's session, "Using Files and Perl Operations." If there is null input, use STDERR (*Standard Error*), which is also covered in more detail in the Sunday Evening session to throw a message and ask the user if they want to quit.

Again, some of the preceding code might seem confusing because I have not gone over it in depth yet. The two important things to notice from the preceding code are

➤ Using print STDOUT is the same as telling Perl to print text because when you use the print command, Perl automatically assumes that you are using STDOUT.

➤ STDIN and STDOUT are the defaults for getting text from the keyboard to the screen.

Using Other Methods to Accept User Input

Following the concept of TIMTOWTDI, Perl has many ways to accept user input. Another common command used to get input from a user is the readline command. Readline is part of the ReadKey module. (Modules are discussed at length in Sunday Morning's session.) However, because it is a commonly used command for input, I am including it here for reference. The syntax is slightly different than the syntax for chomp.

```
$name readline(*STDIN);
```

You can substitute this line directly for chomp, and the script will function exactly the same as long as the user doesn't type in a name that takes up more than one line.

One last common Perl input command is the getc (*get character*) command. It can be used just like the readline or chomp commands, and it also uses STDIN. The only difference is that getc retrieves only one character at a time. You will get a closer look at getc in the next session, "Using Files and Perl Operations."

Storing Information within a Program

Perl has great support for storing text and input to files. It also has two tokens that allow you to store files within an actual running program.

If you insert the token __DATA__ or __END__ into a program file, Perl will not read past those lines when reading the code. Instead, Perl differentiates the data that follows the token as belonging to a separate section and assumes that it will be used by the running program as input. The following code uses a while loop to take in <DATA> and print it. When Perl sees the <DATA> marker, it automatically moves to the end of the script and picks up the text or variables that lie underneath __DATA__ or __END__.

```
While (<DATA>) {
     Print;
}
__DATA__
Text
```

Or:

```
While (<DATA>) {
     Print;
}
__END__
Text
```

In these two examples, Perl will simply print Text.

Program Block

You have covered an incredible amount this morning, and now there are several new Perl pieces you can use to start putting the Trapped game into action. If you look back at the program block from last night, you can see that there are a couple of essential elements that the game needs that we covered this morning, including:

➤ Code that prints information to the screen (print).

➤ Code that takes information from the keyboard(STDIN).

I also introduced the concept of scalars and variables, which can be used in a computer game to keep track of simple values such as health, statistics, speed, direction, rounds of ammunition left, or a number of other game concepts. To add some interest, but also keeping in mind not to add too much complexity, you add a few simple scalars, namely; health, amount of food. Open up the block1.pl we started last night, resave the file as block2.pl, and add these three scalar values somewhere after the commented lines:

```
# Assign Variables
$direction = North;
$food = 10;
$health = 10;
```

The 10 values and North are just starting points; you can play with these later. The next problem to tackle is printing information to the screen. The information given to the player and how it is presented is extremely important for the enjoyment of most games. In Trapped, print out the value of each scalar so the player can keep track of what is going on. This works out to a number of different print statements, spaced out with the new line characters (/n) to make an easy read:

```
print "\n";
print "You are trapped in a cavern\n";
print "You can travel North, South, East, or West";
print "\n\n\n";
print "You are facing $direction\n";
print "You have $food boxes of ramen left\n";
print "Your health is equal to $health\n";
print "\n\n\n";
```

The last thing to cover is user input. At this point the game isn't fleshed out enough to see what user input will actually do, but you can use the standard ending (the STDIN line at the end of each sample program) as a marker for where the user will be pressing keys to make game decisions. Add the STDIN brackets <> and modify the print statement to let the user know that the program expects something:

```
# Add our ending changed to user input
# standard ending
print "\nPress anykey to continue...";

<>
```

And program block 2 is finished. Nothing incredibly fancy, and all using techniques you picked up over the last few hours, but you can see a computer game starting to form. Make sure to add comments like those listed in the following full source code, so that when you revisit this code block in tomorrow morning's session, you will remember what you added. Now that the code actually acts like a program, you may want to try it a few times and work out any kinks.

```
###########################################
#Trapped
###########################################

###########################################
# block1- planning
# What I need:
# Code that prints information to the screen.
# Code that takes information from the keyboard.
# Code that times the display of text/information
# Code that generates a random map
# Code that tracks the player's progress on the map

###############################################
# block 2 - Basic needs.
# We have learned printing information to the screen and
# Taking information from the keyboard and
# Creating scalar variables and
# a standard ending to keep the dos prompt open.
#Initial print action

# Assign Variables

$direction = North;
$food = 10;
$health = 10;

print "\n";
```

```
print "You are trapped in a cavern\n";
print "You can travel North, South, East, or West\n";
print "\n\n\n";
print "You are facing $direction\n";
print "You have $food boxes of ramen left\n";
print "Your health is equal to $health\n";
print "\n\n\n";

# Add our ending changed to user input
# standard ending
print "\nPress anykey to continue...";

<>
```

Summary

You have come a long way since yesterday evening, and now you have a good basis for getting input from both the user and the environment. You now know how to store data in scalars, arrays, hashes, lists, and scripts. Treat yourself to a nice late breakfast or early lunch. When you return, we will focus on Perl math and operators.

Using Files and Perl Operations

- ➤ Handling files
- ➤ Using directories
- ➤ Using mathematical operations

t's Saturday afternoon. By now, the sun is out, you've finished your morning pot of coffee, had a bite of lunch, and you are wide awake and enthusiastic. By the end of today, you will have covered the most important Perl programming components. You are already comfortable with arrays and hashes, which are the basic constructs in Perl. In this chapter, you'll learn how to use files and operators—the second step in determining how Perl works its magic.

Handling Files

Much of Perl's language revolves around altering files. Perl was built around altering text and text files, and you will use these skills later in the book and in programming in general.

You probably understand the fundamentals of file handling. In Perl and in most other programming languages, you use a file in a program by opening it and then creating a file handle that corresponds to it. You can then use the file handle when running operations on the file.

The most commonly used files are text files, and the most common Perl file operations are the ones that read and write lines in text files. You have already used `print` a number of times to write lines on a DOS prompt; using `print` to write to a file isn't much different. In this chapter, you will be using `print` to write lines of text and other data to files.

NOTE

●●●●●●●●●●●●●●●●●●●●●●●●●●●●●●●●●●●●●●

This chapter covers file operations using the most common Perl methods. True to form and the Perl motto ("There Is More Than One Way to Do It"), there are alternative ways of manipulating files. One method that you will likely see is using the Perl IO (input/output) module, which is discussed in the Sunday Evening session, "Learning Advanced Perl Techniques."

●●●●●●●●●●●●●●●●●●●●●●●●●●●●●●●●●●●●●●

The main purpose of files is to store information or data. Scalars, arrays, and hashes all disappear when your Perl program has finished running. Files enable programs to leave lasting legacies.

Perl doesn't really care how a file is structured because it always handles files in the same way. No matter how the file is organized or recorded, Perl can work with it by using file handlers.

Using File Handlers

File handlers are program references to a specific file. They are set up and used in much the same way as scalars. The difference is that when you set up a file handle, you are creating a channel, or a conduit, into a specific file. You can then use that channel to read from the file, send input or output, and run operations on the file.

To set up and close file handles, you use the open and close Perl commands. For example, if you want to create a Perl script that opens the new.txt file, follow these steps:

1. Use the open command to create a file handle to new.txt.

2. Write an or die statement in case the file cannot be opened.

3. When you are finished running operations on a file, you need to close it so that other computer operations can use it. (For example, if Perl had a document open, and then you opened the same document with a word processor, the file could corrupt, or your computer could crash.) You close a file using the close command.

4. Write an or die statement in case the file cannot be closed.

The following Perl code illustrates these steps.

```
open (HANDLE, "<new.txt") or die "Cannot open new.txt";
close (HANDLE) or die "Cannot close new.txt";
```

TIP   Using all uppercase letters when creating a file handle is an optional programming convention used to differentiate the handles from the rest of the Perl commands and script.

The first step in this program is fairly straightforward. The open command takes two parameters contained within parenthesis. The first parameter is the name of the file handle. The second parameter is the mode of access. This is symbolized by the prefix <. There are many different prefixes you can use; some of the most common ones are summarized in Table 3.1. There are also other modes; see the Sunday Evening session, "Learning Advanced Perl Techniques," for more in-depth coverage of open file modes.

In the preceding example, Perl opens the file so that it can accept input if necessary.

TABLE 3.1   OPEN MODE PARAMETERS

Symbol	Mode Explanation
< or none	Opens the file for input
>	Truncates the file and opens it for output
>>	Opens the file for appending or adding
+<	Opens the file for reading and allows write access to the file
+>	Truncates the file and allows write access

The second and third steps are extremely important. The `or die` command is a Perl statement that causes an exit.. The text `Cannot open new.txt` is then fed as a standard error message by the `or die` command, and the message prints to the screen (or whichever device is listening to STDOUT, in this case, the DOS prompt). The `or die` command exits only out of the loop or current command that is running, in this case the `open` file command. Alternatively, you could write that line using the Perl `exit` command, which would exit not only the current loop or command operating, but the entire Perl program:

```
open (HANDLE, "<new.txt") or exit;
```

The third step in this program is the `close` command, which is also very important. When you are working with files, and you want to open them, do what you need to and then quickly close them again. File handling is responsible for a large chunk of programming errors; if you lessen the time you have the file open, you can lower the chance that a programming error will occur.

File handling errors most often happen when multiple programs or processes try to open or change the same file at the same time. Suppose your Perl script opens a large file, such as a log file from a Web server, and deletes records from it. At around the same time, imagine that another program accesses the same log file and tries to write a new entry to it. If you both have the log file open, it might corrupt. This situation could also cause one or both programs to stall or freeze.

Perl has a locking command to help prevent this all-too-common condition from occurring. This command is called `flock` (short for *file lock*) and it gives the Perl program exclusive access to a file, which prevents other programs or processes from interfering or causing errors while you are using the specific file. The syntax of the `flock` command is similar to the syntax of the `open` command. To add `flock` to the code you have already written, you need to include two new lines:

```
open (HANDLE, "<new.txt") or die "Cannot open new.txt";
flock (HANDLE, LOCK_EX) or die "Cannot lock new.txt";
flock (HANDLE, LOCK_UN) or die "Cannot unlock new.txt";
close (HANDLE) or die "Cannot close new.txt";
```

CAUTION On UNIX-based systems, `flock` is a recommended precaution; on Windows systems, it is necessary if you are going to open and alter any files. The `flock` command is also frequently used by certain dynamic Web pages where more than one user can make changes. Internet chat rooms are one good example of multiple users trying to access the same file.

File handling can be extremely error prone. Some programmers even say that file operations are the most error-prone area of programming. In a complex operating system like Windows, this is often the case. When programming file operations, it's usually a good idea to keep the file open for as little time as possible and then close it immediately afterward.

Because file handling can be error prone, I use the `to die` command frequently in this chapter. `To die` is an escape that gives the Perl program a way out in case something goes wrong when another program, process, or user is also trying to access the same file.

Running File Tests

Perl has several file test operators that help it deal with files in a program. These tests cover simple operations, such as checking to see whether a file exists, checking to ensure readability of files, or checking to see whether Perl can write to a specific file. These operations help your program to be error free by checking to see whether certain actions are possible before actually running them. Common file test operators are listed in Table 3.2. Many of the operators listed in table 3.2 refer to Perl functionality that we haven't covered, so do not be concerned if some of them seem puzzling.

For Perl to utilize these statements, you must add a statement to the script. I'll cover statements in detail this evening, but without some sort of program logic you would have a difficult time using these tests. One simple way of utilizing them is to use an `if then` statement.

To get an understanding of how the `if then` statements work, imagine a math problem and read it aloud: If (condition is true), then (do this). In the following code example, I use an `if then` statement to see whether a file exists and is readable and writeable.

```
if (-erw new.txt)
    then {
    open (HANDLE, new.txt)
    }
```

TABLE 3.2 FILE TEST OPERATORS

Test Operator	Action
-r	Checks to see whether the file is readable (based on user permissions only)
-w	Checks to see whether the file is writeable (based on user permissions only)
-x	Checks to see whether the file is executable (based on user permissions only)
-e	Checks to see whether the file exists
-f	Checks to see whether the file is a plain file
-d	Checks to see whether the file is a directory
-o	Checks if file is owned by the user.
-z	Checks the file to see if it has a zero size.
-s	Returns the size of the file if non-zero
-l	Checks to see if the file is a symbolic link
-p	Checks to see if the file is a named pipe
-b	Checks if the file is a block special file.
-c	Checks if the file is a character special file.
-u	Checks to see if the file has setuid bit set.
-g	Checks to see if the file has setgid bit set.
-k	Checks to see if the file has sticky bit set.

TABLE 3.2 (CONTINUED)	

Test Operator	Action
-t	Checks if the filehandle is opened to a tty.
-R	Checks to see whether the file is readable
-S	Checks whether the file is a socket.
-W	Checks to see whether the file is writeable
-X	Checks to see whether the file is executable
-O	Checks if file is owned
-B	Checks to see whether the file is a binary file
-A	Checks the time since the file was last accessed
-T	Checks if the file is a text file.
-M	Gives the age of file in days when script started.
-C	Same for inode change time.

Perl goes through a few steps when running through this code.

1. Perl sees the `if` statement and checks the validity of the condition that is in the parentheses (-erw new.txt).

2. If the condition is true, Perl executes the code that is in the braces after the `then` statement.

3. If the condition is false, Perl skips the code that is in the braces.

Implementing File Permissions

Perl was originally built in a UNIX environment and it normally uses UNIX-style commands to change permissions. Windows, however, uses a completely different type of permission system than UNIX does, which makes Perl permissions difficult to implement.

CAUTION There are a number of original Perl commands that do not port over to Windows very well. The ActivePerl documentation installed on your computer is located by default in C:\Perl\Documents. This documentation discusses these porting problems. In the Sunday Evening session, "Learning Advanced Perl Techniques," I have included a section on Windows and Unix compatibility which discusses techniques you can use to keep your Perl code as portable as possible to both systems.

The bottom line for file permissions is that trouble can result if your Perl program tries to access or alter a file for which it doesn't have permission. This could cause your program to stall, corrupt, or crash.

Ultimately, your computer file system controls file permissions. If you use a Perl program on your machine to open a common file, there is no guarantee that the same program will be able to open that file on a different machine. To ensure that you can work with certain files in Perl, you might need to check or alter the file permissions.

The chmod command normally is used by Perl to alter the permissions of a file. This command generally has the ability to allow or disallow read or write access. (Remember, the file system has the real authority here.)

NOTE On UNIX systems, you normally have the option to change read, write, and execute permissions for a file. I have left the execute option out of this session because the Windows operating system determines a file's ability to execute by its extension. For instance, new.pl and new.exe are executable, whereas new.txt and new.doc are not. Since Windows isn't able to change the executable permission for a file using chmod, I do not discuss executable permissions in this section. However, you will revisit permissions in the Sunday Evening session, "Learning Advanced Perl Techniques." In that session, I will discuss porting programs to UNIX and other operating systems.

Read access to a file refers to the user's ability to look at the file. This book is a good example of read access. You can look at the sentences and read the content, but you cannot alter the content. Write access refers to the user's ability to alter a file. Looking at the contents of this book in a word-processing program would be similar to having write access. Then, you would have the ability to change sentence structure, add pictures, or make any other changes you want.

You can use chmod to change an owner's read or write access to a file. To do so, follow these steps:

1. Call chmod in the same way you would call open or flock.

2. Specify the mode to which you want to change the file.

3. List the file or group of files for which you want to change the permissions.

A code example of using chmod looks like this:

```
chmod (0644, new.txt);
```

The chmod command is similar to the other file-handling commands you have looked at in this section (for example open and close) except for the four-digit number used for input). The 0644 is a mode argument, which is a code for Perl to assign permissions in a specific way. In this case, 0644 tells Perl to assign read and write permissions to the owner of new.txt and that anyone else should have read permissions only for the new.txt file.

The chmod command uses an octal counting system to keep track of permissions. You learned about octal, a counting system that has only the numbers 0-7, earlier in this morning's session. There are four places in the octal code. The first place holds a 0 and tells Perl which counting system to use—in this case, octal. The second place, which holds a 6, refers to the owner of the file. The third place, which holds a 4, refers to group permissions. The last place, which holds another 4, refers to any other permissions. All permissions in chmod can be assigned in this way, using a four-digit number that represents the counting system, owner, group, and other.

On a UNIX system, there are eight basic permission sets, which correspond to octal counting quite nicely. These permission sets are outlined in Table 3.3. In the string 0644, the 6 stands for read and write permissions, and the 4 stands for read permissions. To summarize, the mode 0644 tells Perl (in octal) that the owner of the file has read and write privileges, and everyone else has read privileges.

Because Windows is significantly different than UNIX in terms of permissions, the only numbers Windows will assign in a chmod mode are 4 and 6. The other permissions are covered by the Windows operating system in other ways. (You'll learn more about this in the Sunday Evening session, "Learning Advanced Perl Techniques.")

Common File Commands

Now that you understand the basics of using files, you are going to write code using some of the more common Perl file functions. Built to play with and modify text, Perl contains dozens of built-in commands for manipulating

TABLE 3.3   ASSIGNING OCTAL PERMISSIONS WITH chmod

Octal Number	Access Given
0	None
1	Right to execute
2	Write access
3	Execute and write access
4	Read access*
5	Read and execute access
6	Read and write access*
7	Read, write, and execute access

These permissions are available to be used in the Windows version of chmod; the rest of the permissions are for UNIX-type file systems.

files. A couple of the more common ones we look at here, and a few others we look at in Sunday Afternoon's session, "Putting It All Together."

Using the getc Command

One common command for retrieving characters from a file in Perl is getc (get character). The getc command is similar to the chomp command that you learned about this morning. The main difference between them is that getc only grabs one character at a time. The following code uses getc to grab the first character from a file.

```
$onecharacter = getc (HANDLE);
print $onecharacter
```

Retrieving just one character from a file might not seem useful, but getc is usually combined with a loop to grab many characters or a whole file at one time. (You will get a chance to use loops in this evening's session, "Expressing and Stating.")

In order to write a complete Perl script that retrieves one character from the new.txt file, you need to

1. Use the open command to create a file handle to new.txt.

2. Use the flock command to give your Perl program exclusive access to new.txt by passing flock the LOCK_EX argument.

3. Use the getc command to retrieve the character from the file handle.

4. Remove exclusive access to the file using flock again only passing flock the LOCK_UN argument.

5. Close the file using the close command.

The following Perl script getcexample.pl which you can download from the companion Web site, walks through each of these steps. You can also take a closer look at the Perl script in Figure 3.1. Write and save this file as getcexample.pl.

```
# Create a file handle to new.txt using the open command
open (HANDLE, "<new.txt") or die "Cannot open new.txt";

# your Perl program exclusive access to new.txt using the
  flock command
```

```
flock (HANDLE, LOCK_EX) or die "Cannot lock new.txt";

# the getc command to retrieve the character from the file
  handle
$onecharacter = getc (HANDLE);
print $onecharacter

# Remove exclusive access to the file
flock (HANDLE, LOCK_UN) or die "Cannot unlock new.txt";

# Close the file
close (HANDLE) or die "Cannot close new.txt";

# another print statement telling the reader what to do next
print "Press <ENTER> to continue...";

# Perl waits at these brackets for user input
<>
```

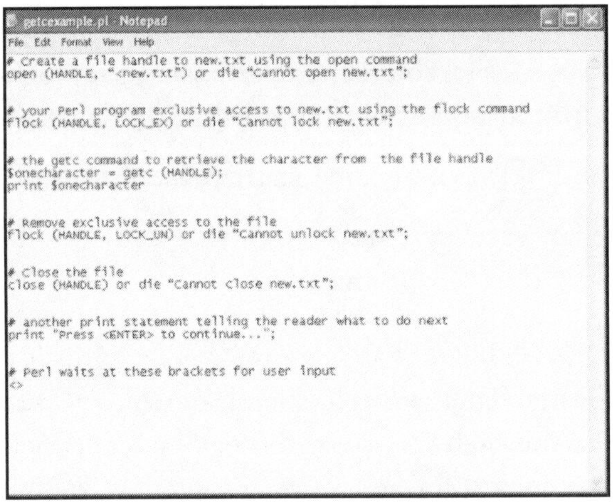

Figure 3.1

The complete getcexample.pl file in Notepad.

Using the Read Command

Although you would normally add a loop so that getc could grab each and every character in a file, Perl has other commands that can do the same or similar things. (Remember, in Perl there is always more than one way to do it.) You could use the read command to retrieve a larger, fixed amount of data from a file. Read takes three arguments—a file handle, a scalar variable, and the number of *bytes* Perl needs to read. A byte is a small amount of memory that can vary depending on the computer hardware architecture. A byte usually translates into a single character, at least when you are working with text files.

If you wanted to alter the getc example that you just created to use read instead of getc to pick up the single character (or single byte, if you want to sound impressive), you could change lines 8 and 9 to read:

```
$onecharacter = read (HANDLE, $buffer 8) or die "Couldn't
   Read HANDLE\n";
```

Using the seek Command

Seek is a useful Perl command that is used to jump to specific sections of a file. Like the read command, seek needs three arguments. It needs to know the name of the file, number of bytes to jump, and the direction to jump toward.

You can use negative or positive numbers when telling seek how far to jump. A positive number tells jump to move forward, and a negative number tells jump to move backward. The positioning is then defined by one last argument—a positioning variable that tells seek to set a new jump point, add the jump to wherever the current jump point is, or set the jump at the end of the file. The following line of code tells seek to jump 10 bytes in the file "HANDLE":

```
seek HANDLE, 10, 0;
```

The 0 given to seek is the positioning variable that tells Perl to set 10 as the new jump point. Now whenever you access HANDLE, Perl will automatically jump to byte 10. If you change the positioning variable to 1, Perl will jump ahead 10 bytes. If you wanted to have seek simply jump 10 bytes forward instead of setting a jump point, you would just change the 0 to a 1 like the following code sample:

```
# this line uses seek to jump 10 bytes up from the current
   seek position
seek HANDLE, 10, 1;
```

You can also use the position variable and negative numbers to use seek to jump back from the end of a file.

```
# this line uses seek to set the place of HANDLE
# to 10 bytes from the end of the file
seek HANDLE, -10, 2;
```

Using the tell command

The `tell` command is used when you are manipulating files to return the position of the file handle within the file, which is normally set by the `seek` command. The syntax for `tell` is:

```
tell FILEHANDLE
```

In the above seek example, you jumped 10 bytes from the end of a file. To utilize tell to then print out your location within the file, you would just add a short `print` statement:

```
# this line uses seek to set the place of HANDLE
# to 10 bytes from the end of the file
seek HANDLE, -10, 2;
# A print statement that shows the location marked by seek
print tell HANDLE;
```

Printing to a File

You have used `print` a number of times today, and now I will show you how to use it to print information to a file. The syntax for using `print` in this way is as follows:

```
print FILEHANDLE list
```

If you need to open a file and print an entry to the file that says "hello", use the same file handling techniques you have utilized thus far this afternoon. The following code:

```
open (HANDLE, ">file.txt") or die ("Cannot open
   file.txt");print HANDLE ("Hello");
close HANDLE;
```

1. Opens the file "file.txt".

2. Assigns file.txt to the file handle "HANDLE."

3. Prints a list to HANDLE.

4. Closes the file.

Using Directories

Directories in Perl are manipulated in much the same way as files are. You first need to open up a handle, and then you can open, close, and read from that directory.

You use the Perl `opendir` (Open Directory) command to open up a directory handle so you can access a directory in a Perl program. The `opendir` command functions in much the same way as the `open` command, about which you just learned.

```
opendir (HANDLE, "folder1") or die "Cannot open directory";
```

After you have opened a directory, you can get a listing of what is inside it by using the `readdir` (Read Directory) command. The following line of code prints out every item in the directory to which the handle refers, all strung together by the `join` command.

```
print join (readdir(HANDLE));
```

One thing Perl programs frequently do is change directories. `Chdir` (Change Directory) is the preferred method to use for this. `Chdir` is similar to the `CD` (Change Directory) command you used in DOS in the Friday Evening session, "Introducing Perl." Like the DOS `CD` command `chdir` is used by typing **chdir** and then providing the command with a path to a directory. For instance, the following line of code uses `chdir` to move to a specific user's Desktop folder.

```
chdir 'C:\Documents and Settings\user\Desktop';
```

CAUTION Both Windows and DOS use a backslash (\) to separate directories. UNIX-type file systems (including HTML) use a forward slash (/) to separate directories. This could cause conflicts in your code if you attempt to port between different platforms.

The Perlport documents that are a part of Activestate's Perl help files (located in your c:\Perl\Docs folder) have information on how to write Perl that is portable, and give suggestions for modules and libraries you can include when programming for more than one platform. This book also covers some helpful modules in the Sunday Evening session, "Learning Advanced Perl Techniques."

Two other common commands are `mkdir` (Make Directory) and `rmdir` (Remove Directory). To make new directors, you use the same permissions mode you used for `chdir`. The following command creates a new directory called NEW, with read and write access for the owner and read access for all other users.

```
mkdir NEW, 0644;
```

Aside from the mode, `mkdir` has the same result as right-clicking in Windows and choosing Make New Directory.

To remove the NEW file using `rmdir`, type the following line of code.

```
rmdir 'NEW';
```

Take a Break

It is only Saturday afternoon, and you have already whipped through most of the basic Perl building blocks, including arrays, scalars, and files. For the second part of this session, you'll need to put on your mathematician's thinking cap. Unfortunately, the way Perl performs mathematical operations is a little different than what you might have learned in your Algebra classes. You had a taste of how differently Perl performs such operations when you learned about counting systems in this morning's session and about octal permissions using `chmod` earlier in this session. Before you leap into Perl mathematical operations, I suggest taking a short break—maybe catch a shrill afternoon sitcom. If, however, you are a glutton for punishment, by all means press on.

Using Mathematical Operations

Perl operations refer to the simple tasks that you perform on files or data, such as applying math, reading, or writing. The Perl commands that make these modifications are often called operands.

Operands can be applied to almost every structure in Perl. You can perform operations on directories, files, scalars, or arrays. Operands also refer to the Perl functions that perform mathematical operations, such as the minus (–) operand for performing subtraction and the plus (+) operand for performing addition.

Working with Basic Operators

Operators are used to manipulate data. The easiest operators to understand in programming are usually the simple mathematical ones, which is why programming books (like this one) often begin explaining operations with simple mathematics, such as addition and subtraction.

One important concept in Perl is *operator precedence.* Basically, operator precedence is the order in which Perl executes operations. If you remember high school algebra, operator precedence is the same as the "order of operations." Consider the following example:

```
print 2 + 2 * 2;
```

You can interpret this code in a number of ways. If you follow the code in order from left to right, you add 2 and 2 and then multiply the result by 2, for an answer of 8. If you read the code from right to left, however, you multiply 2 by 2 and then add 2 to the result, for an answer of 6.

Instead of reading problems in a linear order, Perl actually gives some operators precedence (explained in detail in Table 3.4). In mathematical cases like this code example, Perl always multiplies first, regardless of whether the multiplier is before or after the addition. Even if you reverse the addition and the multiplication, Perl will still multiply first, giving you the same result of 6, for instance:

```
# In Perl
print 2 * 2 + 2;
# is the same as
print 2 + 2 * 2;
```

This can lead to some confusion when you are running multiple complex operations on the same line. However, you can force Perl to run operations in a certain order. If you want to make sure that Perl adds first, before doing any multiplying, you can specify precedence using parentheses ( ). Any operations contained in the parentheses will be executed first. The following code takes the earlier example and uses parentheses to force Perl to add first and then multiply, giving you a result of 8.

```
print ((2 + 2) *2);
```

When you are running multiple equations on a line, you must be careful to include all of the mathematics in one pair of parentheses. If you do not enclose the whole equation, the `print` command will chop off earlier than you would expect. Try running the following code as error.pl.

```
# this is one way NOT to separate operators
print (2 + 2) *2;

# another print statement telling the reader what to do next
print "Press <ENTER> to continue...";

# Perl waits at these brackets for user input
<>
```

In this example, the `print` function will only print 4; it won't realize that the `* 2` is also part of the operation because it isn't included in the parentheses. You might also receive other interesting errors, depending on what Perl distribution you are using.

Table 3.4 shows basic Perl operator precedence. It outlines which operands Perl will act on first when given the choice. The table also displays the session in the book where each operator is discussed.

Precedence	Operator	Session
TABLE 3.4	**PERL OPERATOR PRECEDENCE**	
First	Unary operators such as ! and -	Saturday Afternoon
Second	The assignment operator: =	Saturday Morning
Third	Simple mathematical operators such as *, /, %, and ×	Saturday Afternoon
Fourth	Incremental operators such as ++	Saturday Afternoon
Fifth	Relational operators: <, >, <=, and >=	Saturday Afternoon
Sixth	Logical operators: ==, !=	Saturday Afternoon

C STYLE OPERATIONS

Perl has a lot in common with C programming language where operators are concerned. In fact, Perl mimics the C operator set almost exactly, and many of the lessons you learn in this section will apply to C. Likewise, if you are familiar with C, much of this will be review. For you programming buffs, there are a few main differences between the way C and Perl handle operators:

➤ C is a strongly typed language, and Perl is not. Conversions between types are handled by Perl and are much less of an issue in Perl as in C.

➤ Perl does not have the unary & C address of operator. In Perl you use the \ operator to get a reference.

➤ Perl does not have a unary * C dereference address operator. In Perl you use the dereferencers already mentions ($,@,%,&) to established a typed dereferencer, whereas in C you use unary * and the operator is not typed.

Adding and Multiplying

In Perl, addition, subtraction, multiplication, and division are handled by the +, −, *, and / operators. Two equals signs put together (==) test for equality.

```
# two plus two equals 4
((2 + 2) == 4);
# four times four equals sixteen
((4 * 4) == 16);
# sixteen divided by eight equals two
((16 / 8) == 2);
# two minus 2 equals zero
((2 - 2) == 0);
```

A common mistake beginners make when programming in Perl is confusing the = operator with the == operator. This happens commonly because the Perl way of using equal signs is counterintuitive to the way that math has been taught to most people. In math, you use the lone = sign to make comparisons. In Perl, you use the lone = sign to make an assignment, and to make a comparison you need to have two equal signs (==).

For instance, the following code in Perl doesn't check to see whether 8 is equal to `$number`; it actually changes `$number` to 8.

```
If ($number = 8)
    then {execute}
```

The same equation used in math would check to see if 8 was equal to $number before moving on. In Perl, the $number becomes equal to 8.

CAUTION

◆ ◆

The == operator is covered in more depth in the upcoming "Running Conditionals and Tests" section later in this chapter.

◆ ◆

Perl is very flexible when it comes to operators; you can use them on scalars and other simple data types. When playing with text, you can use a number of *string operators*, which are equivalent to basic math operators. For instance, instead of typing a repetitive `print` statement several times:

```
print "multiply\n";
print "multiply\n";
print "multiply\n";
print "multiply\n";
print "multiply\n";
print "multiply\n";
print "multiply\n";
print "multiply\n";
print "multiply\n";
print "multiply\n";
```

You could write one line that uses an x instead.

```
print "multiply\n" x10;
```

This x operator is sometimes called the string repetition operator.

You can also add strings together by using the concatenation operator, which is just a period (.). Adding strings together puts them on the same line, which is useful if you need to put a few strings together into one scalar.

```
# this code puts three print statements into $onlyone
$name = Small
```

```
$animal = Cat
$owner = My
$onlyone = "$owner"."#name"."$animal";
print "$onlyone\n";
```

Other common string operators include eq (Equals), ne (Not Equals), lt (Less Than), and gt (Greater Than). These operators correspond to the standard numeric and relational operators and can be used on text strings in the same way that the numeric and relational operators can be used on numbers.

Even More Complex Operators

Perl provides plenty of support for other sorts of arithmetic than just basic addition and multiplication. There are commands for determining square roots, cosigns, absolute values, and exponents. Most of these commands are used in almost exactly the same way to make things easier for the programmer.

The common form for writing a line of code that performs one of these operations is

```
$answer = function(number);
```

Function holds the place where the specific command would be, and number holds the place for the number you need to execute the command. If you wanted to determine the trigonometric cosign of 0 and place it into $answer, for instance, you would type

```
$answer = cos(0);
```

The scalar answer should now hold the cosign of 0 or the number 1. If you needed to determine the absolute value of 0 instead, you could use the same structure and replace the cosign operator (cos) with the absolute value operator (abs):

```
$answer = abs(0);
```

Another useful operator is Perl's random number generator command: rand. Rand creates a random number between 0 and the number specified through the argument. For example, the following code creates a random number between 0 and 10 and places the number into $answer:

```
$answer = rand(10);
```

NOTE ●
The rand command included in Perl is actually a random number emulator. Computers have a difficult time creating random numbers, being the logical creatures that they are. Perl has add-on modules that help generate numbers close to truly random. I talk more about rand in the Sunday Morning and Sunday Afternoon sessions.
● ●

In the following code example I take the variable 0 through several complex math functions. Copy the code into a new Perl file called Crazymath.pl and run the program:

```perl
# Assign 0 to $number
$number = 0;
# print the value of $number
print "The number is now equal to $number\n";

# Find the cosign of $number
$number = cos($number);
# print the value of $number
print "The number is now equal to $number\n";

# $number to the power of $number
$number = exp($number);
# print the value of $number
print "The number is now equal to $number\n";

# square root of number
$number = sqrt($number);
# print the value of $number
print "The number is now equal to $number\n";

# cosine of number
$number = cos($number);
# print the value of $number
print "The number is now equal to $number\n";

# sine of number
```

```
$number = sin($number);
# print the value of $number
print "The number is now equal to $number\n";

# another print statement telling the reader what to do next

print "Press <ENTER> to continue...";

# Perl waits at these brackets for user input
<>
```

You can see that each math function uses the exact same syntax. This is one more way that Perl is designed to make things easier for the programmer.

Table 3.5 lists some of the more common built-in Perl math functions. You can use all of these functions with the same code formula.

TABLE 3.5	COMMON PERL MATH FUNCTIONS
Function	**Description**
abs	Determines the absolute value of a number.
atan2	Returns the arctangent of two arguments.
cos	Determines the Cosine of a number.
exp	To the power of a specific number.
int	Truncates a given number into a whole integer.
sin	Determines the sine of a specified number.
sqrt	Determines the square root of a number.
rand	Creates a random number between 0 and the number specified.

Working with Incremental Operators

Incremental operators are used mostly in loops (which I cover in detail in tonight's session, "Expressing and Stating."), but they can also be used to perform quick, shorthand math. The increment operator is two addition signs together (++); the opposite operator, the decrement operator, is two minus signs together (—).

The increment operator automatically increases a value by 1 and the decrement operator automatically decreases a value by 1. Run the following code as increase.pl.

```
# set a value to x and then print it
$x = 5
print "$x\n"
# increment x by 1
$x = $x++
print "$x\n"
# decrement x by 1
$x = Sx--
print "$x\n"

# another print statement telling the reader what to do next
print "Press <ENTER> to continue...";

# Perl waits at these brackets for user input
<>
```

The DOS output will display $x first as 5, then as 6, and then again as 5.

These operators are shortcuts for the two longhand common operations:

```
$number = $number + 1;
$number = $number - 1;
```

These shortcuts work just like their mirrored C commands. These next two lines mean the same thing in Perl as the two lines of script above:

```
$number++;
$number--;
```

Alternatively, you can place the auto increment and decrement commands in front of the variable:

```
++$number;
--$number;
```

The difference here is that the operator is run before $number can return any value. For instance, if you had assigned `$number` the value of 5, this command returns the number 6 to `print` and STDOUT:

```
#assign 5 to $number
$number = 5;


# this print line produces the number 6
print ++$number;
```

If you auto increment `$number` after the scalar, the `print` command returns the number 5 first, then `$number` becomes incremented:

```
#assign 5 to $number
$number = 5;


# this print line produces the number 5 then increments
  $number to 6
print $number++;
```

Working with Relational Operators

Relational operators perform comparisons. Real-life relational operators are less than, equal to, and greater than. Relational operators normally check a condition and then return a binary answer of 0 if the condition is false and 1 if the condition is true.

Relational operators are used often when running loops, which I will cover in more detail in the Saturday Evening session, "Expressing and Stating." A common occurrence is for a loop to check to see whether a value is greater than a certain number each time it runs and whether the value is high enough to end the loop. The following line of code provides an example.

```
if (x > 10) {exit};
```

The most common relational operators are less than (<), greater than (>), less than or equal to (<=), and greater than or equal to (>=), and are outlined in Table 3.6:

Operator	Comparison
<	Left is less than right.
>	Left is greater than right.
<=	Left is less than or equal to right.
>=	Left is greater than or equal to right.
==	Left is equal to right.
!=	Left is not equal to right.
<=>	Compares whether left is less than, equal to, or greater than and returns as -1, 0, or 1 respectively.
lt	Same as < (short for less than).
gt	Same as > (short for greater than).
le	Same as <=.
ge	Same as >=.
eq	Same as ==.
ne	Same as !=.
cmp	Same as <=>

TABLE 3.6 COMMON PERL RELATIONAL OPERATORS

Relational operators are also sometimes referred to as comparison operators or equality operators.

Symbolic Unary Operators

Perl has four *symbolic unary* operators. A symbolic unary operator is an operator that takes one argument. Whereas relational operators compare two numbers, unary operators operate on the logical values of a number. The four symbolic unary operators are

➤ ! Logical negation

➤ – Arithmetic negation

➤ ~ Bitwise negation

➤ \ Creates a reference

These operators work on truth values.

Reviewing Unary and Binary

In Perl operations, binary takes on a slightly different definition than we have been using. A binary operand is one that takes two arguments. So far, you have used mostly binary operations. The x>10 comparison is a binary operation because there are two pieces of input—the x and the 10. Other examples of binary operations are 1 + 1, x = = 5, and 4 * 4.

Perl also has a few unary operations. These are operations that take only one argument. As you saw in Table 3.4, unary operations take precedence over any other sort of operation. The common unary operators are the bitwise negation (~), logical negation (!), and negative sign (–).

The negative sign is the easiest operator of the three to explain. In the following equation, Perl will always resolve the –4 first.

```
2 + -4 * 2
```

For Perl, the negative sign is an operator that turns a positive 4 into a negative 4, and Perl knows that it needs to understand which numbers are negative before it can resolve any other mathematics. This is why the negative sign has such a high precedence.

Logical negation is represented by the exclamation mark (!). This high-precedence operator reverses a condition. You can use it to change an "if this is true" statement, such as:

```
if (true)
```

to an "if this is false" statement by just adding the !.

```
if !(true)
```

In this way, logical negation is similar in function to the negative sign, except that it is used to reverse statements instead of numbers.

Running Conditionals and Tests

Conditionals and tests, which are sometimes called logical operators, are another important part of programming. Like many of the operations I have introduced in this chapter, logical operators are commonly used in looping or statements and will be discussed in greater detail in tonight's session.

Logical operators are low-precedence operators that Perl uses to check or evaluate statements. Many of these operators are based on classic C language style operators. The most common logical operator is the equivalency statement, symbolized by two equal signs(==).

You already looked at equivalency briefly in the "Adding and Multiplying" section earlier this afternoon. However, equivalency is used more frequently when running logic style tests, like the following:

```
if (x = = 10) then {execute}
```

Here, if is used to determine whether x is the same as the number 10. A second common logical operator is the logical or statement, which is represented by two straight lines or pipes (||). logical or might look like this:

```
if (x == 10) || (c == 10) then {execute}
```

In this case, if continues executing if either the first condition (x==10) or the second condition (c==10) is true.

A third common operator in this category is logical and, represented by two ampersands (&&). Perl uses logical and to keep track of two conditions that both must be met, such as in the following example:

```
if (x == 10) && (c == 10) then {execute}
```

Perl evaluates the left side (x == 10) first. If the left side resolves as true, Perl then checks the right side (c == 10). If the right side is also true, then Perl goes on to execute.

Working with Input Output Operators

One last common operator is the input output, or I/O operator. I/O is represented by angle brackets <>. When you put two angle brackets together, you create an input output construct. You have been using this particular construct since the Friday Evening session, "Introducing Perl," as a mechanism to make Perl wait for input before closing a DOS prompt. You have also used this same code in this morning's session:

```
# another print statement telling the reader what to do next
print "Press <ENTER> to continue...";

# Perl waits at these brackets for user input
<>
```

The I/O operator is actually short for <STDIN> (Standard In), Perl's standard input file handle. Perl keeps <STDIN> as its default file handle to keep track of all outside input that comes into the running program, unless you specify to use something else. So when you use the brackets (<>) to make Perl wait for user input, you are actually, in unique Perl shorthand, setting up a file handle called <STDIN> that takes charge of input that comes in from the DOS prompt.

<STDIN> is used regularly in loops to take user input or to grab information from other programs or the operating system. The most common use of <STDIN>, however, is for taking input from the keyboard.

In the example code that you have been using for each program you write, Standard In, represented by <>, waits for user input and then continues. With a few modifications, you can change this to allow Standard In to take the input and print it to the DOS prompt.

1. Enclose <STDIN> within parentheses, like this: (<>).

2. Use the while command to create a loop, like this: (while (<>)).

3. Add a print statement—(while (<>) {print;})—so that when Perl takes <STDIN>, whatever is typed gets printed to the DOS screen.

When you have finished, the code should look like this:

```
# Changing our standard ending to standard input
while (<>) {
    print;
}
```

Write up this program and save it as stdin.pl. When you run it, any text you type will be put into the DOS prompt, as shown in Figure 3.2.

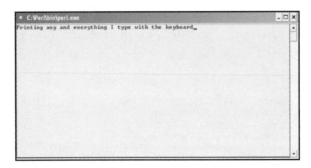

Figure 3.2

Using <STDIN> to take input from the keyboard.

Because the stdin.pl program takes all input received from the keyboard, you have a way to turn off the typewriter. This is actually poor programming because you always want to leave a means of exiting in case something goes wrong. On Windows, you can force the DOS prompt to close by clicking on the X at the upper-right corner of the window stdin.pl is running from, which may or may not cause Windows to send you an error message (depending upon what platform you are running).

The normal way to fix this problem is to leave one keypress available to end the program, like Q for quit, or leave the Esc key free to shut down the program. The easiest way to do this (without going in depth into loops, which are covered in tonight's session) is to switch from using the while command to the until command:

```
# Changing our standard ending to standard input
until (<>) {
    print;
}
```

The until command is almost the opposite of a while command. This script will let you type on the keyboard, displaying what you type as you go, until you send input into <STDIN> by committing with the Enter button (I cover the `until` loop in much greater detail in this evening's session).

To make this program complete, you should include a few comments and print statements to let the user know what exactly is happening, and how to exit the program. The complete listing, which you should test out by creating a new Perl file called untilstdin.pl, follows and is also available as part of the Saturday morning source files on the companion Web site:

```
# changing our standard ending to standard input
print "This program acts like a standard typewriter\n";
print "Hit keys on the keyboard to see them print to the
    screen\n";
print "Hit the ENTER key to quit\n";


until (<>) {
  print;
  }
```

Programming Block: Parsing to a File, RNG

Now it is time to look over the Programming Block from the Saturday Morning session, "Variables and Other Fun Stuff," and see how to apply what was covered in this chapter. Open block2.pl and resave the file as block3.pl so that there is a new copy.

Only a few more things are necessary to finish the game. One important piece is the random map, a feature for game replay-ability, and now is a great time to build the random maps.

Next, I add to the game in this block the mathematical operations needed to run the game. These additions mainly consist of game variables that change while you are playing the game.

To start, add comments for the changes you want to make within the program code:

```
##################################################
# block 3
# Any math that needs to be done
```

```
# Random number generator

# Any variable changes
```

Next, take a look at the existing variables to see what needs to be changed:

```
$direction = North;
$food = 10;
$health = 10;
```

The direction scalar must change based on where the player is facing. The change will most likely be determined by the last move the player made, which will not be tracked until you have an actual game loop. Therefore, I'll move on to the next variable.

The amount of food should decrease as the player moves, symbolizing the energy that it takes to wander throughout the mazelike cavern system. In this example, for every move, the player loses two units of food. The code would look something like this:

```
# While making a move lose one food unit
$food = $food - 2;
print "You have $food boxes of ramen left\n";
```

Health is the last variable and should stay the same unless a mishap occurs to the player, for example, being attacked by rabid bats or trying to move when the player is out of food. In this example, for each mishap the player's health is decreased by 1, and when health equals 0, the game ends.

```
# if a mishap occurs, lose one health
$health = $health - 1;
print "Your health is equal to $health\n";
```

Place these pieces into block3.pl and test to make sure everything is working properly; the full source should look like this:

```
###############################################
#Trapped
###############################################

###############################################
# block1- planning
```

```perl
# What I need:
# Code that prints information to the screen.
# Code that takes information from the keyboard.
# Code that generates a random map
# Code that tracks the player's progress on the map

##############################################
# block 2 - Basic needs.
# We have learned printing information to the screen and
# Taking information from the keyboard and
# Creating scalar variables and
# a standard ending to keep the dos prompt open.
# Initial print action
# Assign Variables

$direction = North;
$food = 10;
$health = 10;

print "\n";
print "You are trapped in a cavern\n";
print "You can travel North, South, East, or West\n";
print "\n\n\n";
print "You are facing $direction\n";
print "You have $food boxes of ramen left\n";
print "Your health is equal to $health\n";
print "\n\n\n";

##############################################
# block 3
# Any math that needs to be done
# Random number generator
# Any variable changes

# While making a move lose one food unit
```

```
$food = $food -2;
print "You have $food boxes of ramen left\n";

# If a mishap occurs, lose one health
$health = $health -1;
print "Your health is equal to $health\n";



# Add our ending changed to user input
# standard ending
print "\nPress an arrow key to continue...";


<>
```

The output of block3.pl should be identical to Figure 3.3:

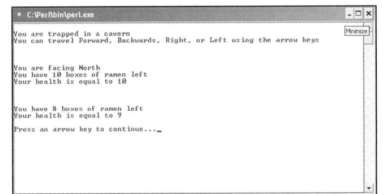

Figure 3.3

block3.pl shows initial food and health and then decrements both variables.

Finally, it's time add the random number and map generator. Because there are only four possible ways to go at any given time, the correct way to go can be represented by a number ranging from 0 to 3, with north being 0, east 1, south 2, and west 3. Place these values into scalars, like so:

```
# Possible directions
$north = 0;
$east = 1;
$south = 2;
$west = 3;
```

Now, plan out a map as an example. Say the way out of the cavern is to go north, then east, then north again, and then west. These directions can now be translated by their number values:

```
north = 0
east = 1
north = 0
west = 3
```

Therefore, the way out can actually be represented by a string of numbers: 0103. In order to create a random map, use the rand command to produce four numbers between 0 and 3, which you can do by using the following code:

```
# The way out is
$turn1 = rand(3);
$turn2 = rand (3);
$turn3 = rand(3);
$turn4 = rand(3);
```

For now, you will have the sample game print the way out so that you can make sure everything is working correctly:

```
print "The way out is $turn1$turn2$turn3$turn4\n";
```

If you save and run block3.pl a few times, you will notice that the way out is different each time you run the program. You will also notice that rand is not giving you just a 0,1,2 or 3, but that the numbers are using a floating point and may be something, such as 0.08926892, 1.34732933, and 2.99763093 (see Figure 3.4).

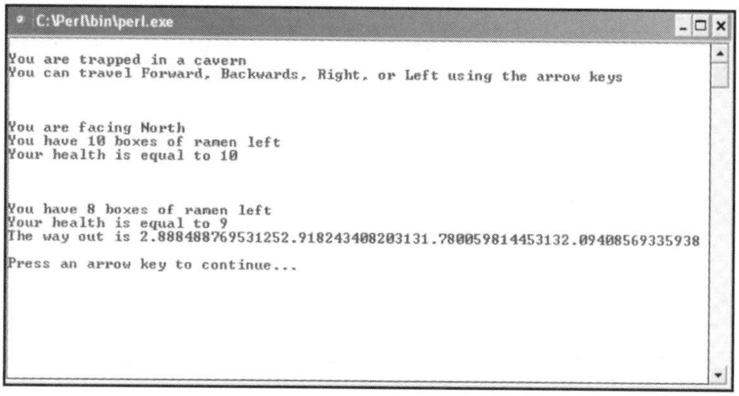

Figure 3.4

The command rand produces unexpected output by including numbers past the decimal point.

This is easy to fix. You just need to explain to Perl that you need a whole integer, which is enforced by including an int command within the rand statements. Change the random statements to the following:

```
# The way out is
$turn1 = int rand(3);
$turn2 = int rand (3);
$turn3 = int rand(3);
$turn4 = int rand(3);
```

You now have just about everything you need to complete the Trapped game. All that is left to do is organize the program in a logical way, which is the focus of this evening's session. The full source of block3.pl is included here and is also available for download (as block3final.pl, the block3.pl covers earlier changes) with the other sample programs from the Web site.

```
################################################
#Trapped
################################################

################################################
# block1- planning
# What I need:
# Code that prints information to the screen.
# Code that takes information from the keyboard.
# Code that generates a random map
# Code that tracks the player's progress on the map


####################################################
# block 2 - Basic needs.
# We have learned printing information to the screen and
# Taking information from the keyboard and
# Creating scalar variables and
# a standard ending to keep the dos prompt open.
# Initial print action

# Assign Variables

$direction = North;
```

```perl
$food = 10;
$health = 10;

print "\n";
print "You are trapped in a cavern\n";
print "You can travel Forward, Backwards, Right, or Left
   using the arrow keys\n";
print "\n\n\n";
print "You are facing $direction\n";
print "You have $food boxes of ramen left\n";
print "Your health is equal to $health\n";
print "\n\n\n";


##################################################
# block 3
# Any math that needs to be done
# Random number generator
# Any variable changes

# While making a move lose one food unit
$food = $food -2;
print "You have $food boxes of ramen left\n";

# If a mishap occurs, lose one health
$health = $health -1;
print "Your health is equal to $health\n";

# Possible directions
$north = 0;
$east = 1;
$south = 2;
$west = 3;

# The way out is
$turn1 = int rand(3);
$turn2 = int rand (3);
$turn3 = int rand(3);
```

```
$turn4 = int rand(3);

print "The way out is $turn1$turn2$turn3$turn4\n";

# Add our ending changed to user input
# standard ending
print "\nPress an arrow key to continue...";


<>
```

Summary

It's late Saturday afternoon, and already you have picked up most of the basic building blocks of Perl. You understand how Perl sorts through files and directories, and you've had a chance to play with basic Perl operations, which include everything from math and logic to input. In this evening's session, which covers statements and loops, you will put these pieces together and make Perl bow before your programming expertise, as you start writing programs that use all these blocks together. For now, take a break, have an early supper, and bask in the glory of your newfound programming knowledge.

Expressing and Stating

- ➤ Understanding statements
- ➤ Understanding Perl loops
- ➤ Working with routines and subroutines
- ➤ Understanding Perl declarations
- ➤ Programming Block: The Game Loop

It's Saturday night and you have the discipline and drive to keep cooking with Perl. You are finally at what I like to refer to as the meat of the cookbook. This chapter is all about program statements and loops. Until now, you have been learning about different Perl ingredients. Now I am going to help you put the ingredients together into actual recipes. Perl uses statements and loops to control and order the flow of a program and to create complete code blocks that actually perform tasks.

Understanding Statements

All Perl code, including what you have written so far, is made up of statements. Statements, however, come in a couple of different forms. So far you have used mostly *simple statements*. Simple statements are expressions that perform specific actions. Simple statements in Perl usually take up a single line of code and end in a semicolon (;).

Compound or complex Perl statements generally consist of more than one line of code and use many expressions. You have also used compound statements, although not as often as you have used simple statements. Compound statements in Perl are usually separated by braces ({}) and hold multiple simple statements.

Compound statements are often referred to as program blocks. The program blocks that you have built at the end of each chapter are good examples. The last two chapters have each held a related group of instructions, the pieces of which will eventually be put together in a large program.

Program blocks aren't always separated by braces, but their separation often defines a *scope*. Scope is the influence of certain variables or commands.

Blocks are often used to hold variables and commands in one part of a program so that they are inaccessible to other parts of the program.

A third type of statement is called a conditional statement (sometimes referred to as a *branch*). Branches are lines or blocks of code that might or might not run, depending on the flow of the program. Programmers generally use branches to initiate actions that are dependent on user input.

Branches are also called control structures by programmers familiar with *structured programming*.

A Look at Structured Programming

Structured programming is a method of programming designed to help make large programs easier to read. It is a predecessor to object-oriented programming, which I will cover in detail in the Sunday Morning session, "Objects and Object-Oriented Programming." Structured programs are usually illustrated in simple graphs that have a top-down approach and flow. Figure 4.1 illustrates a structured-programming graph in which the ovals represent starting and ending points, the squares represent program blocks, and the diamonds represent branches. As I go through each of Perl's branching and looping statements in this chapter I will use structured-programming flowcharts to illustrate them.

The main idea behind structured programming is to divide and conquer. As computers, technology, and software have advanced, programs have become larger and more difficult to write and maintain. Structured programming breaks down complex programs into simple tasks. The rule is that if a task is too complex to be described simply, then the task needs to be broken down further. When the task is small enough to be self-contained and easily understood, then the task can be programmed.

You've had a lot of experience writing simple statements in the last few chapters. This chapter focuses on writing program blocks and conditional statements, starting with common statement commands: if, else, elsif, and unless.

If is the foundation of all conditional command statements. You will find yourself using the if command over and over as you program in Perl, as well as in other programming languages. The if command checks a specified condition which is usually listed in parentheses following the if statement. If the condition is true, the if command executes a code block that follows.

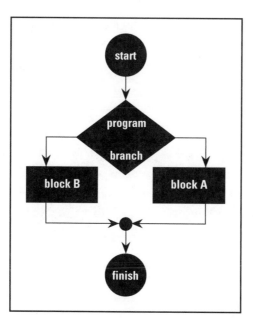

Figure 4.1

A simple structured-
program flowchart.

If the condition is not true, the code block is skipped. In Perl the if statement takes the general form of the following code:

```
if (this condition is true) {then this happens}
```

Perl's if statement is illustrated in Figure 4.2, which depicts the flow of a program going through an if statement. The flow goes through the diamond

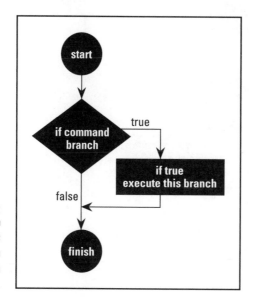

Figure 4.2

A generic example
of a program
flowing through an
if statement.

branch, which executes the code block (the square) if the condition is true or continues to the ending oval if the condition is false.

Using if by itself is useful, but not as useful as using it with other statements, such as the else command.

Using Else

The else command usually follows an if statement. When the if statement returns a value of false, the code block held by else executes. This creates a fork in the program, where either the if block or the else block is executed. When using else and if together in Perl, the general syntax looks something like this:

```
if (this condition is true)
{then this happens}
else {this happens instead}
```

This code syntax is one way of creating program flow in Perl. The series of if and else statements allows code to make decisions based on variables or input. When the program flow has two possible execution choices, it is known in structured programming as a *double selection*. The if/else statement is illustrated in Figure 4.3.

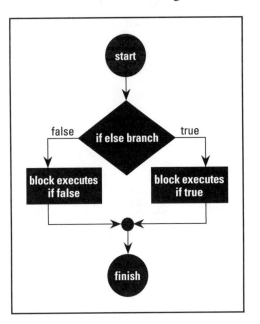

Figure 4.3

The top-down flow of an if/else statement. The false and true branches both execute blocks of code.

A double selection can be limiting because there are only two forks that the program can take. If you need to program for multiple paths, you can use the elsif command.

Using Elsif Statements

After running an if statement, Perl will look for an else statement that follows it. If Perl doesn't find an else statement, it will check for an elsif command. The elsif command will execute if the specified condition (which is held in parentheses, just as in an if statement) is considered true; otherwise, Perl will continue executing the remainder of the program.

You can use multiple elsif statements in a row to create one long string of conditions for which to check. However, only one else statement can follow an if. In Perl the syntax for elsif statements looks like this:

```
if (this first condition is true)
{then this first program block runs}
elsif (this second condition is true)
{then this second program block executes}
elsif (this third condition is true)
{then this third program block runs}
else {this happens instead}
```

Figure 4.4 displays a typical elsif program structure. This is a powerful program structure because it allows you to mold decision trees, multiple paths, or branches that a program can use depending on computer or variable input. When you put an elsif program structure together with operators from this afternoon's session, you can turn simple Perl scripts into powerful complex statements.

One simple application of a decision tree would be to have Perl determine whether a number is less than or equal to a certain value. To create a compound script that deduces a number value, follow these steps:

1. Place the number to compare against into a scalar.

2. Use a series of if and elsif statements to separate the program branches.

3. Use greater than, less than, and equal to operator as conditions for if and elsif statements.

4. Use print after the if and elsif statements have deduced the number.

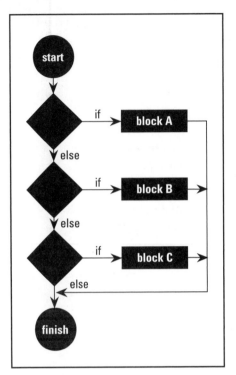

Figure 4.4

You can use an
elsif statement
to create several
branches in a
program flowchart.

Assigning the number to a scalar is simple, since you have been using scalars for almost a full day now. In a new Perl script called Number.pl, assign the number 5 to a scalar called number.

```
# Assign a value to number
$number = 5;
```

Now you need to build the if and elsif blocks. The first possibility is that the number is less than five; the second is that the number is greater than five; and the third is that the number is equal to five. To handle these three possible solutions, build an if statement followed by two elsif statements.

```
# Assign a value to number
$number = 5;
# Set up the program blocks
if (){
}elsif (){
}elsif (){
}
```

After the program blocks are built, you can add conditions for executing each of the three blocks of code. You can use the less than and greater than operators you learned about in this afternoon's session to determine whether $number is less than, greater than, or equal to the value 5.

```
# Assign a value to number
$number = 5;
# Set up the program blocks
if ($number == 5){
}elsif ($number > 5){
}elsif ($number < 5){
}
```

Now you need to fill in the actual program blocks between the braces to determine what will actually happen when Perl discovers the value of $number. One simple way to handle this would be to include print statements that explain what Perl discovered.

```
# Assign a value to number
$number = 5;
# Set up the program blocks
if ($number == 5){
    print "The number is equal to 5\n";
}elsif ($number > 5){
    print "The number is greater than 5\n";
}elsif ($number < 5){
    print "The number is less than 5\n";
}
```

One customary code convention is reserving the last else statement in a group to cover errors in the program. For instance, what if $number was accidentally assigned a string? In that case, Perl would skip all of the elsif statements, and the program would end without displaying any text to the user, which is not graceful. To make the program more elegant and safe, add one final else statement with a catch-all phrase.

```
}else {
    print "Perl could not determine the number.\n";
}
```

Put all the code together, add your patented ending, save the program, and run it. You can also try assigning different values to $number to test how accurately your script runs.

```perl
# Assign a value to number
$number = 5;
# Set up the program blocks
if ($number == 5){
    print "The number is equal to 5\n";
}elsif ($number > 5){
    print "The number is greater than 5\n";
}elsif ($number < 5){
    print "The number is less than 5\n";
}else {
    print "Perl could not determine the number.\n";
}

# another print statement telling the reader what to do next
print "Press <ENTER> to continue...";

# Perl waits at these brackets for user input
<>
```

Using Unless Statements

Unless works just like an else statement except that the conditions are opposite. Unless executes the program block that follows it only if the condition is false. (Some Perl programmers call an unless statement a "reverse if.") Else statements can follow unless statements, just as they can follow if statements. Figure 4.5 shows the unless statement in action. Unless is also used in the following code example to shorten the previous guessing game.

```perl
$number = 5;
unless ($number == 5) {
    print "The number is definitely not five\n";
}else{
    print "the number must be 5\n";
}
```

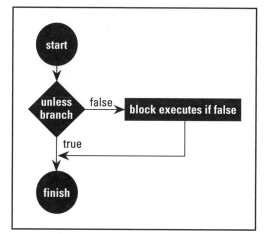

Figure 4.5

An `unless` structure shown as a flowchart. The block is executed only if the condition is false; otherwise, the program flow continues.

THE UNPOPULAR GOTO COMMAND

If you are going through someone else's code, you might run into the `goto` statement. Programmers generally frown upon using `goto` statements, although they were very popular in the early days and in basic languages.

`Goto` statements are frowned upon because they make code choppy and hard to read. This is due to the nature of the `goto`—it tells Perl to jump to another section of code. You can recognize `goto` statements in Perl by their syntax, which looks like this:

```
if ($programmer == bad) {goto UNHAPPYPLACE}
```

Although programming with `if`, `unless`, and `else` seems cumbersome at first, you get used to writing and reading it. The code that you have written so far is not difficult to follow, especially if you have good commenting habits. Code that uses many `goto` statements quickly becomes difficult to read because you have to jump to different places in the code.

You generally will not see `goto` in code very often because loops are more elegant and easier to read. Loops are also less likely to cause error-prone conditions or endless loops. Still, you might run into `goto` and you might even find a legitimate use for the command, although many programmers contend that anything you can do using `goto` can be done using loops and statements.

Different Types of Perl Loops

Computers excel at running quick calculations repetitively, and loops were created to take advantage of this benefit. Loops keep executing a command until they are stopped by some previously set condition.

Loops generally use blocks to hold the code that they execute. When you run a loop, you run a separated program block contained in braces until some condition changes or is met.

At the end of the last session, I introduced you to the `while` loop and you used it to capture the standard input `<STDIN>` of the keyboard, creating a typewriter-like effect. Then you changed the `while` loop into an `until` loop, with the same effect of capturing keyboard strokes. These examples illustrated loops in action. Both the `while` command and the `until` command looped, gathering all the strokes of the keyboard while looping, until the loop exited. In this section, I explain `while` and `until` loops in more depth and cover the other common Perl loops.

Using the While Loop

The `while` loop is considered the easiest of the Perl program loops to implement and learn. It is used most often to grab input from the command line using standard input or the `<>` operator, which was introduced this morning and covered briefly this afternoon.

The `while` loop is designed to execute the same code for as long as a specific condition remains true. For this reason, the `while` loop is a common backbone for e-commerce. While the customer is still purchasing items, a `while` loop can keep track of what they are buying and how much it costs. The `while` loop is also a common backbone for games. As long as a ship hasn't been destroyed, the program will keep sending aliens at it. Figure 4.6 shows a `while` loop as a structured-programming flowchart.

Recalling the script for `elsif` commands that you wrote a few moments ago, you can rewrite this program as a `while` loop to save time and effort and even improve the script a bit.

```
$number = 5;
$guess = 1;
while ($guess != $number){
```

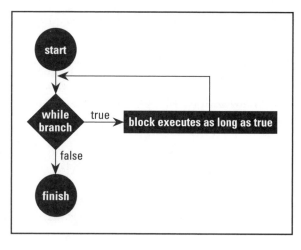

Figure 4.6

Notice how the arrow from the program block brings you back to the beginning of the flow as long as the condition remains true.

```
        $guess++
    }
print "The number is $guess";
```

Stepping through this code line by line, you can see that the following steps take place.

1. Perl assigns the number 5 to `$number`.

2. Perl creates `$guess` and assigns the value 1 to it.

3. Perl hits the `while` loop and checks the condition, which in this case is whether or not `$guess` and `$number` are the same.

4. If the values are the same, the `while` loop will exit. Since they are not equal (symbolized by the `!=` operator), Perl enters the loop and runs through the code, increasing `$guess` by one using the `++` incremental operator. After running through the loop once, `$guess` is equal to 2.

5. Perl starts the loop over and checks the condition. `$guess` is now equal to 2, and `$number` is still equal to 5. Since they are not equivalent, the `while` loop runs again.

6. Perl continues running through the `while` loop until `$guess` is equal to `$number`. Perl then exits the loop and runs the `print` line that displays the guess.

Now you have a much-improved script and because of the `while` loop, you can code it with half the number of lines.

A partner in crime to the `while` loop is the `until` loop (which you used for the first time in the last session). The `until` loop is the opposite of a `while` loop. Instead of executing a block of code when a given condition is true, it executes a block of code when a given condition is false. In Perl, the `until` loop syntax looks like this:

```
until (this condition is false) {do this}
```

In all other cases, `while` loops and `until` loops are implemented the same way. Both are extremely common in Perl because they are easy to use in short, simple, single use scripts. `While` and `until` may also be used for overarching program exit control, where they can constantly watch for a user who needs to exit or leave the program, for example:

```
while (the user does not want to quit) {run the program}
```

Using the For Loop

The `for` loop is probably the most common loop in programming. `For` is essential because it gives programmers fine-tuned control over repetitive actions. When it comes to running routines or actions over a list, an array, or a series of different items, the `for` loop truly excels.

Many beginning programmers initially experience difficulty in grasping the `for` loop structure. Unlike the `while` loop, which takes only one condition, the `for` loop needs three separate conditions to execute properly. Since `for` loops are common, many programming languages have shortcuts associated with them, which adds to their mystique and makes them difficult to decipher. Used in the right way, however, the `for` loop is extremely powerful, particularly when you are running repetitive actions or you need to make changes to items within arrays.

A formal `for` loop takes on the following general structure.

```
for (expression1; expression2; expression3) {the familiar
    code block that executes}
```

Figure 4.7 displays the structured-program flow of a `for` loop. Notice that there are two programming blocks; the first is the code that executes as part of the loop expressions, and the second is the block that the loop executes.

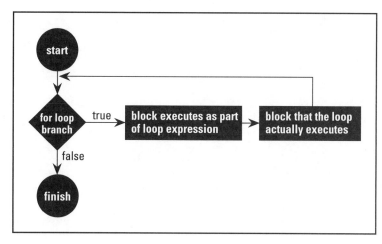

Figure 4.7

The flow of a
`for` loop.

When this structure runs, the following steps take place.

1. Perl sees the `for` loop and immediately executes `expression1`. This is the only time Perl runs `expression1`.

2. `Expression2`, which is normally a condition of some sort, is checked. If the expression/condition is false, Perl immediately exits the `for` loop. If the expression/condition is true, Perl continues through the loop.

3. Perl executes `expression3`. Unlike `expression1`, Perl will execute `expression3` each time it runs through the loop.

4. Perl executes whatever code is in the block, and then returns to Step 2.

Because `expression1` is only executed once, it is normally used to initialize a counter. This counter is usually a variable that begins its life when the loop is started and increments each time the loop is run.

The same variable is set in `expression2` as a condition for exiting the loop. `Expression3` increments the variable. For example, if you wanted to set a `for` loop to execute a `print` statement 10 times, you could set the initial variable to 1 in `expression1`, have the condition test whether the variable has hit 10 yet in `expression2`, and have `expression3` increment the variable each time the loop runs.

As an example, here is a `for` loop that prints "looping" 10 times.

```
for ($loop = 1; $loop <= 10; $loop++){
    print "looping\n";
}
```

Following are the steps of the `for` loop in this example:

1. Perl recognizes the `for` loop and goes to `statement1` ($loop = 1). Perl creates $loop and assigns it the number 1.

2. Perl then checks to see whether the second statement is true before continuing. Perl sees that $loop <= 10 is a true condition, so it continues. If $loop were equal to 10 or greater, Perl would immediately exit the `for` loop.

3. After it runs the code block (the `print`), it executes the third statement ($loop++), which increments $loop by 1.

4. Perl then runs whatever code is in the `for` loop code block, which in this case is a `print` statement.

5. Perl then returns to Step 2.

Using the Do/While Loop

Many programming languages other than Perl have a loop known as `do/while`. This loop has the flow shown in Figure 4.8. Perl does not possess an independent construct that acts as a `do/while` loop, but it is possible to use the `while` loop with a `do` statement to achieve the same effect.

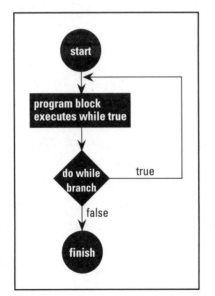

Figure 4.8

A flowchart that illustrates a typical `do/while` loop.

To set up a do/while loop, you first set up a do programming block. The do command is similar to other structures at which you have looked at:

```
do (this};
```

In a simple script like this, do tells Perl to execute whatever is within the do block. You can add a while command to turn this script into a typical do/while structure.

```
do {this} while {this is true}
```

A practical example of this concept is a variation of the while loop you looked at in this afternoon's session, where you used a while loop to print output onto the screen using <STDIN>. You can accomplish the same effect using a do/while construct.

```
do {    print;} while (<>);
```

Keep in mind that this is an artificial construct and not a true loop. When you learn common loop commands such as next, redo, and last in the Sunday Afternoon session, "Putting It All Together," they will not function correctly with do/while.

The do/while construct is not as common as other types of loops in Perl. The main reason do/while in Perl exists is for programmers who transition into coding Perl from other languages (like C) where do/while is an established, commonly used type of loop.

Using the Foreach Loop

Perl's foreach loop is one of my favorite loops. It is an amazing shortcut when you need to make changes or modifications to a number of different scalars, particularly ones held within an array. The foreach loop uses the same structural flowchart as the for loop (see Figure 4.7), but it has a few significant differences.

A for loop that prints every scalar in an array would look something like this:

```
# Assign scalars to an array called array (remember arrays
  from Chapter 2)
@array = ("My", "Cat's", "Name", "is", "Small");
# Set up a for loop that goes through each part of @array
for($loop = 1; $loop <= $#array; loop++){
```

```
        # Print each part of the array as the loop hits it
        print $array[$loop];
}
```

Although this construction works, it can be difficult to read, and Perl's `for` loop is not optimized to run through arrays. The Perl compiler optimizes the `foreach` loop to run more quickly through arrays than regular loops, and the code looks much cleaner.

```
# Assign scalars to an array called array (remember arrays
   from Chapter 2)
@array = ("My\n", "Cat's\n", "Name\n", "is\n", "Small\n");
# Set up a foreach loop that goes through each part of @array

foreach $entry (@array){
        # Print each part of the array as the loop hits it
        print "$entry";
}
```

Another great feature of the `foreach` loop is that it can run through several different arrays at once.

```
# Assign scalars to an array called array (remember arrays
   from Chapter 2)
@array1 = ("My\n", "Cat's\n", "Name\n", "is\n", "Small\n");
@array2 = ("My\n", "Second\n", "Cat's\n", "Name\n", "is\n",
   "Sidney\n");
@array3 = ("My\n", "Third\n", "Cat's\n", "Name\n", "is\n",
   "Jasmine\n");
@array4 = ("My\n", "Fourth\n","Cat's\n", "Name\n", "is\n",
   "Hailey\n");

# Set up a foreach loop that goes through each part of each
   array

foreach $entry (@array1, @array2, @array3, @array4){
        # Print each part of the array as the loop hits it
        print "$entry\n";
}
```

The `foreach` loop, like the `for` loop, is useful for iterating through a list or an array of items. Since the `foreach` loop has been optimized by the Perl compiler to run through arrays quicker than the other types of loops, it is with arrays that you are most likely to use or encounter it.

Take a Break

Whew, statements and loops—and you probably haven't even had dinner yet! Not bad for a Saturday evening. As you start cranking through pieces, you can see how each section builds on the last. The scalars with which you were just becoming comfortable this morning should be almost second nature to you as you tackle these more advanced programming structures and building blocks. This might be a good time for break. When you come back, you will undertake your third programming block and cover the basics of writing your own subroutines.

Working with Routines and Subroutines

Along the lines of program flow is the concept of program routines and subroutines. Routines help organize your programs as you create them. The divide and conquer ideology is possible only if you can split your programs into small, manageable pieces, and subroutines are one mechanism Perl possesses to allow you to split programs apart.

Programmers split their programs into pieces when developing for a variety of reasons, including these:

➤ Small pieces of code are easier to build than large pieces.

➤ Small pieces of code are easier to maintain than large pieces.

➤ Small pieces of code are easy to debug when problems arise.

➤ Small, focused pieces of code can be ported to other applications and projects.

Creating subroutines is the starting point of splitting a large program into small pieces. A big project is broken down into small, focused pieces or components.

Using Simple Routines

A routine is a collection of related features that are saved as a generic, reusable script. You can create a number of Perl scripts that you use frequently or might need in the future and save them as reusable routines that you can draw upon and insert into future projects.

No particular syntax or special commands are needed in Perl to designate routines. Routines are used in a general sense to refer to finished programs or program pieces that you can use and add to your existing code and projects. Any script you have written so far can be saved and used as a routine. Numerous routine collections have been written for Perl.

The Perl community provides Perl routines and other useful resources for programmers in the form of *packages* and *modules*. Perl packages are sections of code that exist in their own space, which are shut-off and unusable from the rest of the program unless Perl is specifically told to go to a package and use the functions within it.

Perl *modules* are groups of packages that can be added to your Perl distribution (the actual added installed Perl files) and add functionality. If Perl were a car, Perl modules would be the additional options you could add (all-weather tires, booming sound system, heated seats) that add additional features, bells, and whistles.

I will provide an overview of a few Perl modules in the Sunday Evening session, "Learning Advanced Perl Techniques," and I also provide an overview of packages Sunday morning with "Objects and Object-Oriented Programming" because packages are the cornerstone of object-oriented programming in Perl. In the meantime, I encourage you to save everything you program in your Perl projects, from this book and elsewhere, so that you aren't reinventing the wheel each time you take on a new challenge.

Using Subroutines

Subroutines are user-defined commands. Subroutines allow you to have multiple routines, or separated functions, within one Perl script. Perl lets you write code, name it, and then call and use the code just like any other function. This is great for professional programmers because it allows them to separate code, recycle it in chunks, and take it with them to use later.

To roll your own subroutine, you use Perl's `sub` command, name the subroutine, and then enclose actual action code within a program block. Here I created a subroutine called `small` which can be used to print out a series of statements:

```
sub small{
    printf "My cat Small\n";
    printf "is indeed\n";
    printf "A creature of curiosity and wit\n";
}
```

Subroutines can be initialized anywhere within your Perl code, although programmers have a tendency to place them at the beginning of their code. (This is a common coding convention that is considered courteous to those who later try to follow your code.) This is good practice because many other languages require that you declare things like subroutines early in a program.

Subroutines that you create are considered global in scope and are also capable of using any existing global variables. To call your own subroutines, you need to use the ampersand (&) in your script to warn Perl that you are going to use a subroutine.

```
&small;
```

One great feature of subroutines is that they can automatically return the value of the last calculation they were performing. In the `simpleaddition` subroutine, the sum value of 20 will be remembered and can be referenced by other common Perl commands.

```
sub simpleaddition{
    10 + 10;
}
print &simpleaddition;
```

In this context, the term *last value* refers to the last value evaluated, which is not necessarily the last line of the subroutine.

Subroutines can take in and send out information in the form of arguments. To give an argument to a subroutine, which Perl enthusiasts like to call *passing*, you put the argument in parentheses when you call the subroutine.

```
&mysubroutine(argument0, argument1);
```

The two arguments are passed to &mysubroutine. These arguments are assigned to a special default array (much like Standard In) named @_.

So when you send the two arguments to &mysubroutine, Perl performs the following array assignment automatically and invisibly:

```
@_ = (argument0, argument1);
```

You can use @_ like an array to access arguments while you are in the subroutine. In the preceding example, argument0 is the first entry in the array, and you could access it by typing:

```
$_[0]
```

Or, you could access both arguments by using

```
$_[0], $_[1]
```

You can pass a scalar to a subroutine instead of a simple value by just including scalars instead of numbers to a subroutine call. For instance, the following code sends two scalars to the subroutine collect:

```
sub collect
{
foreach (@_){}
}
collect($scalar1, $scaler2);
```

It is important to realize that when a subroutine is passed a scalar value, the subroutine actually receives a reference or pointer to the original value. This means that if you pass a subroutine a scalar and then modify that scalar, the subroutine will receive the modified value.

Subroutines can sometimes get you into trouble when information is passed to or from the program block. This is because there is no error checking. If you are in a subroutine and you try to call the 200th entry ($_[200]) in an array that only has 10 entries, you will get an UNDEF error when you run the code. If your subroutine calls for two arguments, and you don't feed it two arguments when you run the code, neither you nor Perl will realize your subroutine will need two arguments before you actually run the program.

Not only can you pass simple scalars to subroutines using @_, you can also pass arrays, lists, or hashes. In this next piece of code, the subroutine `collect` grabs a hash passed to it:

```
sub collect
{
%retreivedhash = @_;
}
collect (%senthash);
```

It's important to realize that if you pass a subroutine two or more arrays or hashes they are pushed together into one long list within the @_ default array.

If you are building a subroutine that takes in a random or undetermined number of arguments, you can determine the length by checking the length of the @_ array. Since the @_ default array is just like any other array in Perl, you can subject it to all the neat tricks you learned to play on arrays in this morning's session. In this case, to determine how many arguments exist within the @_ array, you can use the $#_ command:

```
sub collect
{
print "The number of passed arguments is equal to $#_ +1"\n";
}
```

What if a subroutine needs to have a few arguments to run correctly, and the user forgets to pass the subroutine any arguments? No problem, you can give subroutines default arguments using the ||= operator. The ||= operator syntax looks like this:

```
argument ||= value;
```

If you needed the `collect` subroutine to possess at least one argument that has a value of 1, you could arrange it using this code:

```
sub collect
{
$value = @_;
$value ||= 1;
}
```

If an argument is not sent to collect, the scalar $value will initially have the value 1, which will be overwritten if collect is sent an argument.

Subroutines in Perl are capable of sending back arguments as well as receiving them using a simple return statement. In the preceding example, if I wanted collect to return $value, I could just add a return line to the code, like so:

```
sub collect
{
$value = @_;
$value ||= 1;
return $value;
}
```

Subroutines are also capable of using returning lists:

```
sub get
{
return a, b, c ,d, e, f, g;
}
```

Or returning an array using the @_ default array:

```
sub get
{
return @_;
}
```

And finally, returning a hash:

```
sub get
{
return %hash;
}
```

Using References with Subroutines

Because the @_ default array flattens arrays and hashes when passed into a subroutine, your subroutines can sometimes experience conflicts when you are passing them more than one array or hash at a time. This problem can

DETERMINING WHETHER A SUBROUTINE EXISTS

When working with a large program or smaller programs that have been split up into different sections, it's nice to be able to check and see if a subroutine has already been defined. Perl provides support for this action with the `defined` function, whose syntax looks like this:

```
defined subroutine;
```

A simple example would be to execute a piece of code if a certain subroutine, say the `simpleaddition` subroutine, was already in place:

```
$number = &simpleadditon if defined simpleadditon;
```

In version 5.6, Perl also added the command `exists` which performs the same function, so you could also use this line of code:

```
#number = &simpleaddition if exists simpleaddition;
```

be solved by passing a subroutine a reference instead of the actual arrays. Say you had two arrays:

```
@array1 = (a, b, c,);
@array2 = (1, 2, 3,);
```

Normally you would pass these into the default @_ array if they needed to get into a subroutine, but then you are stuck with one array and all the items meshed together:

```
sub collect
{
$value = @_;
print $value;
}
sub (@array1, @array2);
```

If you ran this subroutine, $value, you print out "abc123", and you are left with one meshed array instead of the two different ones you started out with. The alternative is to use a reference. To turn the arrays you pass into the subroutine into references, you simply need to add a \:

```
sub (\@array1, \@array2);
```

Now Perl will know you wish to pass two references to arrays into your subroutine, and you can collect them inside the subroutine using one line of code and adding a print statement:

```
($value1, $vlaue2) = @_;
print $value1;
print $value2;
```

Altogether, the code would look like this when finished:

```
# Assign the two arrays
@array1 = (a, b, c,);
@array2 = (1, 2, 3,);


# Create the subroutine
sub collect
{
# collect the arrays values sent to the subroutine
($value1, $value2) = @_;
print $value1;
print $value2;
}


# Call the subroutine with your two arrays
sub (\@array1, \@array2);
```

You can also return arrays by reference using the same technique:

```
return \@array;
```

So if you want to return the two arrays passed to `collect` in the above example, you could add the following line of code to the end of the subroutine:

```
return @value1, @value2;
```

The final source would look like this:

```
# Assign the two arrays
@array1 = (a, b, c,);
@array2 = (1, 2, 3,);


# Create the subroutine
```

```
sub collect
{
# collect the arrays values sent to the subroutine
($value1, $value2) = @_;
print $value1;
print $value2;
# return the two arrays
return @value1, @value2;
}


# Call the subroutine with your two arrays
sub (\@array1, \@array2);
```

Different Types of Perl Declarations

Now that you have loops and other Perl program structures at your beck and call, you need to add scalars, strings, and operations into your programs again. The questions now are how to access the different scalars that are in different blocks and how to limit the values you used in your loops so they do not alter the rest of the program.

Perl uses a concept called *scope* (which I briefly defined in this morning's session) to determine a scalar's realm of influence. If you do not specify the scope when you assign a value, Perl by default assumes the scope is global.

Working with Global Declarations

Every scalar you have used since this morning's session has been a global variable. This means that the scalars have been available anywhere in the script. Even though Perl automatically assumes a scalar is global in nature unless you define it otherwise, in some instances you might want to explicitly define a variable as global in your code.

To specifically designate a scalar as global, you use the `our` command. When you are making a scalar declaration, you just add `our` to the beginning of the statement to ensure that the scalar is global.

```
# normal scalar values
$a = 1;
$b = 2;
```

```
$c = 3;
# scalar values specifically designated as global
our $a = 1;
our $b = 2;
our $c = 3;
```

◆ ◆

CAUTION Using global as the default setting for variable scope is the mainstay for Perl, but it is backwards for most other programming languages. Just about every other programming language you learn after Perl will automatically assign a limited scope to a value when you initiate it. For this reason, it might be good idea to start using the our command, even if it does mean a little extra typing.

Along the same lines, Perl is one of the few languages that does not force you to declare variables and their scope before you use them. In fact, there is a Perl pragma (more about pragmas in Sunday Evening's session) called strict that forces programmers to declare variables and their scope before using them.

◆ ◆

Other programming languages will often refer to global variables as *public variables*, implying that they are accessible to the general public of the program. Variables that are not globally accessible are conversely referred to as *private*.

Working with Scoped Declarations

Most of the time, you are not going to want scalars that are global in scope. As the number of variables that your Perl program needs to track grows, the program will run slower and take up more space in your computer memory. To cut back on this program bloat, Perl and other programs have declarations that make variables private and limit their accessibility.

Perl includes commands to designate two types of private variables—lexical and dynamic. Private variables are created by adding a short declaration when you assign a scalar, just like when you use the global our command.

Dynamically-scoped variables are assigned by the local command and they exist while the program block in which they were created also exists. If you created a local scalar within a for loop block, it would exist as long as that for loop was executing and it would be usable by that program block and any program blocks launched by the block in which it was created.

```
#assigning dynamic scalars with the local command
local $a = 1;
local $b = 2;
local $c = 3;
```

Lexical variables can only exist within a certain program. They are the most limited of Perl's scope commands. You limit scalars to their current block using the my command.

```
#assigning lexical scalars with the my command
my $a = 1;
my $b = 2;
my $c = 3;
```

The following code illustrates scope by using the local, my, and the our commands and then shows where each scalar is accessible based on their scope.

```
# assign a global variable
our $global1 = 10;
if ($global == 10){
    # assign a lexical and dynamic variable within a program
block
    local $local1 = 10;
    my   $dynamic = 10;
    # print the scalars that are accessible within this
block
    # This should be all of them
    print "$global1\n";
    print "$local1\n";
    print "$dynamic1\n";
    # Start a nested block to go deeper
    if ($global == 10){
        # print which scalars are available in this block.
        # Both the global and the and the dynamic are, but
not the lexical
```

```
        print "$global1\n";
        print "$local1\n";
        print "$dynamic1\n";
        }
    # left the inner program block,
    # printing should show each scalar accessible again
    print "$global1\n";
    print "$local1\n";
    print "$dynamic1\n";
}
# Now outside of the program block,
# the only scalar accessible should be the one that is global
print "$global1\n";
print "$local1\n";
print "$dynamic1\n";
```

You will receive errors for trying to print out-of-scope scalars when you are running this program, but with some modifications (including removing the `print` statements that access these out-of-scope scalars) the program will be executable.

Programming Block: The Game Loop

Finally, the moment you have been waiting for. Now that loops are securely fastened under your belt of knowledge, it is time to finish up the programming blocks and test drive an actual Perl computer game. To get started, open your block3final.pl program and resave it as block4.pl.

The block3final.pl has few significant pieces to finish. You have most of the pieces that control game play, but no loop that keeps track of the player on the map or continues to loop until the player wants to quit. You now have the tools to accomplish this with your newfound Perl expertise of structures and loops.

First, organize the block4.pl. Take all the comment blocks you wrote and place them at the top of the script. Feel free to add the list of things you need to finish in this chapter (basically the game loop and anything else left undone). Then, take the "Possible Direction" variables and "The Way

Out" variables and place them at the top of the script with the rest of the variables. The beginning of the code script (after the initial comments) should look like this:

```
# Assign Variables
$direction = North;
$food = 10;
$health = 10;
$turn = 1;

# Possible directions
$north = 0;
$east = 1;
$south = 2;
$west = 3;

# The way out is
$turn1 = int rand(3);
$turn2 = int rand (3);
$turn3 = int rand(3);
$turn4 = int rand(3);
```

These are the global variables—variables that the program needs no matter where it is in the course of events. If you were using scope, you would be assigning your to each of these variables. For now, they are just fine as is.

Next, you need to place the rest of the game within a loop. For this example use a for loop, and set up the loop with a turn expression that keeps track of which turn it is. Because your random maze generator generates only four turns, the loop should exit after four turns. This for loop should look like this:

```
for ($turn = 1; $turn <= 4; $turn++){}
```

The only exception is that the rest of the program should exist within the brackets of the for loop. Place all these pieces together and run the block4.pl. The code at this point in time should look like this:

```
###########################################
#Trapped
```

```
###########################################

###########################################
# block1- planning
# What I need:
# Code that prints information to the screen.
# Code that takes information from the keyboard.
# Code that times the display of text/information
# Code that generates a random map
# Code that tracks the player's progress on the map

###############################################
# block 2 - Basic needs.
# We have learned printing information to the screen and
# Taking information from the keyboard and
# Creating scalar variables and
# a standard ending to keep the dos prompt open.
# Initial print action

###############################################
# block 3
# Any math that needs to be done
# Random number generator
# Any variable changes

###############################################
# block 4
# The actual game loop
# Anything else that remains undone.

# Assign Variables
$direction = North;
$food = 10;
$health = 10;
```

```
$turn = 1;

# Possible directions
$north = 0;
$east = 1;
$south = 2;
$west = 3;

# The way out is
$turn1 = int rand(3);
$turn2 = int rand (3);
$turn3 = int rand(3);
$turn4 = int rand(3);

print "The way out is $turn1$turn2$turn3$turn4\n";

for ($turn = 1; $turn <= 4; $turn++){

print "\n";
print "You are trapped in a cavern\n";
print "You can travel North, South, East or West\n";
print "\n\n\n";
print "You are facing $direction\n";
print "You have $food boxes of ramen left\n";
print "Your health is equal to $health\n";
print "\n\n\n";

# While making a move lose one food unit
$food = $food -2;
print "You have $food boxes of ramen left\n";

# If a mishap occurs, lose one health
$health = $health -1;
print "Your health is equal to $health\n";
```

```
}
```

```
# Add our ending changed to user input
# standard ending
print "\nPress any key to continue...";
```

```
<>
```

At this point, the game still doesn't take any user input; it just loops through the print statements in the `for` loop several times before ending. To fix that, we need to wait for a player to choose a direction to travel. An ideal way to do this is with the `readline` command using <STDIN> (which is the computer keyboard by default). Also, add a print line to the following code to make sure that you are receiving the keyboard input you need. This code would look like this:

```
# Need to grab info from the player
$char = readline(*STDIN);
print "$char\n";
```

To collect the information from the player, you need to provide print statements as instructions. To make things simple, have the user press the same keys that the program is already tracking for direction using the following print statements:

```
print "Please choose a direction to travel by pressing:\n";
print "0 for North\n";
print "1 for East\n";
print "2 for South\n";
print "3 for West\n";
```

```
# Need to grab info from the player
$char = readline(*STDIN);
print "$char\n";
```

Now comes the most complex part of the code. As the player makes decisions in direction, the game needs to determine whether the direction is the correct one, and then either reward or punish the player. The easiest way to do this is by using program flow statements. Start with the simplest of conditions: the player chooses the right way during the right turn. This can be a simple `if` statement:

```
if ($turn == 1 && $char == $turn1)
{print "You have chosen wisely!\n\n"};
```

The `if` statement checks to see if, during the first turn ($turn == 1), the player typed the correct direction to travel ($char == $turn1). The two ampersands represent "and" for the if statement, making sure that both conditions are met before printing the success message.

The code logic can be continued in this way for each turn by adding `elsif` statements for every successful move, like this:

```
elsif ($turn == 2 && $char == $turn2)
{print "You have chosen wisely!\n\n"}
elsif ($turn == 3 && $char == $turn3)
{print "You have chosen wisely!\n\n"}
elsif ($turn == 4 && $char == $turn4)
{print "You have chosen wisely!\n\n"}
```

Finally, the consequences of choosing the wrong way out of the maze can be applied to the last `else` statement; another simple `if` statement can be added to check if the player is out of food, and a final `if` statement checks to see if the player has lost and the program needs to be exited. This code piece will also make $turn go backward by one, so that the game will not end until the player's health is below zero, or the maze is successfully navigated:

```
{
# If a mishap occurs, lose one health
$health = $health -1;
print "You have chosen poorly\n";
print "Your health is equal to $health\n";
$turn = $turn-1;
};

if ($food <= 0) {
print "You are out of food!\n";
$health = $health -1;
};

# While making a move lose one food unit
$food = $food -2;
print "You have $food boxes of ramen left\n";

if ($health < 0){
print "You have lost, and remain trapped for all
   eternity!\n";
$turn = 4;



};
```

The game loop is now complete. You can save the block.pl file, run it, and walk through the game loop. Many changes still need to be made. The way out of the maze is still printed at the beginning of the game. The food variable needs some work in order to work with the game correctly. The instructions printed to the screen could be formatted in an easier-to-read way. The code has also become large (over 100 lines) and somewhat difficult to manage. All this is expected: Welcome to the wonderful world of programming. Over the course of the next few sessions, you will make improvements to the script to fix these problems. Following is the full source code for the project as it stands. The code is also available with the Saturday Evening session downloads from the companion Web site (http://www.premierpressbooks.com/downloads.asp):

```
######################################
#Trapped
######################################

######################################
# block1- planning
# What I need:
# Code that prints information to the screen.
# Code that takes information from the keyboard.
# Code that times the display of text/information
# Code that generates a random map
# Code that tracks the player's progress on the map

######################################
# block 2 - Basic needs.
# We have learned printing information to the screen and
# Taking information from the keyboard and
# Creating scalar variables and
# a standard ending to keep the dos prompt open.
# Initial print action

######################################
# block 3
# Any math that needs to be done
# Random number generator
# Any variable changes

######################################
# block 4
# The actual game loop
```

```
# Anything else that reamins undone.


# Assign Variables
$direction = North;
$food = 10;
$health = 10;
$turn = 1;

# Possible directions
$north = 0;
$east = 1;
$south = 2;
$west = 3;

# The way out is
$turn1 = int rand(3);
$turn2 = int rand (3);
$turn3 = int rand(3);
$turn4 = int rand(3);


print "The way out is $turn1$turn2$turn3$turn4\n";


for ($turn = 1; $turn <= 4; $turn++){


print "\n";
print "You are trapped in a cavern\n";
print "You can travel Forward, Backwards, Right, or Left
   using the arrow keys\n";
print "\n\n\n";
print "You are facing $direction\n";
print "You have $food boxes of ramen left\n";
print "Your health is equal to $health\n";
print "\n\n\n";


print "Please choose a direction to travel by pressing:\n";
```

```
print "0 for North\n";
print "1 for East\n";
print "2 for South\n";
print "3 for West\n";

# Need to grab info from the player
$char = readline(*STDIN);
print "$char\n";

if ($turn == 1 && $char == $turn1)
{print "You have chosen wisely!\n\n"}
elsif ($turn == 2 && $char == $turn2)
{print "You have chosen wisely!\n\n"}
elsif ($turn == 3 && $char == $turn3)
{print "You have chosen wisely!\n\n"}
elsif ($turn == 4 && $char == $turn4)
{print "You have chosen wisely!\n\n"}
else
{
# If a mishap occurs, lose one health
$health = $health -1;
print "You have chosen poorly\n";
print "Your health is equal to $health\n";
$turn = $turn-1;
};

if ($food <= 0) {
print "You are out of food!\n";
$health = $health -1;
};

# While making a move lose one food unit
$food = $food -2;
print "You have $food boxes of ramen left\n";

if ($health < 0){
```

```
print "You have lost, and remain trapped for all
    eternity!\n";
$turn = 4;



};


}


# Add our ending changed to user input
# standard ending
print "\nPress an arrow key to continue...";
<>
```

Summary

Bravo, maestro. You have conquered the basic building blocks and structures of Perl and you now have quite a belt of programming tools and knowledge to help you succeed in your next programming venture. Time for some R&R because tomorrow morning, bright and early, you and I are going to tackle advanced Perl, jump into object-oriented programming, and code until our fingers are red.

Objects and Object-Oriented Programming

- ➤ An introduction to object-oriented programming
- ➤ Building a Perl package
- ➤ Using Perl references
- ➤ Using classes
- ➤ Using objects
- ➤ Using methods
- ➤ Using inheritance
- ➤ Program Block: Game Loop

G ood morning, and welcome to your third day of Perl. By now you should be feeling pretty confident with the Perl language. You have built your first Perl computer game, you are familiar with structured programming, and you are more than halfway finished with the programming lessons from this book. This chapter introduces you to a whole new programming paradigm—object-oriented programming, also known as OOP.

One big difference between a beginning Perl programmer and an expert Perl programmer is object-oriented programming. On a simple level, object-oriented programming is just one of the many ways to program (remember TIMTOWTDI). With OOP, you will be doing the same things you have already learned to do in Perl, but the syntax and methodology will be different.

An Introduction to Object-Oriented Programming

Object-oriented programming has been around since the late 1980s and was spread by the advent of C++. OOP is really a way or a style of programming. OOP is also a natural progression of structured programming, a concept with which you should now be familiar.

OOP is mainly used as a tool and method for designing and separating small, reusable software pieces. There are many things that OOP does extremely well, including:

➤ Grouping variables

➤ Grouping sets of functions

➤ Defining and reusing sets of variables

➤ Defining and reusing sets of functions

Like structured programming, OOP has been a front runner in how to organize large programs, except it takes the idea of separating pieces of a program into subroutines even further. OOP abstracts and encapsulates large program pieces and breaks them into smaller, compact, focused pieces. OOP is simply a layer that takes data and subroutines and compartmentalizes them into small, easily managed objects.

Object-oriented programming is a style of programming in which programmers are capable of defining:

➤ The type (variable, integer, character) of a data structure.

➤ The operations and functions that can be applied to a data structure.

When programmers are given this power, data structures can become objects that include the data, the type of data, and the functions that apply to that data all rolled into one. Because these objects contain all of this information, they are incredibly mobile and can be picked up, shared, and passed around into other programs and applications. Common OOP programming languages include C++, C#, Java, Perl, Smalltalk, and some versions of Pascal.

Objects and Object-Oriented Programming

Creating an object in OOP is just a way of gift-wrapping complex code into a simple package. For example, a CD is made up of a complicated blend of plastics and other materials. It holds huge amounts of varied data and is read by a laser pointer whose design is extremely intricate. But when I use a CD, none of the complexity matters; I just put the CD into my computer or CD player, and it magically works.

Complex program pieces are lot like CDs; they often hold huge amounts of data and are very complex. Object-oriented programming takes the complexity of the data and wraps it in an object that has a simple implementation. This implementation doesn't care about complexity; it just makes sure the object does what it is designed to do. To go back to the CD example, when you insert a CD into the correct piece of equipment, such as a drive or a player, the CD runs. In object-oriented programming, the CD is an object, and the player or drive is an *interface*, or a means of interacting with that object (see Figure 5.1).

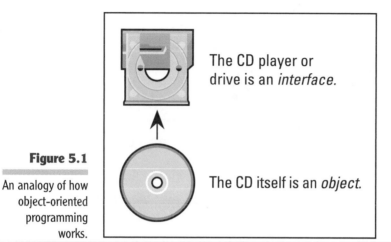

Figure 5.1

An analogy of how object-oriented programming works.

The CD player or drive is an *interface*.

The CD itself is an *object*.

Typical Features of Object-Oriented Programming

OOP is really based on the "divide-and-conquer" strategy. You use OOP to encapsulate data and subroutines into objects, which makes them autonomous, separate, and private. The objects can then interact with your program through an interface you create. The basis for this encapsulation is a structure called a *class*.

OOP uses classes as the top-level, basic building blocks of programming. The class works like a template or blueprint. When you have a functioning class, you can use it as a template to create objects. The programming language is what ties the data and functions of a class together. You can use the class to make the same object over and over. You can also alter the class slightly to make similar objects.

Figure 5.2 is a simple diagram that exemplifies the concepts behind classes and objects. A class is designed to be a blueprint or a template of an object. Once created, the class can act as a factory producing these objects on command. If necessary, the factory production can be altered by the programmer, creating slightly different objects.

Objects enable the programmer to interact with classes in an abstract way using *methods*. Methods are simply subroutines that are built-in to a class

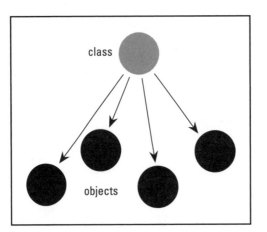

Figure 5.2

The class is a template or blueprint for the objects it creates.

or object. These methods act as functions, routines, or procedures that act when they are called upon. For example, in Perl, a class normally has a method named `new`, and when called upon this `new` method will create an object for the class.

Besides objects, classes, and methods, the object-oriented paradigm also includes several other features, such as *inheritance*. Inheritance basically means that an object or class knows who created it, or who its parent is. Because a class knows where it comes from, it can take on the attributes of its creator. This is technically known as *deriving* one class from another.

Another common feature of OOP is *polymorphism*. Polymorphism refers to taking on many different forms. In OOP, this means that you can use one established interface on many different types of objects.

Extensibility is another OOP feature that is commonly discussed. Extensibility refers to using inheritance to derive from a class, but also adding extra functionality to that class.

You will also see the terms *encapsulation* and *abstraction* tossed around with regard to OOP. Encapsulation refers to the way in which objects separate functionality into small, manageable pieces. Abstraction refers to the way implementation is abstracted from the programmer's view so that a complex object can be utilized in a simple way, despite the object's complexity, because all the programmer has to utilize are simple, abstract methods.

OOP just managed to bring ten fun new programming terms into your Perl world.

➤ **Objects** are structures that encapsulate data or functions and come from classes.

➤ **Interfaces** are a means of interacting with an object from a class. (Interfaces are sometimes called methods.)

➤ **Classes** are structures that encapsulate data and functions and act as blueprints for objects.

➤ **Methods** are a means of interacting with an object or class. (Methods are sometimes called interfaces.)

➤ **Inheritance** is taking on the attributes of a parent.

➤ **Deriving** is the technical term used to describe an act of inheritance.

➤ **Polymorphism** is a feature that enables an interface to interact with many different objects.

➤ **Extensibility** is adding functionality to a derived class.

➤ **Encapsulation** is separating functionality into small, manageable pieces.

➤ **Abstraction** is hiding data or complex features from the implementation.

Ten new programming terms is pretty serious for a Sunday morning. Don't be intimidated by all of the new terms; object-oriented programming is a quick study because it is designed to be an easier way to solve programming problems. OOP was not designed just to bring added complexity and headaches (although you might find some programmers who will argue this point).

Don't worry about digging up flash cards and trying to memorize these terms; that's why I placed them in an easy-to-read bulleted list. Just earmark this page in the book and move on. You can always refer to them later, and these terms will become second nature as you continue to learn about object-oriented programming.

Like many great teachers, most beginning books and tutorials use an analogy to familiarize students with OOP. The typical example is usually a car. If you think of OOP as the process of building a car, and objects as the pieces that make up a car when put together, the terminology begins to make sense.

A car is a pretty complex machine with thousands of different components, but each component has a specific, well-defined use. Tires, stereo, steering, brake system, headlights, engine—all of these can be considered objects. For this example, I'll focus on one car object—the tire.

The tires of a car can be different, depending on whether the manufacturer or customer wants to put normal, radial, or all-weather tires on the vehicle. It doesn't matter to the car what kind of tires it has, because the car has a simple mechanism (like a method or interface) to use the tires. The tires themselves are encapsulated; they are small, manageable pieces that contribute to the entire functionality of the car. The car is exhibiting polymorphism because it can use almost any type of tire; the car's interface to the tires can be used on different types of tires.

All tires share some common characteristics. They are made of rubber, they are round, they spin, they have hubcaps, and they have some sort of tread. In this analogy, the tires' common characteristics would be the data or subroutines that the tire holds. If you were creating tires, you would want to put all of these characteristics into a master blueprint or template. The template would be equivalent to an OOP class (see Figure 5.3).

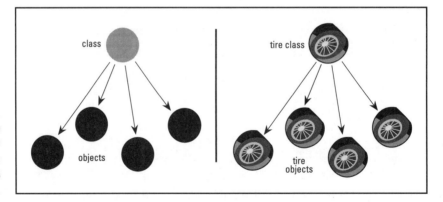

Figure 5.3

A master tire template can create different types of tires.

Imagine that a manufacturer really liked the rubber quality of tire type A, but wasn't so taken with the hubcaps. The manufacturer could take the tire type A template (or class) and use it as a starting point to derive a new type of tire, type B, which has slightly different hubcaps. Deriving the new type of tire is inheritance in action, because the tire takes on most of the attributes of the parent type A tire. Extensibility is also being used, because this newly derived tire type B will have a slightly different and new feature, the hubcaps.

Now take a step back and picture all of the separate parts that make up a car. The tire is only one object, and an actual vehicle would have thousands of different objects. If a car were one long programming script, the script would be too huge to manage effectively. However, if each object was broken down into a small, manageable piece, you can see how building, updating, maintaining, and even changing the programming script would be a much easier job. This manageability is really the essence of object-oriented programming.

Take a look at a practical programming example to illustrate this point. One common task in programming is creating random numbers. Having a class that creates random numbers could be useful, because instead of scripting a random number generator for each project, you could just build a new object for a new project.

The code for creating a random number X in Perl is

```
$number = int rand(X);
```

Placing this code in a class package would look something like this:

```
package RANDOM;
sub new {};
sub number $number = int rand(X);
return 1;
```

When you save this file as RANDOM.pm it becomes a class. The saved RANDOM.pm class can run one of two methods. These methods are the subroutine new, which creates a new object of the type RANDOM, and the subroutine number, which calls the code that creates a new random number.

You can use RANDOM.pm from any Perl program you script by including it with a use command:

```
use RANDOM.pm;
```

When the RANDOM.pm class is included, you can use the class to create a random number object:

```
my $randomobject = new RANDOM;
```

Then you can use the object to run the number subroutine/method whenever you need a random number:

```
$randomobject->number;
```

So now you have a class called RANDOM, which is capable of creating objects that can create random numbers. Using three lines of code, you can import the same random command into any program you ever write in Perl. Admittedly, this may seem strange considering that the random number code is only a single line, but as you familiarize yourself with OOP and continue through this chapter, the practicality will make more sense.

Later in this chapter, you revisit the random number generator code you wrote yesterday afternoon and modify it into an OOP file called MAP.pm. The MAP.pm will be modeled after this code sample but will also include all the steps necessary to create a true class (this example is illustrative and not complete). For now just keep in mind that classes and objects make it easy to reuse code, and realize that you still need to learn Perl's specific syntax for utilizing OOP.

Uses of OOP in Perl

Perl did not start out as a full-blown object-oriented programming language. In fact, the OOP paradigm hadn't quite taken seed yet when Perl first appeared. OOP functionality was added to Perl much later in the language's life. Because OOP for Perl came later, Perl possesses some OOP uniqueness that separates it from other OOP languages (namely Java, C++, C#, Smalltalk, and Python).

The first important difference between Perl and an OOP language like C++ is in syntax. C++ provides special syntax and commands for OOP constructors and for defining a class. Perl does not have any special syntax for these commands. In Perl, a constructor is just a subroutine with a little added oomph, and a class is simply a package, or a collection of code that is contained in it's own space. (You will start building Perl packages in the next section, "Building a Perl Package.") Instead of developing a whole new subset of commands to adopt OOP, Perl just uses the commands it already possesses and adds a bit more functionality to them.

Using the built-in commands, Perl is capable of handling most OOP features, including inheritance, polymorphism, and most of the features you reviewed earlier in this chapter, but it does not have all of the features of the full-blown OOP languages. For you C++ buffs, for instance, Perl has some built-in exception handling, but nothing like C++'s `try-catch-finally`. Perl also does not possess C style templates; from a C++ perspective, all Perl classes are virtual, whereas in C++ you have a choice between virtual and static methods.

NOTE I will try to keep my C++ and Java references to a minimum; however, because they are both such popular OOP languages, they often set the standard, and it is important to keep in mind the family of languages that share OOP. For a good introduction to these languages, you might want to thumb through *C++ Programming for the Absolute Beginner* (Premier Press, Inc., 2001) or *Java Programming for the Absolute Beginner* (Premier Press, Inc., 2001).

The most important difference between Perl's OOP and OOP in other languages is private keywords. Most of the OOP languages have private keywords built into them that keep object and class attributes and methods private. This creates a form of security because these attributes are not readily available anywhere in a program or to a client or user. Perl does not possess this security; it operates from a perspective of trust. Perl assumes that clients will stay out of classes and their implementations; it also believes that the interface the class provides will be used. However, Perl does not enforce this idea by making the class attributes and methods private.

A second important difference in Perl's OOP is terminology and vocabulary. To be honest, OOP terminology tends to vary between languages. When studying different OOP languages, you will see that they often use different terms to describe the same programming constructs. Unfortunately, this helps to enforce the mystique of OOP programmers by making them seem like brilliant, mad geniuses or magicians, especially when they start throwing around terms like base class, generic class, and super class but do not explain that these terms can all refer to the same class.

It is unfortunate that to grasp OOP you need to learn a whole new set of terms, and then learn new subsets of those terms when learning other OOP languages. Since a Sunday morning is not usually the best time to learn a slew of new terminology, I have provided another list for you to earmark in case you get confused by some of the later lessons in this chapter or by OOP lessons in other books. These terms will become second nature as you develop your OOP programming knowledge.

➤ The **parent class** is also referred to as the *base class*, *generic class*, and *super class*.

➤ The **child class** is also referred to as the *derived class*, *specific class*, and *subclass*.

➤ A **class** is basically a Perl package with methods to deal with object references.

➤ An **object** is also called an *instance of a class*. In Perl, an object is a reference to an item in a class.

➤ **Object methods** can also be called *instance methods*.

➤ **Methods** are basically Perl subroutines that accept an object reference or a package name as the first argument.

➤ **Data** can also be called *attributes*.

➤ A **module** is a Perl *package* or a group of packages.

➤ A **function** can also be called a *behavior*.

➤ A **package** is also called a *namespace*. Groups of packages are called *modules*.

Building a Perl Package

The spine of OOP in Perl is the package function. Packages are self-contained units of variables and subroutines that can be used over and over again. Reusability is really the key behind OOP, and packages are the basic building blocks for reusability in Perl.

Packages are built using the `package` command, which has a simple syntax.

```
package Nameofpackage;
```

After you have defined a package, you can add declarations and subroutines just like you would anywhere else in a script.

```
package Nameofpackage;
# Create a subroutine in the package
sub something{ does something }
# Create a variable in the package
$variable = "variable";
```

Packages are important because modules and classes in Perl are based on them. After you create a package in Perl using the `package` command, you normally use the `return` command to end the package.

```
# Creating a package named NEWPACKAGE
package NEWPACKAGE
return 1;
```

`Return` is a function that is used to send a message; the convention for packages is for `return` to send a 1 for successful loading. If NEWPACKAGE is successfully loaded, `return` sends back a 1 to the program that is attempting to load it.

However, a package by itself is not capable of doing much. To make packages useful, you need to include subroutines within them. You should remember how to build subroutines from Chapter 4, "Expressing and Stating." You can use the `sub` command to add a simple printing subroutine to NEWPACKAGE.

```
# Creating a package named NEWPACKAGE
package NEWPACKAGE
sub printing1 {print "Hello my baby.\n"}
return 1;
```

Now you have a package with one subroutine called `printing1` that prints "Hello my baby." In order to utilize NEWPACKAGE, you need to save it as a .pl file, just like any other Perl program. Because NEWPACKAGE is a package, you can now include it and any of its subroutines in your other Perl programs. You include packages in other Perl scripts using the `require` command.

```
require 'NEWPACKAGE.pl';
```

When you include a `require` line, Perl knows that you might be using subroutines or data from the NEWPACKAGE Perl file. Perl will open NEWPACKAGE and make sure it has the appropriate information to continue.

After Perl ensures that your program has the correct Perl package, you can make calls to the subroutines contained within the package by referring to the appropriate name of the package and subroutine, as if the package contents were local to the file. If you want to run NEWPACKAGE's printing subroutine, you can simply refer to the package and subroutine with one line of code.

```
NEWPACKAGE::printing1();
```

Perl recognizes this line as a namespace or package reference. Perl will look for the printing1 subroutine, which is located in NEWPACKAGE. It knows where NEWPACKAGE is because of the earlier require command. If the printing1 subroutine needed any input or variable data to run, the data could be placed within the parentheses.

To increase the scope of this example, you can add a number of print commands to NEWPACKAGE.

```
# Creating a package named NEWPACKAGE
package NEWPACKAGE
sub printing1 {print "Hello my baby.\n"}
# Add more printing subroutines
sub printing2 {print "Hello my darling.\n"}
sub printing3 {print "Hello my ragtime gal.\n"}
return 1;
```

Now you can create a new Perl script that uses all three subroutines.

```
# Creating a New Perl script that utilizes NEWPACAKGE
  subroutines
# Need to Tell Perl to include NEWPACKAGE
require 'NEWPACKAGE.pl';
print "And the Frog sang:\n";
NEWPACKAGE::printing1();
NEWPACKAGE::printing2();
NEWPACKAGE::printing3();
# End
print "Press <ENTER> to continue...";
<>
```

You can test this script by saving it as NPtest.pl. Alternatively, you can download the source files from the book's companion Web site.

In and of itself, NEWPACKAGE admittedly isn't very useful. What makes packages powerful is that they allow you to reuse code. Since NEWPACKAGE has been written, I never again have to code a script in Perl that prints out the chorus of Michigan J. Frog's song. Instead, I can just include a require line to use any of the printing statements I need.

Packages in Perl are very similar to classes, which makes them a perfect introduction to OOP. They are also very similar to modules, which you will learn about in tonight's session, "Learning Advanced Perl Techniques."

NOTE Modules in Perl are simply several packages that are stored in a single file. These files usually end in .pm (short for *Perl Module*). The convention in Perl is to capitalize the names of modules and packages. Thousands of Perl programmers have written unique and helpful Perl modules that other programmers can download and use. In tonight's session, I will spend some time talking about importing useful packages and modules, as well as where to find them.

The scope of a package is important. When you require a package, you can refer and use the package until the end of that particular script file or until another package keyword is used. Unlike global variables in Perl, variables that are contained within a package cannot be accessed by other packages.

Using Perl References

References are the second major foundation of OOP, and they are the basis of objects in Perl. A reference in Perl is a construct that points to or references something else. Programmers use references to access values stored within a variable without having to use the actual variable name. A practical example for a reference is when you are creating an interface to work with the value of pi.

Because pi is an extremely long number (3.14159…), a script that holds a reference for pi could be useful. You can create a variable that holds the value of pi, and then use references to retrieve the variable when you need it. Creating a variable reference involves two simple steps.

1. Assign the variable to a scalar.

2. Set the reference by using the \ indicator.

The code to produce a pi reference would look like this:

```
# Assign your variable to a scalar
$pi = 3.1459;
# set your reference by using the \ indicator
$reference = \$pi;
```

In this script, I bet you are wondering what the difference is between $pi and $reference. The difference is significant because when you create a reference in Perl, it does not hold the value assigned to it—it holds memory of an address to the variable. To illustrate this, create a new script called Pi.pl, add the sample code that assigns a reference to pi, and then add two print statements that print out $reference and $pi. The complete code should look like this:

```
# Assign your variable to a scalar
$pi = 3.1459;
# set your reference by using the \ indicator
$reference = \$pi;
# print values
print "the value of \$pi is $pi\n";
print "the value of \$reference is $reference\n";
# End
print "Press <ENTER> to continue...";
<>
```

Now run the program to see what values the two scalars hold. You will see that $pi is equal to the value you assigned to it: 3.14159. The $reference value, however, is completely different—it looks something like 00x80xx80808. This is because $reference is not concerned with the value of $pi; it is keeping track of where $pi is. The value of $pi is actually stored in the physical memory on your computer, and $reference keeps track of that physical memory by keeping a hexadecimal numeric address that points to the space where the value of $pi is stored.

You can tell Perl to print the actual value of $reference by using a second $ sign.

```
print "The value of reference is $$reference\n";
```

Perl will know that you do not want to print the reference to $pi, but the actual value of $pi instead. This is called *dereferencing*; it is a technique commonly used in OOP.

References are also capable of pointing to arrays and hashes; you just need to remember to insert the \ character, and then assign the arrays and hashes like you have done in the examples in this book.

```
# Build an array
@array = (1,2,3,4);
# Build a hash
%hash = (5=>6=>7=>8=>);
# Assign an array reference
$arrayreference = \@array;
# Assign a hash reference
$hashreference = \%hash
```

You can also have a reference that points to a subroutine. You use an additional character, the ampersand (&), to create a reference to the subroutine or run the subroutine via the reference.

```
# Create a subroutine
sub example {
print "This is a simple subroutine example\n";
}
# Create a reference to subroutine
$reference = \&example;
# Run the subroutine via reference
&$reference;
```

Using Classes in Perl

OOP uses a class to create objects. A class is basically a set of routines that are focused or related in some way. Normally, classes provide users with objects, and these objects know what class they belong to and how to behave.

The name you give a class is important because it is also the name of the file that holds the class. This is the way modules work; I will cover this in more detail in tonight's session, "Learning Advanced Perl Techniques." After the class has a name, you provide it with a way to create objects. You also provide the class with certain mechanisms for it to use when other processes want to use the objects the class creates. Basically, a class is factory that creates objects. As a programmer, you control the objects created by the class and how the class creates them.

In Perl, a class is the same as a package. The only difference between the two is that a class provides methods to other parts of the program. A class also needs to include a constructor to kick-start object creation.

Declaring a Class in Perl

Creating a class is sometimes referred to as *declaring* or *implementing* a class. Creating a class involves naming the class and defining the subroutines that will be included. For an analogy, consider a cat. Every cat has common characteristics—they possess claws, fangs, temperament, fur, and eye color. To create a Cat class, you would need to:

1. Create a package named Cat.

2. Create a way for Cat objects to be constructed.

3. Include all the subroutines that make up cats in the class.

4. Finish the class with a return command.

Coding these steps involves using the package command, creating the subroutines (new, claws, fangs, and fur), and ending with a return line as shown here:

```
package Cat;
# Constructor called new that creates a Cat object
sub new
{ code that creates class objects }
# A few object methods
sub claws{ code for claws in here }
sub fangs{ code for fangs in here  }
sub fur{ code for fur in here }
# end with a return
return 1;
```

This Cat class is detailed in Figure 5.4.

Figure 5.4

The Cat class and corresponding subroutines illustrated as a program block.

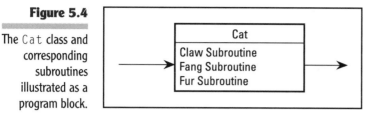

Referencing a Class

Once you have created a class, another script or program can use all of the subroutines within the class by creating an instance of the class (or class object). You can see that a class isn't much more complicated than a package. When your program needs to use a Cat object, you simply call the new subroutine. A programmer who wanted to sound important would call this, "instantiating an object by calling the constructor."

To set up a reference to a class in a script (using Cat as an example), you need to

1. Tell the script to use the Cat class.

2. Create a Cat object by calling the new constructor.

```
# Script includes the cat class by using the use command
use Cat;
# Script creates a cat object (named kitten) by invoking the
   new subroutine
$kitten = new Cat;
```

This new kitten object possesses all of the subroutines that you had in the Cat class. You can now access these subroutines within kitten by using a process known as *running object methods*.

```
# This command runs the fur subroutine within the kitten
   object
$kitten->fur();
# This command runs the claw subroutine within the kitten
   object
$kitten->claws();
```

Creating Your First Perl Class

Organizing program pieces into classes and objects in Perl might seem daunting at first. The key is to think in terms of reusing and packaging code and, of course, to practice. In this section, you will create a simple class that creates a type of tire, like in the example you read about earlier. This class will be used to create the objects in the next section. Start your tire class by following these steps:

1. Create a package named `CreateTire`.

2. Create a new subroutine that will become the tire constructor.

3. Use `return` to end the class.

4. Save the class as CreateTire.pl.

The code should look like this:

```
package CreateTire;
sub new { };
return 1;
```

So far I have not detailed the specifics of how a new subroutine instantiates an object. The new subroutine actually needs to do three things to create an object.

1. Create a local scalar.

2. Use the `bless` command to change the scalar into an object.

3. Use the `return` command to send back a reference to the new object.

In object-oriented programming, the code that creates a new object is called a constructor. In Perl, a constructor is a subroutine in a class that returns a reference to an object that has the class name attached to it. Connecting a class name with a reference is referred to as *blessing* an object.

You have already used references and the `return` command. Perl's `bless` command is a built-in function that turns a reference into an object. Basically, a constructor is just a subroutine that returns a reference to something "blessed" in the class. The syntax for `bless` is simple.

```
bless $reference;
```

In Perl, all objects are blessed. Being blessed allows objects to know where they belong. In Perl, this is the only major difference between an object and a reference. Blessed objects know which package they belong to, and references do not.

To add the functionality to your `CreateTire` package, you need to add three lines of code to the new subroutine.

```
sub new
{
# Create a local scalar
my $tire = {};
# bless the tire to turn it into an object
bless $tire;
# return the new tire object
return $tire
}
```

The entire code listing should now look like this:

```
package CreateTire;
sub new
{
# Create a local scalar
my $tire = {};
# bless the tire to turn it into an object
bless $tire;
# return the new tire object
return $tire
}
return 1;
```

Now that there is a method to create `tire` objects, you can include the subroutines and attributes the tires should possess. These attributes are simply subroutines with default values; they are shown in Figure 5.5.

```
package CreateTire;
sub new
{
# Create a local scalar
my $tire = {};
# bless the tire to turn it into an object
bless $tire;
# return the new tire object
```

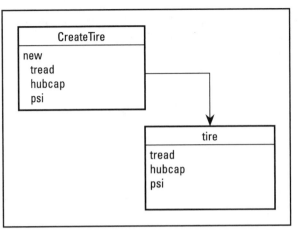

Figure 5.5

The `CreateTire` class/package uses its new method to create `tire` objects. The `tire` objects have the subroutines (methods) of the parent class.

```
return $tire
}

# A few object methods
sub tread{ my $tiretread = wavy; };
sub hubcap{ my $hubcap = metal;  };
sub psi{ my $tirepsi = 40 pounds per square inch; };
# end with a return
return 1;
```

There you have it—your first Perl class. Save the class as Tire.pl. In the next section, you will use the new method you scripted to create and run actual `tire` objects.

Take a Break

Whew. Classes, references, and packages all in one morning, and you haven't even finished the chapter yet. You have covered the basics of OOP, and you have already been introduced to the tough subjects. The next part of this chapter outlines the rest of Perl's OOP abilities, but before you move on to the likes of inheritance and object methods, take a breather. Get up, stretch, fill your coffee cup. You have come along way, but you still have a ways to go.

Using Objects in Perl

Just as packages are the basis for classes in Perl, references are the basis of objects. An object is simply a reference that knows it is within a class. In the

RANDOM.pm example I used in the earlier in this chapter, I illustrated how to create a local instance of the RANDOM.pm class utilizing this line of code:

```
my $randomobject = new RANDOM;
```

The only difference between `$randomobject` and any other scalar is that `$randomobject` knows who its parent is. Because `$randomobject` has a relationship with RANDOM, `$randomobject` can call upon the powers (methods)of RANDOM.

Object methods are simply subroutines that expect references as arguments. Using the same example, the code calling `$randomobject`'s method `number` is:

```
$randomobject->number;
```

The only difference between `number` and any other Perl subroutine is that `number` knows that it needs the reference back to the class which created it. That reference is the object `$randomobject`.

An object is called an *instance* of a class. In this case, `$randomobject` could be called and instance of `RANDOM.pm` The subroutines in an object are called *instance methods* or *member functions* (or sometimes just *methods*). Again, using the random number generator as an example, the methods are `number` and `new`, both contained within RANDOM.pm.

Finally, objects can hold subroutines and data. Sometimes data items are called *data members* or *instance data*. (Classes can also hold data, which is normally called *class data*.)

Declaring an Object in Perl

To create an object, you call a class constructor (usually `new`). To call a class constructor, you need to:

1. Include the class in the script with the `use` command.

2. Create a local variable to hold the object using the `my` command.

3. Use the arrow referencer to have Perl run the new constructor for the specified class.

You have seen the `use` command in action already.

```
use Class;
```

You have also used `my` to create local variables.

```
my $object;
```

The only new Perl you need to learn is how to use the arrow referencer to point to the appropriate class and constructor. You have used the arrow referencer before, but not in this context.

```
Class->new();
```

That's all there is to it. You can put everything together in a few lines of Perl code.

```
use Class;
my $object Class->new();
```

If you want to call the `Tire` class you built in the last section, you can just replace `Class` with Tire.pl.

```
use CreateTire.pl;
my $object Tire->new();
```

If you run this as a script, Perl creates a brand new object named `$object`, which possesses all of the abilities (subroutines and data) that the Tire.pl class possesses.

● ●

NOTE As a programmer, you have the freedom to name a constructor whatever you want. The common convention is to use the `new()` command as the constructor of an object, but you are not forced to use it. You might discover cases where an object constructor is named something completely different. You might also find classes with multiple constructors to make different types of objects.

● ●

Referencing an Object in Perl

After you have built an object, you can reference it like an array or hash. However, objects normally are manipulated with methods, which in Perl are simply subroutines. This is called *dereferencing*, and methods used to access objects are called *object methods*.

MANUALLY TRIGGERING PERL'S BUILT-IN DESTRUCTOR

At some point, an object needs to stop existing. Perl's garbage-collection feature is fast, simple, and reference-based. Perl uses a built-in destructor to end the life of an object. This destructor is a method whose job is to erase an object and clean up the associated memory space. In Perl, you use the DESTROY command to call an OOP destructor, which automatically calls DESTROY when an object goes out of scope. Perl assumes the object is still within scope as long as a reference to the object exists. As soon as the last reference to the object is gone, the object is destroyed. However, if your object contains references to universal variables, the references might still exist after the object is destroyed. If you have stored references in universal variables, object destruction might occur after the program exits.

You can attempt to force DESTROY early or override DESTROY so that objects remain in memory, but this technique is not recommended. However, the DESTROY command is universally accessible as a subroutine call if needed:

```
sub DESTROY{}
return 1;
```

If you need more information about DESTROY, check out the resources in tonight's session, "Learning Advanced Perl Techniques."

Since object methods are basically subroutines, they can be accessed, built, and used just like other subroutines. Referring back to the Tire.pl class, when a new tire object has been created, you can call all the other subroutines in the same way you called the new constructor, by using the arrow referencer.

```
# Create a local scalar that holds the tire psi value
my $localpsi Tire->psi();
```

Now you have a local reference to the psi subroutine. In the tradition of TIMTOWTDI, you can also use colons instead of the arrow referencer.

```
# These two commands are equivalent
my $localpsi Tire->psi();
my $localpsi Tire::psi();
```

The path from the local reference of $localpsi to the existing psi subroutine in the Tire class is detailed in Figure 5.6, which illustrates a program block with a local reference to psi.

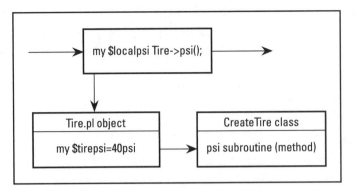

Figure 5.6

A local subroutine is
referenced through
an object and
a class.

CAUTION If you try to call an undefined method for an object, Perl will not complain. Instead, the program will throw an exception while it is running. Perl relies on the programmer or the script to understand the inner workings of an object; it will not check to see whether a method is correct, unlike other OOP languages. In other words, if you use an object incorrectly, Perl will not catch the problem when the program is compiling; it will only notice the problem when the program is running.

Here is an overview of the entire process of creating and using an object in Perl. This process is also summarized in Figure 5.7. The numbers that point to the various steps depicted in Figure 5.7 correspond to the numbers of the steps in this overview.

1. Create a class, which functions as a template for objects.

2. Create a new constructor, which is a simple subroutine (or method) that creates a local instance of the class and returns a reference to that instance.

3. Create an object by calling the new class constructor.

4. The new constructor returns a reference to the new object that was created.

5. When an object has been created and blessed, you can access the subroutines and data within the object, as if the subroutines were local.

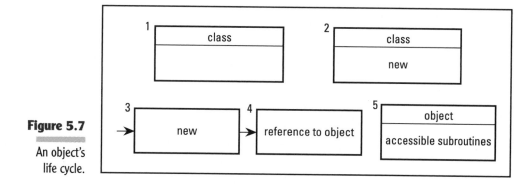

Figure 5.7

An object's life cycle.

Using Methods in Perl

Perl does not provide any special syntax for defining methods. A method is simply a subroutine that expects its first argument to be an object or package. If the argument is a reference, the method expects an object; if the argument is a string, the method expects a package. There are also two types of method calls—class method calls and instance method calls.

Class methods are sometimes referred to as *static methods*. A class method expects a class name as the first argument. This method provides functionality for the class as a whole, not for any individual objects belonging to that class. Many class methods actually ignore the first argument.

An instance method expects an object reference as its first argument. Instant methods are sometimes referred to as *virtual methods*.

Constructing a Method in Perl

You do not need to use a method to access data directly from a class or object. For instance, if an object contained a variable named DATA, you could create a local variable that references DATA.

```
my $localvariable = $object->{DATA};
```

However, this defeats the purpose and power of OOP, so most of the time you will see that a method is included to gather whatever DATA is within the object.

```
my $localvariable = $object->method();
```

After constructing an object for a class, a program can call an object's method by using the arrow referencer, and then treat the method as a subroutine.

```
object->method( argument );
```

Utilizing Methods

Methods can do anything, and every programming trick you have learned so far in this book can be placed within a method. However, you shouldn't reference class data directly from an object method. If you do, you are not building a scalable, inheritable class. The object should be the cornerstone of any operations.

If you go back to the Tire.pl script from earlier in this chapter, you can see that I left a few dummy methods to define later.

```perl
package CreateTire;
sub new
{
# Create a local scalar
my $tire = {};
# bless the tire to turn it into an object
bless $tire;
# return the new tire object
return $tire
}
# A few object methods
sub tread{ my $tiretread = wavy; };
sub hubcap{ my $hubcap = metal;  };
sub psi{ my $tirepsi = 40 pounds per square inch; };
# end with a return
return 1;
```

There are three methods here—tread, hubcap, and psi. Currently each method is assigned a local variable, but each method can actually hold any sort of Perl trick you want to include. For instance, if you wanted to have variable tire treads depending on the time of year and the weather, you could simply include a series of if...else statements in the tread method to determine which type of tread should be created.

```perl
sub tread{
    if ($season == summer){ my $tiretread = "normal"}
    elseif ($season == winter){ my $tiretread =  "studded" }
    elseif ($season == spring){ my $tiretread = "all weather" }
```

```
elseif $season == fall){ my $tiretread = "all weather" }
else { my $tiretread = "normal"};
};
```

When you invoke the tread object method, tread makes sure that the tire tread is appropriate for the season, if specified. The entire code listing looks like this and can be found on the companion Web site:

```
package CreateTire;
sub new
{
# Create a local scalar
my $tire = {};
# bless the tire to turn it into an object
bless $tire;
# return the new tire object
return $tire
}
# A few object methods
sub tread{
    if ($season == summer){ my $tiretread = "normal"}
    elseif ($season == winter){ my $tiretread =  "studded" }
    elseif ($season == spring){ my $tiretread = "all
  weather" }
    elseif $season == fall){ my $tiretread = "all weather" }
    else { my $tiretread = "normal"};
        };
sub hubcap{ my $hubcap = metal;  };
sub psi{ my $tirepsi = 40 pounds per square inch; };
# end with a return
return 1;
```

Using Inheritance in Perl

Inheritance is one of the most powerful parts of OOP because it allows you to use preexisting objects and add new capabilities to them. With inheritance, you can use classes that are derived or built from other classes, which is an excellent form of software reuse. Inheritance boils down to the ability of one class to use the features of another class so that you don't have to rewrite the class.

Perl classes can only inherit methods; you must use your own mechanisms to implement data inheritance. This is another aspect in which Perl is different than most other OOP languages. It is also another example of Perl's uniqueness when it comes to OOP methodology.

How Inheritance Works

Perl implements inheritance with a special construct called @ISA. In Perl, each package can have a variable called @ISA. @ISA functions as a method and is basically a special array that tells Perl where else to look if a specific method cannot be found in the current class or package.

Within each element of the @ISA array is the name of another package or class that Perl can search for methods. These classes are searched in order for any missing called methods. Classes that are listed through @ISA are known as the *base classes* of the current class.

When you attempt to call a method for an object or a class, Perl goes to the class and searches for the method among the subroutines listed. If the method cannot be found, Perl will open up @ISA and look at the classes and packages listed, and then take the first package or class and search for the method there.

In Perl, it is possible to have multiple inheritance, which means that you have more than one parent class listed in the @ISA array. Perl will search these packages in order for the missing method. If Perl cannot find the method in the first class or package listed, it will continue on to the next class or method on the list; it will continue on until the method is found. Although multiple inheritance is possible in Perl, you will not find it used very often. This is because multiple inheritance can greatly complicate programs, which is the opposite of the goals of object-oriented programming.

Implementing Inheritance

@ISA needs to be a package-scoped global array, which means you cannot declare @ISA as a lexical or local array. If you recall from the Saturday Evening session,

"Expressing and Stating," you can declare global arrays using the our command. You declare @ISA the same way you would declare any other global array.

```
our @ISA = ("secondpackage.pl", "thirdpackage.pl");
```

In addition to a default universal array, Perl also has a default universal class. This class, named UNIVERSAL, exists unspoken and hidden in the shadows of Perl OOP. UNIVERSAL is useful because it is possible to place methods in the UNIVERSAL class. These methods can then be accessed through @ISA by every class you create. UNIVERSAL is known as the *universal inheritor*, it acts as an all-encompassing base class to all existing classes.

If the current classes, the base classes, and UNIVERSAL don't contain the methods for which you are looking, Perl makes one final search for a method named AUTOLOAD(). AUTOLOAD is a universal, all-encompassing Perl method. Perl will look for a method you designate as AUTOLOAD first within the current class, then in any base classes, and finally in the UNIVERSAL class. If an AUTOLOAD is found, the AUTOLOAD method is run on behalf of the method that is missing. This method-searching process is depicted in Figure 5.8.

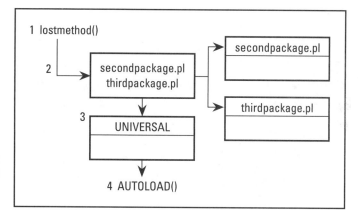

Figure 5.8

Perl searches for a
lost method.

There is a special condition that occurs when a derived class and a base class both have the same method defined. When this happens, Perl will always use the derived version of the method. In OOP, this is called *overriding*, and it is one way to change a child's functionality from its parent's. Overriding is the key that makes code easily changeable in OOP, especially in a case where you need a method or an object to be slightly different than its parent.

Program Block: Using OOP Constructions in Your Program Game Loop

It is time to pull out your block4.pl file and make a few changes. One of the problems you may have experienced in last evening's session was organization. The block4.pl file is over 100 lines long now, making it fairly difficult to manage all at once. OOP is a life saver in this regard, and classes and objects will be perfect for compartmentalizing this little game.

First, open block4.pl and resave it as block5.pl. Second, thumb through the source code and see what could be easily broken out into a small, single-use component. Taking a quick glance, a few sections to break off should be obvious:

➤ The Initial Game Variables

➤ The Random Map Generator

➤ The Main Game Loop

You get the idea. Any component can become modular, as long as it makes sense organizationally.

To start, put the map generator into its own class. To set up a map class you need to follow these steps:

1. Cut and paste the appropriate code into a new Perl package called MAP.pm.

2. Add the `package` command to the beginning of the script (package MAP;).

3. Move the existing code into subroutines, for example: `sub turn1 {$turn1 = int rand(3);};`

4. Add a return command to the end of the MAP.pm file (`return 1;`).

5. Create a subclass called `new`. The MAP.pm file should now look like this:

```
package MAP;
sub new {};

sub turn1 {$turn1 = int rand(3);}
```

```
sub turn2 {$turn2 = int rand (3);}
sub turn3 {$turn3 = int rand(3);}
sub turn4 {$turn4 = int rand(3);}
```

```
return 1;
```

Your new method needs to include the necessary `bless` and `return` commands in order for it to create new map objects:

```
sub new
{
my $map = {};
bless $map;
return $map;
};
```

Put all this together and you now have a callable class called MAP that creates random maps for your application:

```
package MAP;

sub new {
my $map = {};
bless $map;
return $map
}

sub turn1 {$turn1 = int rand(3);}
sub turn2 {$turn2 = int rand (3);}
sub turn3 {$turn3 = int rand(3);}
sub turn4 {$turn4 = int rand(3);}


return 1;
```

Now in order for our block5.pl to call the class and create a map object, there needs to be a few small changes:

1. Place a use statement at the beginning of the file so that Perl can locate MAP.pm (use `MAP;`).

2. Call the MAP.pm file and ask it to create a map object using the new constructor, and then store that object in a local scalar (`my $localmap = new MAP;`).

3. Change the print statements for $turn1 through $turn4 to reference the map object's subroutines (`print "The way out is $localmap->turn1$localmap->turn2$localmap->turn3$localmap->turn4\n";`).

The source for this new, improved block5.pl should be as follows:

```
###########################################
#Trapped
###########################################


###########################################
# block1- planning
# What I need:
# Code that prints information to the screen.
# Code that takes information from the keyboard.
# Code that times the display of text/information
# Code that generates a random map
# Code that tracks the player's progress on the map


##############################################
# block 2 - Basic needs.
# We have learned printing information to the screen and
# Taking information from the keyboard and
# Creating scalar variables and
# a standard ending to keep the dos prompt open.
# Initial print action


##############################################
# block 3
# Any math that needs to be done
# Random number generator
# Any variable changes


##############################################
```

```perl
# block 4
# The actual game loop
# Anything else that remains undone.#includes
use MAP;

# Assign Variables
$direction = North;
$food = 10;
$health = 10;
$turn = 1;

# Possible directions
$north = 0;
$east = 1;
$south = 2;
$west = 3;

my $localmap = new MAP;

print "The way out is $localmap->turn1$localmap-
   >turn2$localmap->turn3$localmap->turn4\n";

for ($turn = 1; $turn <= 4; $turn++){

print "\n";
print "You are trapped in a cavern\n";
print "You can travel Forward, Backwards, Right, or Left
   using the arrow keys\n";
print "\n\n\n";
print "You are facing $direction\n";
print "You have $food boxes of ramen left\n";
print "Your health is equal to $health\n";
print "\n\n\n";

print "Please choose a direction to travel by pressing:\n";
print "0 for North\n";
```

```perl
print "1 for East\n";
print "2 for South\n";
print "3 for West\n";

# Need to grab info from the player
$char = readline(*STDIN);
print "$char\n";

if ($turn == 1 && $char == $localmap->turn1)
{print "You have chosen wisely!\n\n"}
elsif ($turn == 2 && $char == $localmap->turn2)
{print "You have chosen wisely!\n\n"}
elsif ($turn == 3 && $char == $localmap->turn3)
{print "You have chosen wisely!\n\n"}
elsif ($turn == 4 && $char == $localmap->turn4)
{print "You have chosen wisely!\n\n"}
else
{
# If a mishap occurs, lose one health
$health = $health -1;
print "You have chosen poorly\n";
print "Your health is equal to $health\n";
$turn = $turn-1;
};

if ($food <= 0) {
print "You are out of food!\n";
$health = $health -1;
};

# While making a move lose one food unit
$food = $food -2;
print "You have $food boxes of ramen left\n";

if ($health < 0){
```

```
print "You have lost, and remain trapped for all eternity!\n";
$turn = 4;



};


}


# Add our ending changed to user input
# standard ending
print "\nPress an arrow key to continue...";
<>
```

If you run this script, you will see that the game operates as before except that the way out is no longer printed (The way out is 0...). Instead you will see four hash references (The way out is MAP=HASH<0x1827f04>...). This can be fixed easily by creating local instances of the turn scalars and referencing those instead to get the way out of the maze. Code that creates these local instances would look like this:

```
my $localmap = new MAP;
my $localturn1 = $localmap->turn1;
my $localturn2 = $localmap->turn2;
my $localturn3 = $localmap->turn3;
my $localturn4 = $localmap->turn4;
print "The way out is
   $localturn1$localturn2$localturn3$localturn4\n";
```

The second part of your block5.pl program section would be the game variables. At the beginning of block5.pl there is a large group of scalars:

```
# Assign Variables
$direction = North;
$food = 10;
$health = 10;
$turn = 1;


# Possible directions
```

```
$north = 0;
$east = 1;
$south = 2;
$west = 3;
```

These can just as easily be placed in a class, and will help limit the currently cluttered programming block. To separate these variables, you can follow a similar procedure as what you did to create MAP.pm:

1. Cut and paste these lines into a new Perl file named GAMEVARS.pm.

2. Add the `package` command to the beginning of the file.

3. Split the directions and the variables into two subroutines.

4. Add a `return` to the end of the file.

5. Create a new subroutine that blesses and returns an instance of the class.

All said and done, the new GAMEVARS.pm file should look like this:

```
package GAMEVARS;

sub new {
my $gamevars = {};
bless $gamevars;
return $gamevars;
}



# Assign Variables
sub direction {$direction = North;}
sub food {$food = 10;}
sub health {$health = 10;}



# Possible directions
sub north {$north = 0;}
sub east {$east = 1;}
```

```
sub south {$south = 2;}
sub west {$west = 3;}


return 1;
```

Now several changes need to be made to the block5.pl code before the game variables are accessible:

1. A use statement needs to be placed at the beginning of block5.pl.

2. The GAMEVARS.pm new constructor needs to be called by block5.pl to create a local instance of the GAMEVARS.

3. All the variable references within the game loop need to be changed to call upon the local instance of GAMEVARS.

The first two of these steps is easily accomplished by adding a use GAMEVARS; line to the beginning of block5:

```
#includes
use MAP;
use GAMEVARS;
```

Next, create a local instance to the GAMVARS object by adding this line:

```
my $localvars = new GAMEVARS;
```

Then create local instances of each of the game variables you need:

```
my $localhealth = $localvars->health;
my $localfood = $localvars->food;
my $localdirection = $localvars->direction;
```

Now you need to find every instance of a game variable use and switch to use the local variable instead, all of which occur in the body of the for loop.

Resave block5.pl to "gameloop.pl", and your game is now sectioned into one Perl file and two Perl modules.

In the end you did not end up lessening the number of lines of code in the main file. Organizationally, however, this new code is superior. If you need to change any of the initial variables to make the game harder or easier, they are all contained and organized in the easily readable GAMEVARS.pm file. If the game length needs to be increased or decreased, most of the work can be done in the MAP.pm file, and the game loop can be left untouched. And if you ever write any future programs that need similar subroutines, the .pm files are easily exportable.

All of theses changes will make the work you do in the next session, where you really start significantly altering the code, much easier. The source for all these files follows with a few added comments. GAMEVARS.PM:

```perl
# This package holds all of the game variables

package GAMEVARS;

sub new {
my $gamevars = {};
bless $gamevars;
return $gamevars;
}



# Assign Variables
sub direction {$direction = North;}
sub food {$food = 10;}
sub health {$health = 10;}



# Possible directions
sub north {$north = 0;}
sub east {$east = 1;}
sub south {$south = 2;}
sub west {$west = 3;}



return 1;
```

MAP.pm:

```perl
# This package creates a random map

package MAP;

sub new {
my $map = {};
bless $map;
return $map;
}


sub turn1 {$turn1 = int rand(3);}
sub turn2 {$turn2 = int rand (3);}
sub turn3 {$turn3 = int rand(3);}
sub turn4 {$turn4 = int rand(3);}


return 1;
```

gameloop.pl:

```perl
#############################################
#Trapped
#############################################


#############################################
# block1- planning
# What I need:
# Code that prints information to the screen.
# Code that takes information from the keyboard.
# Code that times the display of text/information
# Code that generates a random map
# Code that tracks the player's progress on the map


###############################################
# block 2 - Basic needs.
# We have learned printing information to the screen and
```

```
# Taking information from the keyboard and
# Creating scalar variables and
# a standard ending to keep the dos prompt open.
# Initial print action


###############################################
# block 3
# Any math that needs to be done
# Random number generator
# Any variable changes


###############################################
# block 4
# The actual game loop
# Anything else that remains undone.

#includes
use MAP;
use GAMEVARS;

# Get map variables
my $localmap = new MAP;
my $localturn1 = $localmap->turn1;
my $localturn2 = $localmap->turn2;
my $localturn3 = $localmap->turn3;
my $localturn4 = $localmap->turn4;

# Get game variables
my $localvars = new GAMEVARS;
my $localhealth = $localvars->health;
my $localfood = $localvars->food;
my $localdirection = $localvars->direction;

# Variable assignments for game loop
```

```
$turn=1;

print "The way out is
    $localturn1$localturn2$localturn3$localturn4\n";


# Main game for loop
for ($turn = 1; $turn <= 4; $turn++)
{

print "\n";
print "You are trapped in a cavern\n";
print "You can travel Forward, Backwards, Right, or Left
    using the arrow keys\n";
print "\n\n\n";
print "You are facing $localdirection\n";
print "You have $localfood boxes of ramen left\n";
print "Your health is equal to $localhealth\n";
print "\n\n\n";

print "Please choose a direction to travel by pressing:\n";
print "0 for North\n";
print "1 for East\n";
print "2 for South\n";
print "3 for West\n";

# Need to grab info from the player
$char = readline(*STDIN);
print "$char\n";

if ($turn == 1 && $char == $localturn1)
{print "You have chosen wisely!\n\n"}
elsif ($turn == 2 && $char == $localturn2)
{print "You have chosen wisely!\n\n"}
elsif ($turn == 3 && $char == $localturn3)
```

```
{print "You have chosen wisely!\n\n"}
elsif ($turn == 4 && $char == $localturn4)
{print "You have chosen wisely!\n\n"}
else
{
# If a mishap occurs, lose one health
$localhealth = $localvars->health -1;
print "You have chosen poorly\n";
print "Your health is equal to $localhealth\n";
$turn = $turn-1;
};

if ($localfood <= 0) {
print "You are out of food!\n";
$localhealth = $localhealth -1;
};

# While making a move lose one food unit
$localfood = $localfood -2;
print "You have $localfood boxes of ramen left\n";

if ($$localhealth < 0){
print "You have lost, and remain trapped for all
  eternity!\n";
$turn = 4;



};


}

# Add our ending changed to user input
# standard ending
print "\nPress an arrow key to continue...";
<>
```

Summary

Object-oriented programming is a lot to swallow, especially early on a Sunday morning. It takes some people years to master the intricacies of this unique and powerful programming methodology, so don't be too concerned about memorizing all of the possible OOP terms and thinking in an entirely object-oriented way. Expertise will come in time.

Understanding Perl packages early on will make your life as a Perl programmer much easier, because hundreds of Perl packages exist for programmers to use and reuse for free. Since Perl has been around for decades, almost any program you would want to create has been written already. Often organized Perl programmers place their scripts together in packages or modules and share these scripts with others. There are entire databases and Web resources that are filled to the brim with functioning Perl scripts you can download and use; I will direct you toward many of these in this evening's session.

If there is anything you should remember from this chapter, it's the idea that you do not have to reinvent the wheel. Because Perl possesses OOP-style mechanisms, programmers can easily bundle and share their programs and solutions. When you embark upon a new project in Perl, keep in mind that there might already be a solution out there. And if you keep OOP in mind when you are programming, you will be able to keep solutions in easily portable bundles. One day you too can share your solutions with the next generation of beginners.

Putting It All Together

➤ Expanding the Saturday Morning program block

➤ Expanding the Saturday Afternoon program block

➤ Expanding the Saturday Evening program loop

➤ Expanding the Sunday Morning objects and classes

➤ Putting it all together

I n the past two days you have covered an amazing amount of Perl ground, and now it is time to show off what you have learned. In this chapter, you will use methods and lessons from previous chapters and apply them to the Trapped game program you have been building and other Perl scripts as well. Along the way, I will point out some of Perl's other advanced features and show you how to incorporate them. At the end of this chapter, I will show you how to take the program classes and objects you have created and apply them to other programming projects.

Expanding the Saturday Morning Program Block

To begin, think about the lessons you learned in the Saturday Morning session, "Variables and Other Fun Stuff." You walked through arrays, hashes, lists, and the all-important `print` statement. At the end of the session, you built a programming block that set up the initial variables for the Trapped game, as well as the information that the player needed.

The Trapped program has changed dramatically since then. The `print` statements that inform the player of the game variables have been placed into the main game loop, and in this morning's session you moved most of the game variables into their own class/module named GAMEVARS.pm.

The goal for this section is to modify the main game loop and GAMEVARS.pm so that each game variable is held within an array, instead of in individual scalars. Organizing these values into arrays will help clean up the code and increase the portability of the program modules.

Improving Array Efficiency

Arrays are extremely powerful programming tools. Because Perl has a wide range of built-in tools to deal with arrays, using one to hold the Trapped game variables will open up the flexibility of the game. To review, the basic syntax of an array is as follows:

```
@array = (item0, item1, item2,);
```

Open GAMEVARS.pm. GAMEVARS.pm includes several subroutines that create the game variables.

```
# Assign Variables
sub direction {$direction = North;}
sub food {$food = 10;}
sub health {$health = 10;}


# Possible directions
sub north {$north = 0;}
sub east {$east = 1;}
sub south {$south = 2;}
sub west {$west = 3;}
```

Putting these two groups of variables into two arrays limits the number of subroutines you need to maintain. Doing so will also limit the number of local variables you need to keep track of in the main game loop. Start by modifying the game variables using these steps:

1. The `direction` subroutine is superfluous because you now have a second series of subroutines to deal with possible direction, so remove that subroutine completely.

2. Next, create a new array called `vars` with the remaining two entries and their values:

   ```
   @vars = (10, 10,);
   ```

3. Put this array into a new subroutine called `vars` and delete the old subroutines. The new variable-assigning code should look like this:

   ```
   # Assign Variables
   sub vars {@vars = (10, 10,);}
   ```

Not bad; you just went from four lines of code to two.

4. Do the same for the possible-direction variables. Create a new array called nsew (for north, south, east, west), place it within a subroutine called nsew, and assign the appropriate variables. The code is again two lines:

```
# Possible directions
sub nsew {@nsew = (0, 1, 2, 3,); }
```

5. Because the Perl code is looking less readable, add comments so that the function of the module is obvious when you come back to modify it. The complete GAMEVARS.pm code should look like this:

```
# This package holds all of the game variables

package GAMEVARS;

# The new method for constructing GAMEVARS objects
sub new {
my $gamevars = {};
bless $gamevars;
return $gamevars;
}

# Assign Variables
# Currently the two game variables are health and food
and they are both assigned a value of 10
sub vars {@vars = (10, 10,);}

# Possible directions
# Currently there are four possible directions, N,S,E,
and W, represented by 0, 1, 2, and 3, respectively.
sub nsew {@nsew = (0, 1, 2, 3,); }

return 1;
```

Now that you have modified the GAMEVARS.pm module, you need to make some changes to the main game loop so it can keep up. Save and close GAMEVARS.pm and then open gameloop.pl.

First, there are nearly 30 lines of code in gameloop.pl. At the beginning of the code listing are notes from the earlier session. Because these notes aren't necessary, remove them and place them in a new file called notes.txt (or something similar). Now you should have only the necessary game code and comments.

In looking over the loop, you will see that you need to make several more changes, the first one being the local variable assignments from GAMEVARS.

```
# Get game variables
my $localvars = new GAMEVARS;
my $localhealth = $localvars->health;
my $localfood = $localvars->food;
my $localdirection = $localvars->direction;
```

You need to change these variable assignments to reflect the new arrays. The process is simple enough; you just need to create local instances of the arrays.

```
# Get game variables
my $localvars = new GAMEVARS;
my @localvar = $localvars->vars;
my @localdirection = $localvars->nsew;
```

Now that the game loop has these local instances, you need to change the scalar references to reference the arrays instead. First, you need to change the print statements that show the game status to the player.

```
print "\n";
print "You are trapped in a cavern\n";
print "You can travel Forward, Backwards, Right, or Left
   using the arrow keys\n";
print "\n\n\n";
print "You are facing $localdirection\n";
print "You have $localfood boxes of ramen left\n";
print "Your health is equal to $localhealth\n";
print "\n\n\n";
```

Some of these print statements are left over from earlier versions of Trapped, so remove the unnecessary lines and leave only the ones that actually need to reference the new array.

```
print "\n";
print "You are trapped in a cavern\n";
print "You have $localfood boxes of ramen left\n";
print "Your health is equal to $localhealth\n";
print "\n";
```

Now change the two scalar references to print out the values from @vars instead.

```
print "You have $localvar[0] boxes of ramen left\n";
print "Your health is equal to $localvar[1]\n";
```

Near the end of the game loop, there are several tests to see whether the game variables need to be changed.

```
# If a mishap occurs, lose one health
$localhealth = $localvars->health -1;
print "You have chosen poorly\n";
print "Your health is equal to $localhealth\n";
$turn = $turn-1;
};


if ($localfood <= 0) {
print "You are out of food!\n";
$localhealth = $localhealth -1;
};


# While making a move lose one food unit
$localfood = $localfood -2;
print "You have $localfood boxes of ramen left\n";

if ($$localhealth < 0){
print "You have lost, and remain trapped for all eternity!\n";
$turn = 4;
```

These need to be altered to access the local arrays. You can do this by cutting and pasting the appropriate array references.

```
# If a mishap occurs, lose one health
$localvar[1] = $localvar[1] -1;
print "You have chosen poorly\n";
```

```
print "Your health is equal to $localvar[1]\n";
$turn = $turn-1;
};

if ($localvar[0] <= 0) {
print "You are out of food!\n";
$localvar[1] = $localvar[1] -1;
};

# While making a move lose one food unit
$localvar[0] = $localvar[0] -2;
print "You have $localvar[0] boxes of ramen left\n";

if ($localvar[1] < 0){
print "You have lost, and remain trapped for all
   eternity!\n";
$turn = 4;
```

Save your new gameloop.pl file and run the game to make sure you made all of the changes correctly. The complete new-and-improved game loop code follows:

```
# Get game variables
my $localvars = new GAMEVARS;
my @localvar = $localvars->vars;
my @localdirection = $localvars->nsew;

# Variable assignments for game loop
$turn=1;

print "The way out is
   $localturn1$localturn2$localturn3$localturn4\n";

# Main game for loop
for ($turn = 1; $turn <= 4; $turn++)
{

print "\n";
```

```
print "You are trapped in a cavern\n";
print "You have $localvar[0] boxes of ramen left\n";
print "Your health is equal to $localvar[1]\n";
print "\n";

print "Please choose a direction to travel by pressing:\n";
print "0 for North\n";
print "1 for East\n";
print "2 for South\n";
print "3 for West\n";

# Need to grab info from the player
$char = readline(*STDIN);
print "$char\n";

if ($turn == 1 && $char == $localturn1)
{print "You have chosen wisely!\n\n"}
elsif ($turn == 2 && $char == $localturn2)
{print "You have chosen wisely!\n\n"}
elsif ($turn == 3 && $char == $localturn3)
{print "You have chosen wisely!\n\n"}
elsif ($turn == 4 && $char == $localturn4)
{print "You have chosen wisely!\n\n"}
else
{
# If a mishap occurs, lose one health
$localvar[1] = $localvar[1] -1;
print "You have chosen poorly\n";
print "Your health is equal to $localvar[1]\n";
$turn = $turn-1;
};

if ($localvar[0] <= 0) {
print "You are out of food!\n";
$localvar[1] = $localvar[1] -1;
```

```
};

# While making a move lose one food unit
$localvar[0] = $localvar[0] -2;
print "You have $localvar[0] boxes of ramen left\n";

if ($localvar[1] < 0){
print "You have lost, and remain trapped for all
    eternity!\n";
$turn = 4;

};

}

# Add our ending changed to user input
# standard ending
print "\nPress an arrow key to continue...";
<>
```

Altering the Array

The main benefit to placing all of the game variables into an array is that it makes the game easy to expand. Suppose you wanted to add to Trapped by including more dimensions—things the player can carry, such as water, a light source, or gold. First, you alter the vars array within GAMEVARS.pm by adding values and comments.

```
# Assign Variables
# Currently the three game variables are health, food and
    water and they are all assigned a value of 10
sub vars {@vars = (10, 10, 10);}
```

Then add the game logic required to incorporate the new value.

```
# While making a move lose one food unit and one water unit
$localvar[0] = $localvar[0] -2;
$localvar[3] = $localvar[3] -1;
```

```
print "You have $localvar[0] boxes of ramen left\n";
print "You have $localvar[3] units of water left\n";
```

That's all there is to it. As you will see later this afternoon, you can also add functionality to the game modules using Perl's OOP features.

Handling Leftover Loop Errors

Before you move on to the next section, there are a few loose ends you need to wrap up in the existing game code. When running the code, you have probably noticed that there are multiple unnecessary or repetitive print statements. For instance, with each iteration of the game loop, the amount of food the player has available is printed twice. The game is also printing the map solution with this print statement:

```
print "The way out is
    $localturn1$localturn2$localturn3$localturn4\n";
```

This statement should be taken out unless it is needed to double-check any possible code errors or typos.

To clean up the game loop, follow these steps:

1. Remove one of the food print statements.

2. Comment out the map solution line, but leave it in the code in case you need to come back and test any problems with the game loop.

3. Add an opening print statement. (You can just print the Trapped comments that are already at the beginning of the code.)

4. Add a final end-game statement to the code that announces that the player has ended the game.

The gameloop.pl should now look like this:

```
print "###########################################\n";
print "# Trapped\n";
print "# The Video Game\n";
print "###########################################\n";

# includes
use MAP;
```

```
use GAMEVARS;

# Get map variables
my $localmap = new MAP;
my $localturn1 = $localmap->turn1;
my $localturn2 = $localmap->turn2;
my $localturn3 = $localmap->turn3;
my $localturn4 = $localmap->turn4;

# Get game variables
my $localvars = new GAMEVARS;
my @localvar = $localvars->vars;
my @localdirection = $localvars->nsew;

# Variable assignments for game loop
$turn=1;

# The map solution has been commented out. Remove the pound
   sign if testing is necessary.
# print "The way out is
   $localturn1$localturn2$localturn3$localturn4\n";

# Main game for loop
for ($turn = 1; $turn <= 4; $turn++)
{

print "\n";
print "You are trapped in a cavern\n";
print "You have $localvar[0] boxes of ramen left\n";
print "Your health is equal to $localvar[1]\n";
print "\n";

print "Please choose a direction to travel by pressing:\n";
print "0 for North\n";
print "1 for East\n";
```

```
print "2 for South\n";
print "3 for West\n";

# Need to grab info from the player
$char = readline(*STDIN);
print "$char\n";

if ($turn == 1 && $char == $localturn1)
{print "You have chosen wisely!\n\n"}
elsif ($turn == 2 && $char == $localturn2)
{print "You have chosen wisely!\n\n"}
elsif ($turn == 3 && $char == $localturn3)
{print "You have chosen wisely!\n\n"}
elsif ($turn == 4 && $char == $localturn4)
{print "You have chosen wisely!\n\n"}
else
{
# If a mishap occurs, lose one health
$localvar[1] = $localvar[1] -1;
print "You have chosen poorly\n";
print "Your health is equal to $localvar[1]\n";
$turn = $turn-1;
};

if ($localvar[0] <= 0) {
print "You are out of food!\n";
$localvar[1] = $localvar[1] -1;
};

# While making a move lose one food unit
$localvar[0] = $localvar[0] -2;

if ($localvar[1] < 0){
print "You have lost, and remain trapped for all
  eternity!\n";
```

```
$turn = 4;



};


}


# Add our ending changed to user input
# standard ending
print "Congratulations! You have solved the game and are no
    longer Trapped!\n";
print "\nPress an arrow key to continue...";
<>
```

Expanding the Saturday Afternoon Program Block

In the Saturday Afternoon session, "Using Files and Perl Operations," you learned how to handle files, directories, and Perl operations. You built a random-number generator and used it to create the random map element of the Trapped game. You also started building the basic blocks of the Trapped program loop—in particular, pieces of code that alter the game variables and lower the player's health and food.

In this section, you will revisit the sections of code from the Saturday Afternoon session. You will take a closer look at the rand Perl command and alter the MAP.pm file that increases the random-number generator's portability.

Random Efficiency

I have mentioned that Perl's rand command isn't actually a random-number generator, but rather a random-number emulator. In fact, in some Perl distributions (prior to version 5.004), if you use rand without first *seeding* the command, Perl will give you the same set of numbers each time.

Seeding means providing a random number emulator with a variable. Computers are notoriously bad at creating random numbers, and the rand command doesn't produce numbers that are actually random. Instead, rand references a table of hidden numbers and returns a result. This process makes the result hard to predict, but not truly random.

To demonstrate how bad computers are at generating random numbers, create a new Perl file called truerand.pl and have the file create and print two random integers. You can use MAP.pm as a template.

```
# create two random numbers between 1-10
$number1 = int rand(10);
$number2 = int rand(10);


# Print these two random numbers


print "$number1\n";
print "$number2\n";
```

When you use rand by itself, Perl automatically seeds the random number emulator behind the scenes. It does this by checking the computer system clock and feeding the current time as a seed, which is why you get different number results when you run rand. Try using srand, the Perl command for seed random number, and see what happens when Perl runs rand twice with the same seed.

```
# create two random numbers between 1-10
# Set the seed to 1
srand(1);
$number1 = int rand(10);
$number2 = int rand(10);


# Print these two random numbers


print "$number1\n";
print "$number2\n";


# standard ending
print "\nPress an arrow key to continue...";


<>
```

Save truerand.pl (or download the version from the Web site) and run it. No matter how many times you run the program, you will always get the same two numbers.

For the purposes of the Trapped game, this is not such a big problem. The chances of someone playing the game and noticing that the way out is the same if the game is played at exactly the same time are somewhat slim. The chance of someone wanting to cheat at Trapped is also remote. However, at some point, you might want to reuse the MAP.pm module to create random numbers for another application or program, so it is important to know how Perl comes up with these numbers.

To make MAP.pm exportable, you should allow other programs that use it to provide their own seeds. You should also grant MAP.pm the flexibility to create more than four random numbers. Luckily, Perl is designed for this sort of flexibility.

To change the MAP.pm class into a generic random-number generator, follow these steps:

1. Open the MAP.pm file and resave it as RDOM.pm (short for random).

2. Go through the map references (within the package command and the new method) and replace them with rdom.

    ```
    package RDOM;

    sub new {
    my $rdom = {};
    bless $rdom;
    return $rdom;
    }
    ```

3. This new random class will take in the random seed as a data time. Add a line of code that creates the seed using srand.

    ```
    srand ({DATA_ITEM_1});
    ```

4. Change the localturn subroutines and variables to something a bit more generic.

    ```
    sub random1 {$random1 = int rand(3);}
    sub random2 {$random2 = int rand(3);}
    ```

```
sub random3 {$random3 = int rand(3);}
sub random4 {$random4 = int rand(3);}
```

5. Save the RDOM.pm module.

Now you need to test to make sure the random number generator works as specified. Create a new Perl file called rdomcall.pl. All this file needs to do is:

1. Reference the RDOM class by placing the use command at the beginning of the script.

2. Create an RDOM object using the new constructor.

3. Pass the data item to be used as the seed to RDOM.

4. Print out the random numbers.

You have performed Step 1 several times already.

```
use RDOM;
```

For Step 2 and Step 3, use the my command to create a local instance of the object. The only difference between this code and the earlier my localvars code you used earlier in the game loop is that you add the data item in parentheses to be passed to new.

```
my $object = RDOM->new(100);
```

You accomplish Step 4 by creating local instances of the random1–4 scalars and then printing them out, just like you did in the game block.

```
my $localrandom1 = $object->random1;
my $localrandom2 = $object->random2;
my $localrandom3 = $object->random3;
my $localrandom4 = $object->random4;
```

The two pieces of code are included here and are also available for download on the book's companion Web site.

The complete listing for RDOM.pm:

```
# This package creates random numbers

# declare package
package RDOM;
# new constructer
```

```
sub new {
my $rdom = {};
bless $rdom;
return $rdom;
}

# Sets the seed first
srand ( $_[0] );

# uses rand to create a new number based on the seed
sub {
   random1 {$random1 = int rand($_[1]);}
   return random1;
}
return 1;
```

The complete listing for rdomcall.pl:

```
use RDOM;

my $object = RDOM->new(1);

my $localrandom1 = $object->random1(2, 2);
my $localrandom2 = $object->random1(3, 3);
my $localrandom3 = $object->random1(2, 3);
my $localrandom4 = $object->random1(10, 200);

print "The way out is
   \n$localrandom1\n$localrandom2\n$localrandom3\n$localrandom4\n";

print "\nPress an arrow key to continue...";
<>
```

Expanding the Saturday Evening Program Loop

In the Saturday Evening session, you learned about statements, structured programming, subroutines, and loops. You put together the actual Trapped game loop and ran the completed, functional program for the first time.

In this section you will take a quick look at a few more loop-modifying statements and use these to further enhance the current game loop in Trapped.

Improving Loop Efficiency

In the original gameloop.pl file, there are a few lines that increase or decrease the $turn variable within the loop. Although these commands do work, it isn't always a good idea to internally change a loop's iteration while it is running. In fact, changing a loop while it is running can lead to common programming errors, such as endless loops.

Fortunately, Perl has several built-in commands that allow programmers to navigate within loops. Although I mentioned these commands in earlier chapters, I haven't covered how to use these life savers, which are referred to as next, last, and redo.

The next command is often found within loop environments. It simply forces the loop to stop what it is doing, start over, and increment to the next iteration if possible. The next command is basically a quick way to start the loop over without running the rest of the code in the block.

The last command has the opposite effect. Like next, last skips the rest of the program block when executed, but it also completely exits the loop, regardless of whether the loop is in its final iteration.

Finally, there is the redo command. Redo works exactly like the next command except that when the loop starts over, it does not increment to the next iteration. The loop simply takes a step back and repeats the same iteration.

Handling Changes to the Game Loop

Looking over the existing game loop, you can probably already see places where these loop control commands should replace the current method of changing the $turn variable. First, there is the code that checks for the ending of the game:

```
if ($localvar[1] < 0){
print "You have lost, and remain trapped for all
  eternity!\n";
$turn = 4;
};
```

Instead of incrementing $turn to the end of the loop, you could use last to create an exit point in the game code.

```
if ($localvar[1] < 0){
print "You have lost, and remain trapped for all
  eternity!\n";
last;
};
```

Now when the player's health is less than zero, the loop exits with a "You have lost" statement.

The second time the game ends is when the player chooses the correct direction during turn 4.

```
elsif ($turn == 4 && $char == $localturn4)
{print "You have chosen wisely!\n\n"}
```

Up until now, you have waited for the loop to exit and then thrown a success print statement to the player. Using last, you can set up this elsif for the winning print statement and an exit from the game loop.

```
elsif ($turn == 4 && $char == $localturn4)
{print "You have chosen wisely!\n";
print "Congratulations! You have solved the game and are no
  longer Trapped!\n";
last;
}
```

The loop iteration is also changed when a mishap occurs, and the player chooses the wrong direction in which to travel.

```
# If a mishap occurs, lose one health
$localvar[1] = $localvar[1] -1;
print "You have chosen poorly\n";
print "Your health is equal to $localvar[1]\n";
$turn = $turn-1;
};
```

This isn't the most elegant way to repeat a loop, especially with the redo command at your disposal. Using redo instead of decrementing $turn is another way to go back and make sure the player picks the appropriate way out.

```
# If a mishap occurs, lose one health
$localvar[1] = $localvar[1] -1;
print "You have chosen poorly\n";
print "Your health is equal to $localvar[1]\n";
redo;
};
```

The changes discussed in this section are listed completely in the following code. This code is also available on the companion Web site, under the filename gamelooptwo.pl.

```
print "########################################\n";
print "# Trapped\n";
print "# The Video Game\n";
print "########################################\n";

# includes
use MAP;
use GAMEVARS;

# Get map variables
my $localmap = new MAP;
my $localturn1 = $localmap->turn1;
my $localturn2 = $localmap->turn2;
my $localturn3 = $localmap->turn3;
my $localturn4 = $localmap->turn4;

# Get game variables
my $localvars = new GAMEVARS;
my @localvar = $localvars->vars;
my @localdirection = $localvars->nsew;

# Variable assignments for game loop
$turn=1;

# The map solution has been commented out. Remove the pound
  sign if testing is necessary.
```

```
# print "The way out is
    $localturn1$localturn2$localturn3$localturn4\n";

# Main game for loop
for ($turn = 1; $turn <= 4; $turn++)
{

print "\n";
print "You are trapped in a cavern\n";
print "You have $localvar[0] boxes of ramen left\n";
print "Your health is equal to $localvar[1]\n";
print "\n";

print "Please choose a direction to travel by pressing:\n";
print "0 for North\n";
print "1 for East\n";
print "2 for South\n";
print "3 for West\n";

# Need to grab info from the player
$char = readline(*STDIN);
print "$char\n";

if ($turn == 1 && $char == $localturn1)
{print "You have chosen wisely!\n\n"}
elsif ($turn == 2 && $char == $localturn2)
{print "You have chosen wisely!\n\n"}
elsif ($turn == 3 && $char == $localturn3)
{print "You have chosen wisely!\n\n"}
elsif ($turn == 4 && $char == $localturn4)
{print "You have chosen wisely!\n";
print "Congratulations! You have solved the game and are no
    longer Trapped!\n";
last;
}
```

```
else
{
# If a mishap occurs, lose one health
$localvar[1] = $localvar[1] -1;
print "You have chosen poorly\n";
print "Your health is equal to $localvar[1]\n";
redo;
};

if ($localvar[0] <= 0) {
print "You are out of food!\n";
$localvar[1] = $localvar[1] -1;
};

# While making a move lose one food unit
$localvar[0] = $localvar[0] -2;

if ($localvar[1] < 0){
print "You have lost, and remain trapped for all
  eternity!\n";
$last;
};

}

# Add our ending changed to user input
# standard ending
print "\nPress an arrow key to continue...";
<>
```

Expanding the Sunday Morning Objects and Classes

In this morning's session, you learned all about object-oriented programming and how to build Perl packages and modules. You also learned the importance of separating pieces of code into small, manageable bits, and you took more than 100 lines of game code and separated the file into three more manageable pieces—one main game loop and two additional modules.

You also learned about inheritance, but I talked only briefly about the extensibility feature in OOP. Extensibility is basically the next level of inheritance. You can create a new object that inherits the properties of a parent but also has its own added attributes.

For instance, you can create a new package called VARS.pm, which inherits from the base class GAMEVARS.pm. Create a new file and name it VARS.pm. You only need to do a few things for this new package to inherit all of the features of GAMEVARS.pm.

1. Enter the usual `package` command at the top of the VARS.pm file.

2. Use the `require` command to open GAMEVARS.pm.

3. Use the `@ISA` array to bring in all of the available methods that GAMEVARS.pm possesses.

You can code this clone file using only a few lines of Perl.

```
# the usual package command
package VARS;
# using require to read the original GAMEVARS.pm file
require GAMEVARS.pm
# Use the @ISA array to make all of GAMEVARS's methods
  available
@ISA=("GAMEVARS");
```

You can now replace all instances of GAMEVARS.pm in the game loop with the new VARS.pm file. Switching the files won't cause havoc because the two files are identical in functionality.

The ability to create twin versions of packages isn't extremely useful, but the power comes from the extensibility of these packages. VARS.pm has all of the super powers of GAMEVARS.pm, but you can alter the base code for VARS.pm to add new functionality without altering the GAMEVARS.pm parent. Currently, both GAMEVARS.pm and VARS.pm hold two arrays— one for player variables and one for map directions. If you want VARS.pm to have an additional array that contains a list of possible objects a player can pick up in Trapped, it is as simple as adding another subroutine.

```
# Add a new subroutine that holds objects a player can pick up
sub playerobs {@playerobs = ("torch", "lantern", "ice pick",
    "water skin",); }
```

This new package can do everything its parent can. In addition, the new package has added functionality. Now you should be able to see how OOP and Perl can make your life as a programmer extremely easy. Everything you have already scripted is inheritable and extendable for future projects.

Take a Break

It's Sunday afternoon, and you are well on your way to being a Perl guru. You have taken apart your first full-length Perl application and put it back together, shiny and brand new, with added functionality and extensibility. Along the way, you learned about several advanced features of Perl, and you are now capable of spewing OOP speech like a seasoned veteran of a major software company. Go ahead and take a break—perhaps a short walk—and bask in the glory of being a guru. When you come back, you will be using the techniques you've learned and the code you have written to create a few more Perl games.

Putting It All Together

Back already? So far you have used your Perl skills to create only one really operable program. Although running your first real program in a specific programming language is surely a thrill, you probably are a bit tired of playing the same game over and over.

What's great about Perl programming and OOP in particular is that everything you learn and do builds upon itself. As you gain programming experience and take on new challenges, you will find yourself digging through old files and projects. You will look at the way you solved problems in the past, apply new techniques, and come up with even better solutions.

Looking at the Trapped program, you now have several large sections of code that can be reused. Think of these different pieces as tools that you can alter subtly to tackle new domains and issues. Take an inventory of what you have built so far, and you will discover that you have at your disposal the two most important things for programming simple computer games:

➤ A functioning game loop with established entrances and exits

➤ A random-number generator

Using these two pieces, you can simulate almost any text-based computer game.

Creating Your Second Complete Perl Program

Remember the Magic 8 Ball? A toy from the 1970s, the Magic 8 ball was like a snow globe. You asked a question, shook the ball, and an answer would appear in the glass on the bottom of the ball. The Magic 8 Ball has been mimicked in computer game tutorials for many years, and there are numerous Perl applications that do so as well by returning random answers to questions.

This application uses the `rand` function in a new way—to demonstrate how you can take the principles you have learned and apply them elsewhere. Start by creating a new Perl file called 8ball.pl.

This application has two parts—the main application structure that prints an answer and a random-number generator that chooses between 0 and 7 (for eight possible answers). The random-number generator is only one line of code, so you should start there. As you might recall, Perl will automatically seed the number when `rand` is used. All you need to do is specify a range and force `rand` to use an integer, which is exactly what you did when you created the MAP.pm file.

```
$turn1 = int rand(3);
```

Using the same syntax, you can set up `rand` to create a value between 0 and 7.

```
$random = int (rand 8);
```

Now add a comment to the beginning of the script that identifies it. You should also add a few `print` statements to be read by the user of the program.

```
###############################################################
# 8 ball code base
```

```
#############################################################

print "The Mysterious Magic Eight Ball!\n";

print "Please type a question and when finished press enter
    for your answer.\n";

$random = int (rand 8);
```

Now you can construct the main application structure. The 8-ball program simply prints one of eight possible answers, which are chosen at random. You have already used rand to build the mechanism for determining the number of the answer, so the loop simply needs to compare the number ($random) to a list of possible answers. One easy way to do this is by using an elsif structure.

```
if ($random == 0) {print}
elsif ($random == 1) {print}
elsif ($random == 2) {print}
elsif ($random == 3) {print}
elsif ($random == 4) {print}
elsif ($random == 5) {print}
elsif ($random == 6) {print}
elsif ($random == 7) {print}
```

When the two code segments are put together, the code for 8ball.pl looks like this:

```
#############################################################
# 8 ball code base
#############################################################

print "The Mysterious Magic Eight Ball!\n";

print "Please type a question and when finished press enter
    for your answer.\n";

$random = int (rand 8);
if ($random == 0) {print}
```

```
elsif ($random == 1) {print}
elsif ($random == 2) {print}
elsif ($random == 3) {print}
elsif ($random == 4) {print}
elsif ($random == 5) {print}
elsif ($random == 6) {print}
elsif ($random == 7) {print}
```

All that is left for you to do is add the text to each `print` statement and cut off with a `<STDIN>` so the DOS prompt doesn't disappear instantly when you are running 8ball.pl. All of the pieces put together make up this complete script listing, which is also available for download on the companion Web site. Take a look at 8ball.pl in action see Figure 6.1

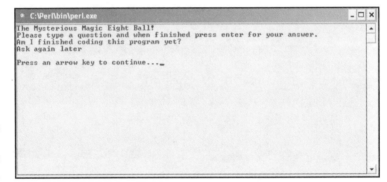

Figure 6.1

The magic 8ball.pl answers a question posed to it.

Here's the source code:

```
###############################################################
# 8 ball code base
###############################################################

print "The Mysterious Magic Eight Ball!\n";

print "Please type a question and when finished press enter
    for your answer.\n";

$random = int (rand 8);

$question = <>;
```

```perl
if ($random == 0)
{
print "Most Likely\n";
}
elsif ($random == 1)
{
print "Probably\n";
}

elsif ($random == 2)
{
print "Maybe\n";
}

elsif ($random == 3)
{
print " Outlook not so good\n";
}

elsif ($random == 4)
{
print "Future is shady\n";
}

elsif ($random == 5)
{
print "Ask again later\n";
}

elsif ($random == 6)
{
print " Perhaps\n";
}

elsif ($random == 7)
```

```
{
print "Definitely\n";
};

print "\nPress an arrow key to continue...";
<>
```

Creating Your Third Complete Perl Program

The game loop you have written is versatile and can be used in similar games. Looking at the basic structure of gameloop.pl, you can see that it follows a certain order of events:

1. Initializes any necessary game variables.

2. Prints information for the player.

3. Accepts input.

4. Applies input.

5. Repeats until a winning or losing condition is met.

This simple formation could be the basis for almost any game that can be played on a computer. In this section, you will turn your game loop into a number-guessing game. You have written most of the pieces for this game already, so the necessary steps are simply:

1. Cut and paste any necessary pieces from code that already exists.

2. Add or replace any necessary game variables.

3. Reword any necessary dialogue.

4. Set up winning and losing conditions for exiting the game loop.

Create a new Perl file and call it GuessMe.pl. Then cut and paste the `for` loop from gameloop.pl into this new file and strip out everything except for the `readline` section that gets information from the player. The new loop should look like this when you are finished:

```
# Main game for loop
for ($turn = 1; $turn <= 4; $turn++)
```

```
{
# Need to grab info from the player
$char = readline(*STDIN);
}
```

You will need to cut and paste a few other pieces to get the game running. Start by cutting and pasting the rand call to generate a random value from MAP.pm.

```
$turn1 = int rand(3);
```

Also, you need to cut and paste an ending <STDIN> to keep the DOS prompt from exiting.

```
# standard ending
print "\nPress a key to continue...";
<>
```

Now initialize a few variables. A number uses two variables for guessing—one that holds the random number and one that holds the range of the random number.

```
$range = 10;
$number = x;
```

Now alter the rand command you pasted from MAP.pm and place the random value in $number and use the $range value to determine the maximum value of the number. Because rand starts at 0, add a +1 to the final value.

```
$number = int rand ($range)+1;
```

Now you need to create the dialogue. Use print statements to add something simple outside of the loop to show that the game has started.

```
print "###########################################\n";
print "#GuessMe\n";
print "###########################################\n";
```

Add a print statement within the loop to tell the player that it is time to guess.

```
print "I'm thinking of a number between 1 and $range\n";
print "Type in a guess and hit enter\n";
```

You're almost done; the existing code is still fairly short and it looks like this:

```
print "######################################\n";
print "#GuessMe\n";
print "######################################\n";

# game variables
$range = 10;
$number = int rand ($range) +1;

# Main game for loop
for ($turn = 1; $turn <= 4; $turn++)
{
print "I'm thinking of a number between 1 and $range\n";
print "Type in a guess and hit enter\n";

# Need to grab info from the player
$char = readline(*STDIN);
}
# standard ending
print "\nPress a key to continue...";
<>
```

All that is left for you to do is set up winning or failing conditions. You can do this using an if statement.

```
if ($char == $number){
    print "You're Correct\n";
    last;
    }
```

Finally, add a print statement at the end of the game outside of the for loop to confirm the value of the actual number.

```
print "The answer is $number";
```

The entire script is shown here in its entirety. It is also available for download on the book's companion Web site. You can also view guessme.pl in action in Figure 6.2.

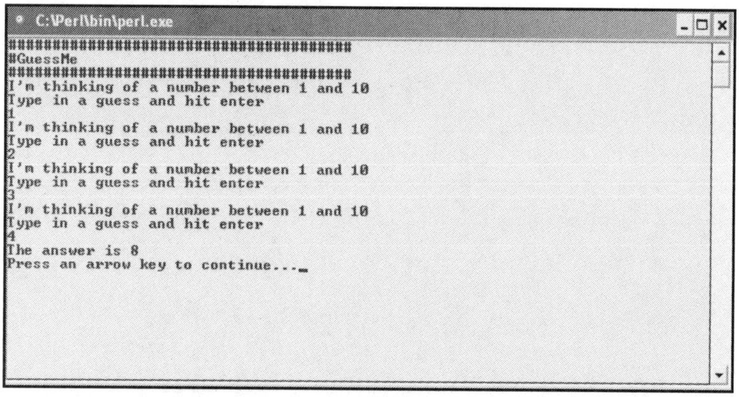

Figure 6.2

The simple
guessme.pl
program outsmarts
the author
yet again.

```perl
print "###########################################\n";
print "#GuessMe\n";
print "###########################################\n";


# game variables
$range = 10;
$number = int rand ($range) +1;



print "$number\n";

# Main game for loop
for ($turn = 1; $turn <= 4; $turn++)
{
print "I'm thinking of a number between 1 and $range\n";
print "Type in a guess and hit enter\n";

# Need to grab info from the player
$char = readline(*STDIN);

if ($char == $number){
    print "You're Correct\n";
    last;
```

```
        }

}
print "The answer is $number";

# standard ending
print "\nPress a key to continue...";
<>
```

Considering Other Possible Applications

Now that you have seen the versatility of loops and random-number generators, you can dream up dozens of other creative Perl games. You can write gambling games, such as Craps or 21 using these same basic tools, as well as games like tic-tac-toe and hangman. There are also Web sites where you can download existing copies of Perl games; I will cover some of those sites in tonight's session.

Perl isn't only about fun and games. There are plenty of serious and professional programs and scripts in use today, particularly in the realm of the World Wide Web and as tools for system administrators. Generating a random number might be the basis for a simple game, but it is also the basis for generating random keys in the exchange of secure data using encryption. Game loops are necessary for taking turns in a game environment, but almost every computer application utilizes a loop as a controller for accepting input or running repetitive actions.

Now try a few short but serious Perl applications. In Saturday Afternoon's session you looked at creating a mock typewriter (and called it sdtin.pl). How about taking a look at typewriter's counterpart, the calculator?

The stdin.pl file was basically a `while` loop that took in all keyboard input, as shown here:

```
# changing our standard ending to standard input
while (<>)
{
print;
}
```

You are going to use a modified version of this `while` loop to create a new Perl application called calc.pl. Create a new file and copy the source code for the `while` loop from the stdin.pl file, or rewrite the lines of code.

The first thing to change is the existing print line, which simply prints whatever goes into `STDIN` (`<>`). You want the file to print the answer to a mathematical equation. Change the print line to `print "Answer = $output\n";`

```
while (<>)
{
print "Answer = $output\n";
}
```

Your `while` loop will now print whatever is sent to `$output`. You also need to take in the mathematical question, which is easily accomplished using Perl's default variable `$_`, because `<STDIN>` goes here unless otherwise specified. Add the line `$input = $_;` to your `while` loop:

```
while (<>)
{
$input = $_;
print "Answer = $output\n";
}
```

Since the code is growing is size, adding a few comments is a good idea:

```
# The while loop takes (<stdin>)
while (<>)
{

# Perl's default variable $_ places <stdin> into the scalar
   $input
$input = $_;

# print the scalar $output to the screen as the answer
print "Answer = $output\n";
}
```

So far so good. Now you need to add the chomp command to take care of those pesky end of line characters. You can do this by chomping the scalar $input:

```
# The while loop takes (<stdin>)
while (<>)
{

# Perl's default variable $_ places <stdin> into the scalar
   $input
$input = $_;

# chomp end of line characters
chomp( $input );

# print the scalar $output to the screen as the answer
print "Answer = $output\n";
}
```

Almost finished—just a few more steps to go. You need your calculator to evaluate when the user has finished typing. This can be accomplished with an unless loop utilizing the last command like so:

```
unless ( $input ) { last }
```

In this context, the loop unless waits until <STDIN> has reached an end. An end is signified by a return from the user:

```
# The while loop takes (<stdin>)
while (<>)
{

# Perl's default variable $_ places <stdin> into the scalar
   $input
$input = $_;

# chomp end of line characters
chomp( $input );

# waits until return hit by user
```

```
unless ( $input ) { last }

# print the scalar $output to the screen as the answer
print "Answer = $output\n";
}
```

Finally, the input needs to be evaluated and sent to output. This is done using the two scalars `$input` and `$output` and the `eval` function.

The `eval` statement is a new Perl command that is short for evaluate, and is capable of evaluating blocks and statements in Perl. The syntax for `eval` is:

```
eval expression;
```

Perl already knows how to add, multiply, subtract, and divide using the `+*-/` operators; the `eval` command in the following line of code just tells Perl to go ahead and do so:

```
# go ahead and evaluate what has been entered
$output = eval( $input );
```

The calc.pl file can now be executed. Go ahead and run calc.pl and try typing in some basic math commands, such as 1+1 or 2*2 and hitting enter:

```
# The Perl Simple calculator

# The while loop takes (<stdin>)
while (<>)
{

# Perl's default variable $_ places <stdin> into the scalar
  $input
$input = $_;

# chomp end of line characters
chomp( $input );

# waits until return hit by user
unless ( $input ) { last }

# go ahead and evaluate what has been entered
```

```
$output = eval( $input );

# print the scalar $output to the screen as the answer
print "Answer = $output\n";
}
```

To make the calc.pl file useful to someone else, you will probably want to add a few `print` statements explaining how to use it. The full source code for the completed calc.pl file is shown here and is also downloadable from this book's companion Web site. You can also look at Figure 6.3 for a visual example.

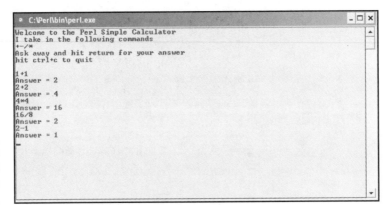

Figure 6.3

Several calculations performed by the calc.pl program.

```
# The Perl Simple calculator

# A few introductory print statements
print "Welcome to the Perl Simple Calculator\n";
print "I take in the following commands\n";
print "()+-/*\n";
print "Ask away and hit return for your answer\n\n";
print "hit ctrl+c to quit\n\n";

# The while loop takes (<stdin>)
while (<>)
{

# Perl's default variable $_ places <stdin> into the scalar
    $input
```

```
$input = $_;

# chomp end of line characters
chomp( $input );

# waits until return hit by user
unless ( $input ) { last }

# go ahead and evaluate what has been entered
$output = eval( $input );

# print the scalar $output to the screen as the answer
print "Answer = $output\n";
}
```

Here is another example before you move on to more advanced Perl. The following program creates random words. The program does this by creating four random letter combinations, rotating vowels and consonants. All this takes are a couple of split arrays and a few numbers generated by rand.

Split is the opposite of the join command, and it splits a string or expression based on a pattern you feed it. You will need to split lines for this new program, one for vowels and one for consonants:

```
# Create array of consonants
@con=split(/ */, "bcdfghjklmnpqrstvwxyz");

# Create array of vowels
@vow=split(/ */, "aeiou");
```

Take a close look at the split array command:

```
split(/ */,
```

Split will be using an * or wildcard character to choose from the list that follows. In the @con array, split will choose one of the consonants listed, and in the @vow array, split will choose one of the vowels present. Creating a print statement that prints one at random can be accomplished with one line of code:

```
print $con[int(rand(21))];
```

This may look complex at first because of all the brackets and parentheses, but it really is fairly simple. Working in to out, the sequence goes like this:

1. The number 21 is being given to rand, which tells rand to create a number from 0–20.

2. The random number is handed to the $con scalar/array reference.

3. The $con scalar splits the array based on the random number, pulling that numerical reference (0–20) from the list.

4. Print then prints the letter associated with the reference (from 0–20) from the @con array.

You will need to print twice: once for the consonants and once for the vowels. This can all be placed on one line of code:

```
# print statement
print $con[int(rand(21))], $vow[int(rand(5))]
```

Now all that is left is a loop that repeats this process. You can actually copy the for loop used within the game loops you have written:

```
for ($turn = 1; $turn <= 4; $turn++)
```

For now, change the loop so that it loops only twice instead of four times, and place print statement within the for loop's brackets:

```
# For loop that mimics the gameloop
for ($turn = 1; $turn <=2; $turn++)
{
# print statement
print $con[int(rand(21))], $vow[int(rand(5))]
}
```

That's the long and short of it. Save this file as words.pl. If you run the program from a DOS prompt, you will see it generate a random four letter word.

```
# random word generator


# Create array of consonants
```

```
@con=split(/ */, "bcdfghjklmnpqrstvwxyz");

# Create array of vowels
@vow=split(/ */, "aeiou");

# For loop that mimics the gameloop
for ($turn = 1; $turn <=2; $turn++)
{
# print statement
print $con[int(rand(21))], $vow[int(rand(5))]
}
```

HOW THOSE RUMORS GET STARTED

Ready for Perl guru-dom? Here is something you won't see everyday:

```
@c=split(/ */, "bcdfghjklmnpqrstvwxyz");@v=split(/ */, "aeiou");
for ($turn = 1; $turn <=2; $turn++){print $c[int(rand(21))],
$v[int(rand(5))]}
```

This is the same as the words.pl program, except that the array names have been shortened to just one letter, and most of the white space has been taken out so that the code fits on two lines. Now, look at this code snippet:

```
while (<>) {$i = $_;chomp($i);unless($i){last}$o = eval($); print "$o\n";}
```

This is one line of code, but it is perfectly legal Perl syntax. It is the calc.pl code with each name shortened to one letter and without spaces, comments, or wordy `print` statements. It is code snippets like these that give Perl programmers a bad name, but also where the rumors that any program is replaceable by one line of Perl code come in.

Shortening these programs also illustrates why commenting and carefully spacing your source code is important. Try coming back to this chapter in a few months and read this calculator code line and you will see why comments and coding conventions are so necessary.

Summary

In the past few hours, you have improved your Perl skill set dramatically by adding only a few simple new features. You should now have a strong grasp on how to organize simple applications, and you have a few games you can play. In tonight's session, I will get a bit more serious and show you how Perl is used in a wide range of real-world applications and as a daily tool for programmers worldwide.

Learning Advanced Perl Techniques

- ➤ Using modules, packages, and libraries
- ➤ Perl and the Internet
- ➤ Perl security
- ➤ Debugging
- ➤ Understanding Windows and Unix compatibility
- ➤ Using databases
- ➤ Beyond this book
- ➤ Perl 6

n the past couple of days, you have greatly developed your programming skill set. Not only have you learned basic Perl programming, but you also have a strong grasp of how to organize simple applications. You even have few completed computer games to show for it! Now it is time get a bit more serious and learn how Perl is used in a wide range of real-world applications and as a daily tool for programmers around the world.

This chapter could easily be called "Perl in the Real World." It is meant to be a gateway to Perl resources. Not only will I cover some of the advanced topics that I have avoided for most of the weekend, such as CGI, security, and modules, but I will also attempt to provide alternative sources of information about Perl. The community of Perl programmers is huge and growing. Right now, Perl itself is undergoing immense changes that were prompted and driven by this community. For the Internet junkie, the wealth of information and resources available is outstanding.

To begin this evening's session I will cover how you can access online numerous prebuilt Perl functions, objects, classes, and programs through established modules, packages, and libraries maintained by the Perl community.

Using Modules, Packages, and Libraries

In this morning's session, "Objects and Object-Oriented Programming," you created your own Perl packages and modules for grouping functions together in an object-oriented method. A *Perl package* is a self-contained unit of functions or variables used within a Perl script. A *Perl module* is simply a collection of related functions or a package that has been bunched into its own file and saved with the .pm extension. Packages and modules are designed to be used by other programs.

A *Perl library* is a collection of modules or packages. Like books on a bookshelf, you can search Perl libraries for the functionality, classes, or groups of variables you need. Then, you can import what you need to your machine or Perl scripts. The ability to import libraries of functionality is an important concept in programming and is used in most other modern languages as well. The advantage is that when you need to create a program or solve a problem in Perl, established techniques and shortcuts probably exist.

Working with Packages

Packages group and organize global identifiers. Packages have nothing to do with security or privacy, which is important to remember later in this chapter when I discuss Perl security. Package variables are always global, and code compiled in one package can freely alter and examine variables in another package.

When you create a package in Perl you are basically creating a unique space. This space includes only the code that you designated as belonging there. You can create multiple packages within the same physical file, or a package could include many different files. I spent quite a bit of time covering packages in this morning's session, but here is a quick refresher. You need two lines of code to designate a package, a `package` declaration at the beginning of the package, and a `return statement` at the end of the code, as shown in this code example:

```
# declaring a package
package simplepackage;

# subroutines within the package
sub printing
{
print "Very Simple Package\n";
}

# return statement
return 1;
```

Now you simply save the file as simplepackage.pl, and voila, you are the proud owner of a new Perl package. When you need to use the printing subroutine within simplepackage.pl, you write a `require` or a `use` command, and then call the specific subroutine, like so:

```
# a use or require statement to include simplepackage
require 'simplepackage.pl'


# a call to the subroutine printing within the simplepackage
  namespace
simplepackage::printing();
```

I didn't cover some of the more advanced package commands this morning. For instance, packages do not have to be inhibited by file boundaries. You can have several packages within one file or one package that is spread across several different files.

You can separate packages in the file by using the package constructor command BEGIN and the package destructor command END. Both the constructor and the destructor are utilized as subroutines:

```
sub BEGIN
{
print "my package has begun!\n";
}
sun END
{
print "My package has come to an end\n";
}
```

In this code sample the BEGIN subroutine initializes a package, and the END subroutine finishes the package. Using these two commands you could declare multiple packages within the same file using the `package` command. The following code, for example, creates two simple packages, package1 and package2, within the same file:

```
package package1;
sub BEGIN
{
print "my first package has begun!\n";
}
```

```
sun END
{
print "My first package has come to an end\n";
}


package package2;
sub BEGIN
{
print "my second package package has begun!\n";
}
sun END
{
print "My second package has come to an end\n";
}
```

The `package` command and the package constructors and destructors are also capable of splitting a single package across multiple files. Say you had two files called file1.pl and file2.pl, and you wanted pieces of package1 in both files. You would initiate package1 in the first file with this code:

```
package package1;
BEGIN{}
sub subroutines()
return 1;
END{}
```

In the second file, you would initiate the second part of package1 in the same way:

```
package package1;
BEGIN{}
sub moresubroutines()
return 1;
END{}
```

When you need to import this spread package into a source code file, you just need to be sure you include both files with the `require` command:

```
require 'file1.pl'
require 'file2.pl'
```

And then you can call upon either set of subroutines as if the routines where all placed together:

```
package1::subroutines();
package1::moresubroutines();
```

Working with Modules

Every module has a public interface—a set of variables and functions used to access the module from the outside. The `require` and `use` commands enable you to import a foreign module into a program you have written.

The `require` command loads a package module during run time; the `use` command loads the package immediately. `Require` ensures that a package hasn't already been loaded, as a redundancy check to avoid including the same package or module twice.

The `use` command works like the `require` command, but `use` also offers compile-time loading and automatic importing. You should be sure to keep track of which modules you are loading at compile time.

Having `use` or `require` import a function from one package to another is basically a form of aliasing. They make two different names for the same thing in different places.

NOTE There are a few programming conventions for Perl packages and modules. These aren't mandatory like most programming conventions, but you will come across them frequently when you're dealing with packages and modules.

First, it is a common convention to capitalize modules and packages. You will find names in all capitals, such as `CGI.pm`, but you will rarely find lowercase module names, such as `cgi.pm`.

Also, at the end of a Perl module you will normally see the line:

```
return 1;
```

This line tells the program to return a 1 when a `use` or `require` function call is successful.

ActivePerl comes with a built-in Perl Package Manager (PPM) to help Perl programmers download, install, and keep track of different Perl modules.

This program is located in your C:\Perl\bin folder if you used the default installation choices when you installed ActivePerl. The program is called ppm.bat, and its purpose is to download, install, verify, and remove Perl packages and modules, as shown in the following steps.

1. Open your C:\Perl\bin folder.

2. Locate the ppm.bat icon.

3. Double-click on it to run the Perl Package Manager (see Figure 7.1).

4. A DOS prompt will open and display the PPM interactive shell.

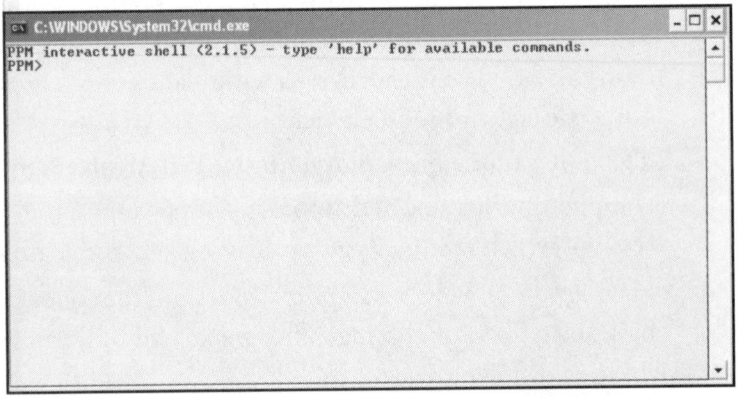

Figure 7.1

A DOS prompt displays the Perl Package Manager interface.

Typing **help** at the PPM prompt (PPM>) will produce a list of commands to which the PPM will respond. To find a particular Perl package, you can use the search option. For instance, in this morning's session, "Objects and Object-Oriented Programming," you learned about some of the other Perl random-number modules that exist. If you type in **search random**, a list of different Perl modules that have built-in random functionality will be returned (see Figure 7.2).

Installing one of these packages is easy; simply type **install** and the package name. If you want to download and install the Data-Random package, type **install Data-Random**. The PPM also has a verify command that helps you make sure you are running the latest and greatest version of a specific module. If you want to ensure that your Data-Random module is up-to-date with the latest version of the module, type **version Data-Random**, and the PPM tells you whether your version was current.

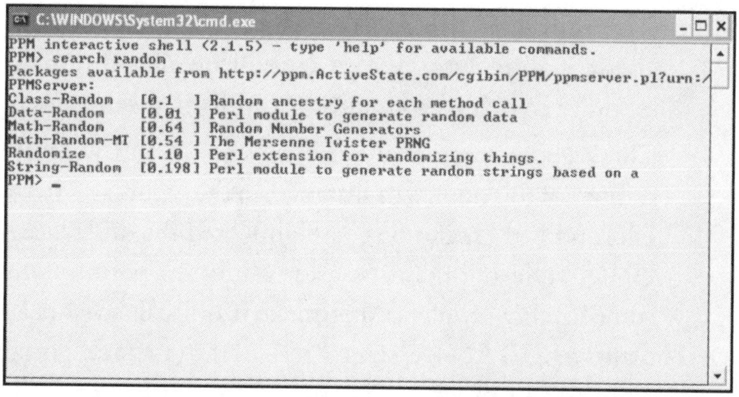

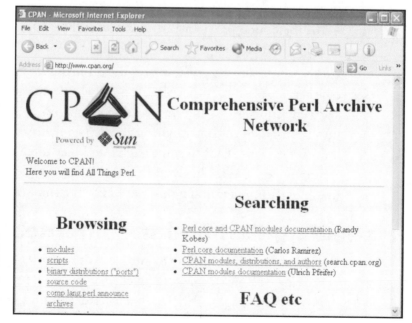

Figure 7.2

The PPM returns a list of modules that match the random search criteria.

Finding Common Modules and Packages

The PPM finds all of these modules and packages from a community-supported online archive of Perl modules, packages, and distributions. The collection is called The Comprehensive Perl Archive Network, or CPAN for short. The PPM is simply a local .bat file that searches CPAN for the requested modules. CPAN, shown in Figure 7.3, is an amazing resource that is perhaps the most important Perl collection in existence. In the archive located at http://www.cpan.org, you will find almost every flavor of Perl in existence, along with numerous useful modules, advice, documentation, and Perl FAQs.

Figure 7.3

The homepage of CPAN, the Comprehensive Perl Archive Network.

Keeping with the TIMTOWTDI motto, CPAN offers numerous alternatives to writing Perl code from scratch. You'll find hundreds of modules covering thousands of Perl coding solutions.

Think about some of the difficulties you had writing Perl code in earlier sessions of this book. For instance, in the Saturday Afternoon session, "Using Files and Perl Operations," I highlighted the differences between Perl-based UNIX-style permissions and Windows permissions, as well as other compatibility problems that make it difficult to port Perl between the two platforms. CPAN has several modules to increase portability and flexibility when you are programming on a Windows platform. (Try searching for win or win32 using the PPM.) You can find a zipped group of Windows extensions for Perl at http://www.cpan.org/authors/id/GSAR/libwin32-0.151.zip.

In this morning's session, I discussed several alternatives to the rand command. CPAN has a handful of useful modules that have random number-generating capability or boost Perl's existing capabilities, including

➤ Data-Random

➤ Math-TrulyRandom

➤ Randomize

➤ String-Random

All of these modules help Perl to create truly random (or close to truly random) numbers.

CPAN is by far the most widely recognized and used archive of Perl modules, but there are plenty of other places online where you can find Perl modules and Perl scripts. Most Internet hosting companies provide CGI and Perl tutorials for their customers who utilize Perl on their Web sites. Most major universities utilize CGI to some degree and they often host Perl Web sites and resources. You are likely to find Perl scripts online anywhere you can find programming training tutorials or script examples.

Understanding Perl and the Internet

Perl is renowned for its ability to integrate with HTML, but it is also capable of utilizing FTP (*File Transfer Protocol*), manipulating e-mail, and generating dynamic Web pages. Perl has been used to build countless Internet applications and to automate common administrative system tasks, such as browsing Web pages for broken links or checking to make sure Web pages and Web servers remain available.

Most of Perl's Internet capabilities come from modules you can download from CPAN. However, Perl and CGI are often used together, and the CGI.pm module is included in most distributions by default.

Using CGI

A common preconception among those unfamiliar with CGI is that it is a programming language with its own library of commands and functions. CGI is actually a protocol, or a way of doing things, *not* a programming language. It is the common way that Web servers talk to the programs with which they need to interact. Any script that sends or receives information to or from a Web server needs to follow the CGI protocol in order to be understood. CGI scripts are commonly written in Perl but are also written in C, Visual Basic, AppleScript, and a number of other languages. Figure 7.4 shows how a typical Web browser requests and receives a Web page through CGI.

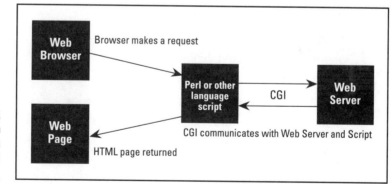

Figure 7.4

Flow chart of a typical CGI interaction.

CGI is most commonly used as a gateway that allows you to execute code on a Web server and return the results to a Web browser. This code execution is normally prompted by a user action, such as pushing a button, selecting an item from a list, entering information into a form, or performing an action in a game.

A CGI program executes normal Perl code just like any other program. The only difference is that the program is usually called by a Web browser.

Everything you have done in Perl so far in this book is applicable to a Web page using CGI. You can print to a browser window using standard out (<STDOUT>) and you can take in information from an HTML page using standard in (<STDIN>). You can also utilize Perl's standard error (<STDERR>) to send error messages directly to a Web server's error log.

NOTE You need to have an ISP (*Internet service provider*) to provide you with a Web server to upload any Web pages using CGI. Normally, FTP is used to upload CGI pages, so you need a working knowledge scripting HTML, using FTP, and implementing CGI. In addition, your ISP must support the CGI protocol. (Many ISPs actually do not support the CGI protocol.) Finally, the CGI scripts you create must have the appropriate permissions on the Web server to run correctly.

A Perl CGI program is a Perl script that has been renamed with the .cgi extension. You can create a script in Perl, change the file extension from .pl to .cgi, and place it on a Web server that supports the CGI protocol. The Web server will realize that the file is slated for Web use and can utilize the file accordingly.

The CGI.pm module is designed as an object-oriented module; it comes with its own custom controls to create Web pages and Web-executable scripts. To utilize the module, call CGI.pm's new method to create a CGI object and then call on CGI's various methods.

To illustrate, create an example CGI Perl script. Create a new Perl file and name it examplecgi.pl. To get CGI into the Perl script, follow these steps:

1. Include CGI.pm by utilizing the use command.

2. Create a local CGI object by calling the new method.

This is easily accomplished with just a few lines of code, by treating CGI.pm as if it were any other sort of OOP Perl module.

```
# include the CGI.pm module with use
use CGI;

# create a local instance of a CGI object
$local = new CGI;
```

CGI.pm has a number of methods that allow it to create and manipulate HTML pages. The header command is the method that tells Perl to start an HTML page. You can call the header command using your local object, like this:

```
print $local->header,
```

Remember that the print command in CGI sends data to a Web browser using <STDOUT>.

Perl also needs to know where to start the HTML page and where to end it. You can use CGI.pm's start_html and end_html methods to accomplish this.

```
$local->start_html,
$local->end_html;
```

Notice that each line of the CGI methods end with a comma, except for end_html, which ends with a semicolon.

Finally, you need the Web page to actually do something. For simplicity, printing a simple Hello should suffice. Add this line of code between the start_html and end_html methods:

```
$local->h1('Hello and welcome to Perl CGI'),
```

The h1 method works just like an HTML header command (<h1>) and in this case prints out the statement "Hello and welcome to Perl CGI" as the browser's header 1 text. The entire source code follows; this code is also available with the Chapter 7 downloads from this book's companion Web site (http://www.premierpressbooks.com/downloads.asp) as examplecgi.pl.

```
# Include the CGI.pm module with use
use CGI;

# Create local CGI object
$local = new CGI;

print $local->header,
$local->start_html,
$local->h1 ('Hello and welcome to Perl CGI'),
$local->end_html;
```

Perl has built-in functionality to test CGI scripts without uploading the scripts to a Web server. Perl automatically prints out the script as HTML code that a browser would have to read. Run this script from a DOS command line, and you will see that it looks something like this (see Figure 7.5):

```
Content-Type: text/html; charset=ISO-8859-1
<?xml version="1.0" encoding="utf-8"?>
<!DOCTYPE html
        Public "-//W3C//DTD XHTML Basic 1.0//EN"
        "http://www.w3c.org/TR/xhtml-basic/xhtml-
  basic10.dtd">
<html xmlns=http://www.w3c.org/1999xhtml lang-"en-US>
<head>
<title>Untitled Document</title>
</head>
<body>
<h1>Hello and welcome to Perl CGI</h1>
</body>
</html>
```

To run this program as a DOS command you need to revisit these steps (originally outlined in Friday Evening and Saturday Morning's session):

1. Click on the Start menu.

2. Click on Run. The Run dialog box appears, containing an Open line.

3. Type **command** at the Open prompt.

4. Navigate to the appropriate directory (the directory containing the shortxml.pl file) using the CD (change directory) command.

5. Type **shortxml.pl** on the command line and hit enter.

Perl CGI is a lengthy topic, and entire books have been written on programming that combine these two environments. There are also numerous online resources for putting together Perl CGI scripts. The World Wide Web Consortium and the University of California at Berkeley both host CGI libraries, and there are also a handful of script archives that carry CGI source code for downloading. Several of these online archives are outlined in Table 7.1. This table is also a Web page you can download from this book's companion Web site (cgi.html).

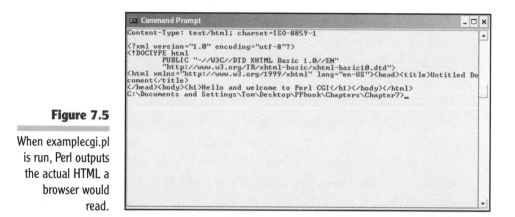

Figure 7.5

When examplecgi.pl is run, Perl outputs the actual HTML a browser would read.

TABLE 7.1 ONLINE CGI ARCHIVES		
Organization	**Web site**	**Location of CGI Files**
University of California at Berkeley	http://www.berkeley.edu	http://cgi-lib.berkeley.edu
The National Center for Supercomputing Applications	http://www.ncsa.edu	http://hoohoo.ncsa.uiuc.edu/cgi
Matt's Script Archive, Inc.	http://www.worldwidemart.com	http://www.worldwidemart.com/scripts
World Wide Web Consortium Overview.html	http://www.w3c.org	http://www.w3.org/Tools/
Cold Spring Harbor Laboratory	http://stein.cshl.org	http://stein.cshl.org/WWW/CGI

◆ ◆

CAUTION   Because there are a number of security concerns surrounding Web hosting, I bring up CGI again later on in this chapter in the "Perl Security" section. Whenever you open up your scripts to be accessed by the online community, you are taking significant risks. These risks can be mitigated with appropriate security measures while scripting, but there are also issues that need to be addressed by the Web Server administrators or by the department that runs the servers.

Before you upload any code you have written, you should make sure you have permission from the people in charge of your Web server. Without care and precaution, malicious attackers may be capable of utilizing your scripts to cause serious damage. Even with care and precaution there is still some degree of risk, so communicating with your host is essential. Because most ISPs and established companies have rules for CGI and Internet development, it shouldn't be difficult to find these rules. Normally a quick e-mail or short Web site search will give you the results you need to ensure your Perl scripts comply with your host's rules.

◆ ◆

Here is a walk-through of a simple, common CGI use: the Web counter. A *Web counter* keeps track of how many times a Web page has been visited and displays that number to the person browsing the Web page. The CGI Web counter is a simple example of dynamic Web content because the content changes for each viewer. To run a CGI Web counter, you need three files:

➤ An HTML Web page that calls the CGI Perl script and displays the results

➤ A CGI Perl script that does the work

➤ A counter file that has the actual counter number

Start with the HTML page. Using Perl to create the Web page, you need to do the following things:

1. Import CGI.

2. Create local instance of CGI.

3. Use `print` to send the browser a header.

4. Use `start_html` and `end_html` to signify the beginning and end of the HTML page.

5. Display a $count variable that holds the number of times the Web page has been visited.

You have gone through steps 1 and 2 once already in this section. The code for these steps looks like this:

```
# Import and create local instance of cgi
use CGI;
$local = new CGI;
```

Steps 3 and 4 are accomplished with a simple `print` statement and a few method calls you just picked up:

```
print
$local->header,
$local->start_html(),
$local->end_html,
```

The only real new piece is displaying a scalar value in Step 5, which can be done using a few CGI->header methods:

```
$local->center($local->h1('Counter')),
$local->center($local->h3("Current count: ", $count)),
```

This will display two lines of HTML, the first in heading 1 and the second in heading 2. These steps have been put into one script called counterhtml.pl and can be downloaded with this chapter's files at the companion Web site. The full source code looks like this:

```
print
$local->header,
$local->start_html(
-title=>'Web Counter',
),
$local->center($local->h1('Counter')),
$local->center($local->h3("Current count: ", $count)),
$local->end_html,
```

Now you need to create the Perl script that does all of the work. Create a new script and name it counter.pl. In order for the counter to work, this script needs to do the following steps:

1. Tell the Web server that the script runs where to find the Perl distribution (explained shortly).

2. Import and create a local instance of CGI.

3. Open a file that keeps track of the number of Web site visits. (You will call the file COUNT in this example.)

4. Assign COUNT to a local scalar and increase COUNT by one.

5. Close the file that keeps track of the number of Web site visits.

Step 1 is accomplished by writing one line of code at the top of the script. The code will depend on what kind of Web server the script will reside on, but on most Unix-flavored servers the line would be:

```
#!/usr/bin/Perl
# This line tells the Web server where to go to run Perl, and
    may vary depending upon the server.
```

You used the open and close commands in the Saturday Afternoon session. In CGI, they work pretty much the same way. In this example, you will be opening counter.dat, which will be the file that holds a value equal to the number of times a Web site has been visited. You will then assign counter.dat to the COUNT filehandle:

```
# Use open to open up the file that keeps track of the number
    of hits
open (COUNT, "<counter.dat") or die "Could not open the
    counter file.";
```

After you open counter.dat, assign the value to a scalar and then immediately close the file to avoid any mishaps:

```
Assign the count to a local variable
$count = <COUNT>;


# Always close the file immediately afterwards.
close COUNT;
```

Now, increment the $count value:

```
# Increment the count variable

$count = $count +1;
```

And finally, open up counter.dat, assign the new number, and close counter.dat again:

```
# Open the counter.dat file and increase it with the new number

open (COUNT, ">counter.dat");
print COUNT $count;
close COUNT;
```

This entire file is available on the companion Web site, and the full source code follows:

```
#!/usr/bin/perl
# server needs to know where Perl is stored. This varies
    depending upon the server

# Import
use CGI;

# create local instance
$local = new CGI;

# Use open to open up the file that keeps track of the number
    of hits
open (COUNT, "<counter.dat") or die "Could not open the
    counter file.";

Assign the count to a local variable
$count = <COUNT>;

# Always close the file immediately afterwards.
```

```
close COUNT;

# Increment the count variable

$count = $count +1;

# Open the counter.dat file and increase it with the new number

open (COUNT, ">counter.dat");
print COUNT $count;
close COUNT;
```

NOTE The counter.pl file is included for download from the companion Web site for reference and illustrational purposes. The file will not run on your home computer without all the appropriate files and Web server settings.

Using Perl with XML

XML is a scripting language that was developed by the World Wide Web Consortium (W3C). XML is similar to HTML except that instead of using existing, predefined HTML tags, such as <head> or <h1>, XML is flexible so that you can define your own tags. Although XML is beyond the scope of this book, this section will provide a quick introduction to how Perl and XML are integrated.

XML was developed in 1996 by W3C. It is derived from the same parent as HTML—SGML (*Standard Generalized Markup Language*). The driving paradigms of XML are

➤ The content must be separate from the presentation.

➤ The language must be highly portable.

➤ The language must be easy for both human and machines to read.

XML is driven by programmer-defined tags. These tags hold data and describe the data that they contain. XML tags allow programmers to structure data any way they want; this has helped to make XML the most popular language for structured data exchange. Databases today commonly are capable of utilizing XML to deliver information.

An application can easily utilize XML through a parser. An XML parser is required to read any XML document; most major languages, such as Perl, Java, and Python, have built-in XML parsers.

Perl comes with a minimal built-in XML parser in the form of an included module named `XML::parser`. Most of the modules needed to do extensive work with XML must be downloaded. The two primary XML modules, `XML::DOM` and `CGI::XMLform`, are both available through PPM. If you search on CPAN, you will find a handful of Perl modules that have been built to provide XML support.

The Perl `XML::DOM` module provides an interface for manipulating XML documents in accordance with the DOM (*Document Object Model*), which was also developed by the W3C.

When Perl has the required modules, generating XML is similar to generating HTML or CGI. Perl is capable of utilizing the `print` or `write` commands to parse XML data or structures through standard out `<STDOUT>`.

To parse an XML document, you follow the same principles you learned to utilize any other object-oriented module, as outlined next:

1. Include the appropriate XML module with the `use` command.

2. Create an XML parser object using the `new` method.

3. Use the parser's `parsefile` method to parse an XML document.

For instance, to utilize the `XML::DOM` module, you first utilize the `use` command.

```
use XML::DOM;
```

Then you create an instance of the parser object for `XML::DOM`.

```
my $localparser = new XML::DOM::Parser;
```

Finally, you use the `parsefile` method to parse the XML file.

```
my $localfile = $localparser->parsefile ("file.xml");
```

When put together, these three lines of code import the XML::DOM package, create a local instance of the parser for XML::DOM, and parse "file.xml" into the $localfile scalar.

```
use XML::DOM;
my $localparser = new XML::DOM::Parser;
my $localfile = $localparser->parsefile ("file.xml");
```

How about a simple XML example to whet your appetite? You can start with a simple XML document that Perl loads via the XML::DOM parser and prints. To do this, you need to perform the following steps:

1. Create a simple XML document.

2. Import the XML::DOM module.

3. Create a local instance of XML::DOM's parser so that you have something capable of parsing XML.

4. Parse the XML document into a local scalar.

5. Print out the local scalar.

Remember that XML is based on user defined tags. In the document you are about to create only two tags are used (to keep thing simple): <MESSAGE> and <HELLO>. When you code these tags, they look identical to the tags you were introduced to with HTML in Friday Evening's session. In this example, you will have <HELLO> placed within <MESSAGE>:

```
<MESSAGE>
<HELLO>
</HELLO>
</MESSAGE>
```

Notice how the tags use a </> to signify that they are ending, just like in HTML. Now put in the text you want to display in your XML document:

```
<MESSAGE>
<HELLO>
Hello and Welcome to XML.
</HELLO>
</MESSAGE>
```

When XML looks at this document, XML will format the string "Hello and Welcome to XML" with the rules assigned to both the `<HELLO>` and `<MESSAGE>` tags. In the meantime, you need to slap an indicator at the top of the file that lets the world know that the file is an XML document, after which the complete file should look like this:

```
<?xml version="1.0"?>
<MESSAGE>
<HELLO>
Hello and Welcome to XML.
</HELLO>
</MESSAGE>
```

This `xml version=` tag enables you to specify which brand of XML you are using to create this document. This complete file is available as shortxml.xml on the companion Web site.

For the Perl file, create a new Perl source file and name it shortxml.pl. The first thing you need to do is import and use the appropriate module:

```
# Import XML::DOM
use XML::DOM;
```

Then, like the example above, you must create a local instance of the XML::DOM parser.

```
# Create a local instance of DOM's parser
my $localparser = new XML::DOM::Parser;
```

Now you can use the parser to assign the contents of shortxml.xml into a local scalar. This can be done using the `parsefile` method within XML::DOM::Parser:

```
# Open the xml file into a local scalar
my $localscalar = $localparser->parsefile ("shortxml.xml");
```

Finally, add the print statement that displays the file. The entire source example can be downloaded form the Web site and looks this when completed:

```
# Import XML::DOM
use XML::DOM;

# Create a local instance of DOM's parser
```

```
my $localparser = new XML::DOM::Parser;

# Open the xml file into a local scalar
my $localscalar = $localparser->parsefile ("shortxml.xml");

# And print
print $localscalar;
```

If this sets off your curiosity to learn more about XML, there are plenty of online resources available. The W3C is the first place to look for more information on both XML (http://www.w3c.org/XML) and DOM (http://www.w3c.org/DOM).

NOTE Some of the lines of code within the shortxml.pl file available for download have been commented out. This is because the shortxml.pl file is meant to be a template only and is not designed to run on a desktop machine.

C Is for Cookies

When Internet commerce (or e-commerce) first hit the scene, the biggest problem companies had with online shopping was session tracking. When a Web page is closed, an HTTP session ends, and it is extremely difficult to pass data from one Web page to another Web page. This made shopping through multiple Web pages a puzzle, with the only solution being a method for the client computer, Web server, or Web browser to store information. Cookies emerged as the primary way for a client computer to store data while browsing the Internet.

Cookies are small text files that a Web server sends to a browser. The browser then saves the cookie in a file on the client computer. Cookies have long been considered a privacy issue because they have been used to track Web activity and browser movements, sometimes without the consent of the customer.

Whether you approve or disapprove of the use of cookies, they play an important part in Internet commerce because they enable a programmer to store data on a visitor's computer. Because Perl has been optimized for the Web, creating a session cookie is fairly simple when you use Perl's `CGI.pm` module. To create a cookie using Perl, you simply:

1. Import the `CGI.pm` module with the `use` command.

2. Create a local instance of a CGI object using the `new` command.

3. Create a cookie by calling the `cookie` method.

In the section "Using CGI", you walked through the steps necessary to import the `CGI.pm` module into a script, so the only unfamiliar part at this point is utilizing the `cookie` method. The code to create a cookie looks like this in Perl code:

```
$localcookie = $cgiobject->cookie{}
```

Cookies can contain several different variables, including:

➤ Domain

➤ Name

➤ Expires

➤ Path

➤ Secure

➤ Value

These are set with the basic syntax of:

```
-variable=>'value',
```

Suppose you want to include three variables within the cookie to hold the cookie name, value, and expiration. You simply add these lines to the code.

```
$localcookie = $cgiobject->cookie
{
-name=>'myfirstcookie',
-value=>'page1',
-expires=>'+1h'
}
```

The expire value in this example, which is set to `+1h`, is one hour. You can also set a cookie expiration value in minutes, days, or years by using `m`, `d`, or `y` in place of the `h`, respectively.

Cookies can be written only within a header, although you can read cookies from anywhere within your code.

```
print $local->header(-cookie=>$myfirstcookie);
```

To read a cookie, you use the CGI `cookie` method and pass it the name of the cookie.

```
%readcookie = #local->cookie('myfirstcookie');
```

Altogether, the code that allows you to create a simple cookie with the three parameters and read it looks like the following code snippet. This code is also downloadable as cexample.pl:

```
# Import CGI with the use command
use CGI;
# Create a local CGI object
$local = new CGI;
# Call upon the CGI cookie method to create a cookie
$mycookie = $local->cookie
(
# Set cookie values
-name=>'myfirstcookie',
-value=>'page1',
-expires=>'+1h'
)
# Cookie has to be created within the header of a Web page
print $local->header(-cookie=>$mycookie);
# Grabs the cookie for reading
%readcookie = #local->cookie('myfirstcookie');
```

When you run this code via the DOS command line, you will receive limited information (see Figure 7.6). This is because the code is designed to be run on a Web server, not a local computer.

NOTE   The shortxml.pl file is included for download from the companion Web site. The file will not run on your home computer without all the appropriate files, necessary XML modules, and Web server settings.

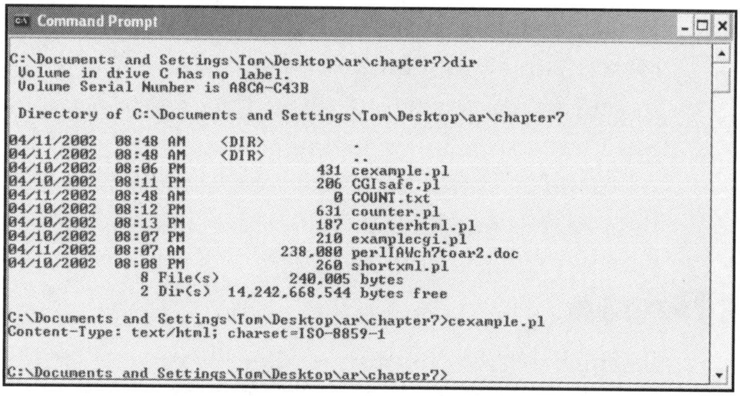

Figure 7.6

The Perl program displays limited information when executed on a DOS prompt.

Working with Sockets

A *socket* is one end of a commutation between two programs running on a network. To work with sockets, you use ports on an Internet server or computer. You specify an Internet server and a port to connect to on that server, and then you establish a connection. After the connection is established, you can use that socket just as you would use a Perl file handle in most cases.

When you browse the Web, your browser uses sockets to make connections. Normally, a Web server opens one port to listen for Web page requests. (Port 80 is the normal port opened for Web browsing.) When your browser goes to a specific Web site, it requests a Web page through port 80 on the server that hosts that Web site.

When port 80 on the server is hit with a request, that end of the request is called an *open socket connection.* The Web server then sends a Web page in HTML format back to your computer. Your computer takes in the HTML through a socket of its own and then gives the HTML to your browser, which reconstructs the Web page for you to view.

For the most part, all Internet and TCP/IP (*Transport Control Protocol/Internet Protocol*) traffic works this way. When you send e-mail, your e-mail client communicates to an e-mail server using socket connections. When you receive e-mail, you receive it from a server through socket connections. FTP (*File Transfer Protocol*) clients utilize socket connections, as do instant messengers, multiplayer video games, streaming media, and every other application that relies on the Internet.

Perl, being the Internet child that it is, was built to utilize and manipulate sockets. Perl has two built-in commands, `send` and `recv`, that can be used to send data back and forth through socket connections. This data is called *byte streams* when it is traversing through a socket connection. Perl also has several modules that are capable of dealing with sockets on different levels; some of these modules are outlined in Table 7.2.

Take a Break

So much to learn, and so little time. As you can see, Perl is truly a child of the Internet age, with plenty of Internet-based features and functionality and even a World Wide Web support base. You are about to embark on the last stretch of advanced Perl, in which you will learn about security, debugging, and the up-and-coming changes for Perl 6. Now is a good time to take a break and reflect upon what you have learned—just a quick one before the final stretch.

Understanding Perl Security

Security needs to be taken seriously, particularly when you are developing applications for the Web. Someone who is capable of cracking an online Perl

TABLE 7.2 PERL SOCKET MODULES	
Module	**Use**
`IO::Socket`	Setting up client/server, TCP/IP, UDP, and socket connections
`Net`	Utilizing common Internet protocols, such as `Net::FTP` and `Net::Telnet`
`Mail`	Retrieving and sending mail using `Mail::POP3Client` or `Mail::Mailer`
`LWP`	The `LWP` is short for Library WWW Perl, and provides Web-based automation and browser capabilities.

script might also be able to compromise the Web server on which the script runs. From there, they might compromise other parts of the network on which the Web server runs. A Perl script compromise could mean downtime for the Web site on which it runs, server downtime, loss of revenue, money, and effort spent to fix or recover from the attacks, and serious liability issues.

These issues are some of the reasons why you might have trouble locating a Web host for your CGI and Perl scripts. The problem with allowing CGI to run on a Web server is that CGI poses a considerable security risk. It grants access to files and directories on the Web server, and malicious attackers could use this access to take advantage of security holes or simply overuse the scripts to cause machine deadlock. This might even happen mistakenly by a consumer.

All of these issues make it very important to take security precautions. There are a number of precautions you should take to protect a server that needs to run CGI, and there are precautions you should take when you are designing even small Perl scripts and applications. Perl security is possibly a whole book in itself, but this section will outline a few starting points and will point you to a number of existing online resources.

Trust and Taint Checking

The first rule of security is, "Never trust anyone." In programming, this usually translates into, "Never trust data received from anywhere—whether it be a user, a customer, a Web server, or another program." Many security problems arise when you make assumptions about data, especially if you assume the data is safe to use. When writing code you should:

➤ Never assume a user will do what you ask.

➤ Always be suspect of data that comes into your program.

➤ Always be suspect of code someone else has written.

One of the biggest security holes in Perl is that users can pass unchecked data. Usually an exploiter will look for a CGI script that accepts data and try to use the script to execute system commands on the machine or the shell. To assist programmers in avoiding suspect data, Perl has a built-in functionality called *taint checking*.

Taint prevents this particular code exploit by automatically tagging any variable assigned from outside the program, in particular anything that is received from standard in (`<STDIN>`) as "tainted" and therefore unsafe. With taint enabled, a program cannot use tainted data to affect anything outside the actual script. Data that has been marked as tainted spreads the mark to any other data it comes in contact with. Therefore if you use a tainted variable to change a second variable within the script, the second variable also becomes marked as tainted.

Taint basically halts any data being sent through `eval`, `system`, `exec`, or `open` calls. Taint also stops you from calling any external program without first setting a `PATH` environment variable. To turn on taint, you need to use a `-T` switch. You can use `-T` at the DOS command line to turn on taint when you are running a program. The following command uses Perl to open program.pl with taint enabled.

```
Perl program.pl -T
```

On a Web server, taint should be added to the path the Web server uses to search for the Perl distribution. If Perl is located within the usr/local.bin folder (which is usually the case on a UNIX system), then each Perl script on that Web server should begin with the line:

```
#!usr/local/bin/perl -T
```

ActivePerl recommends that all Perl script used online or on a Web server should have taint enabled.

Using Pragmas

Pragmas are arguments that Perl's compiler uses to set options. The two most commonly used pragmas in Perl also happen to be ones that catch unsafe code—the `strict` and `warnings` pragmas. When Perl is set up to use these pragmas, the Perl compiler will check for, issue warnings against, and disallow certain programming constructs and techniques. In Perl, pragmas are set up at the beginning of a script with the `use` command.

```
use strict;
use warnings;
```

The `strict` pragma checks for unsafe programming constructs. `Strict` forces a programmer to declare all variables as package or lexically scoped variables, to use quotes around all strings, and to call each subroutine explicitly.

The `warnings` pragma sends warnings when the Perl compiler detects a possible typographical error and looks for potential problems, such as variables that have not been initialized.

I have met Perl programmers who swear that the `strict` pragma is an absolutely necessary piece of any code, regardless of the size or function of the script. These pragmas help by forcing programmers to use more secure coding techniques, such as setting a scope for all variables. They also help to uncover possible bugs or mistakes in code, which is a necessity because attackers frequently exploit bugs.

Perl possesses a number of other pragmas that can be set to do compile checking, although they aren't used as commonly. These pragmas include `autouse`, `constant`, `diagnostics`, `integer`, `lib`, `locale`, `overload`, `sigtrap`, `subs`, and `vars`. Information on these pragmas can be found within ActiveState's ActivePerl documentation, located in your C:\Perl\Docs folder.

Understanding File Permissions

I talked about file permissions in the Saturday Morning session, "Variables and Other Fun Stuff," and this afternoon's session, "Putting It All Together." Perl scripts that are used on Web servers usually have some sort of permissions associated with them. Normally, a Perl CGI script operates as a normal user or an anonymous agent on a Web server. The permissions that your script possesses should be carefully considered. For instance, suppose your script has read and write capabilities to open files and parse data into them. If the script is attacked and compromised, the attacker will have read and write privileges over those same files.

Security gurus usually exercise a policy of "least privilege" to combat this sort of problem. This means that a script should only have the minimum permissions required for it to do its job. If possible, a script should only have the permissions it requires when it actually has to perform the job. You should also take care to prevent a script from being overwritten by an attacker, which means that you should carefully set the permissions of those who use the server on which the script resides.

Web server permissions are usually not the main focus of the Perl CGI scripter; that task usually belongs to the server administrator. Therefore, you should address your script permission needs with the local administrator of the machine on which you are running the script. You will also want to pay attention the administrative policies for CGI and Web scripts when you start developing scripts to run on a particular Web server.

CGI Security Issues

Web programming gives you a lot of power, but it also exposes your computer and programs to attacks from anywhere on the planet. The most common exploitation in CGI is for an attacker to attempt to use your script to execute a command on the server that hosts the script.

Hackers will try to force pipe commands through a known CGI script, hoping for an opening. They will try to force the script to take commands that the script does not expect. Commonly these commands take the form of two calls: `system` or an `exec` call.

The `system` command is a shortcut to executing a call or command from Perl to the underlying operating system. With `system`, you can call the same commands and programs that your cooperating system could call. For instance, if I wanted to use the `system` command to open up my Word.exe program, I could use something like the following:

```
system "c:\Program Files\Word.exe"
```

The `exec` command is short for execute, and operates in much the same way. Although the temptation to utilize `system` or `exec` is strong due to the power they wield, you should use these commands in CGI with caution, and only when absolutely necessary.

A CGI interface should be set up so that nothing can be executed inadvertently. Tainted data is one way Perl facilitates this. When you use tainted data with CGI, Perl will not allow you to pass any data that has come from outside of the script into a `system`, an `exec`, or similar calls. You should never pass unchecked data to an external program.

DoS (*Denial of Service*) attacks are also common problems for Web servers. Denial of Service attacks occur when the number of work requests sent to a Web server exceeds the server's ability to process the requests and renders the server unable to process any new work requests. Perl CGI has a few built-in countermeasures to prevent DoS attacks. For example, you can use the $CGI::POST_MAX variable to limit the size of a post from a form. You can also disable uploads by setting the variable $CGI::DISABLE_UPLOADS to 1. This can be done utilizing the following code (available as CGIsafe.pl on the companion Web site):

```
# load the necessary pieces utilizing use
use CGI qw( :standard );
use CGI::Carp 'fatalsToBrowser;
# Limit the size of any post to 512 bytes
$CGI::POST_MAX = 512;
# Turn off any uploads
$CGI::DISABLE_UPLOADS = 1;
```

NOTE   The CGIsagfe.pl file will not run correctly on your home machine. The file is not a complete program; it is merely a template illustrating how to turn on safety features when:

➤ The appropriate cgi modules have been downloaded and installed.

➤ The code is included in an actual working Perl script.

➤ The template is included on an appropriate Web server where Perl and CGI are supported.

Understanding Other Security Issues

One mistake that programmers make is assuming that certain language functions have security built-in to them. One particular example in Perl is the package function. Packages are used to group and organize global identifiers, and some programmers might assume that an identifier in a package can be isolated or protected. Packages, however, have nothing to do with security or privacy, and there are no security checks to ensure that a program or user is utilizing a particular package appropriately.

There is also a big risk in using prewritten scripts. As a rule, you might want to read through and check for security issues on any scripts you download from the Internet, unless they are retrieved from a trusted source such as CPAN.

One final useful tip is to remove or strip *metacharacters* from any input your script receives. Metacharacters are the special key characters, such as $, @, {, and }, that Perl uses to recognize specific command and program structures. For programs that accept user input, it is best to only allow regular letters and numbers as input. This can be accomplished by using pattern matching to check for or remove metacharacters from a string:

```
$scalar =~ /(^[\w]+)\@([\w.]+)/;
```

This line seems garbled at first, but the concept is pretty simple. =~ is a *binding operator*. A binding operator binds a scalar to a specific pattern match. This $scalar is being bound to the patterns established on the right side this code snippet, which are held within slashes / /.

The /w is a match word character command, and makes sure that $scalar holds true to binding only alphanumeric characters. Another way to ensure the proper pattern is being matched with our =~ binding operator is: You could ensure a word or phrase matches only alphabetical characters using this code snippet.

```
$scalar =~ /([A-Za-z]+)/;
```

Resources

There are numerous security organizations, companies, and institutions that provide online resources and instructions to help you learn secure coding techniques. A brief listing of resources can be found in Table 7.3. There is also a downloadable Web page on the Web site that includes these resources as links.

Debugging

Sometimes, despite your brilliance and this handy Perl reference, you will find yourself unable to figure out exactly what is wrong with a Perl program you have written. When a Perl script goes bad and you are uncertain of the cause, these suggestions can help you find the elusive hidden typo or syntax error. Just remember that syntax errors are the most common errors!

➤ Use the `warnings` pragma. `Warnings` point out common misspellings and possible syntax errors.

➤ Use `print` statements often to print out each variable or scalar after any change. These `print` statements can be simply commented out of the production code and enable you to follow the structure of a program while it is running.

➤ When debugging CGI, make sure that the script is executable and capable of running locally first and then worry about getting the script to work on a server.

➤ Make sure your file has the proper permissions to do what you want it to do.

Along the lines of debugging, here is a list of common novice programmer errors.

➤ Testing a program all at once, instead of incrementally after each piece has been written.

➤ Using the wrong metacharacter or prefix dereferencer. For instance, using a % to establish an array instead of an @.

➤ Forgetting to place a semicolon at the end of a statement.

➤ Forgetting to place braces around a block of code (especially the closing brace). These characters almost always come in pairs: ( ), " ", ' ', <>, { }, and [ ].

➤ Placing the wrong brace at the end of a statement, such as {block{ instead of {block}.

➤ Confusing \ with / and vice versa.

➤ Using one equal (=) sign when two (==) are needed.

➤ Typing `elseif` instead of `elsif`.

➤ Using uppercase when lowercase is necessary, or vice versa. Almost all Perl commands are in lowercase, and most coders use some uppercase letters in Perl for their naming conventions.

➤ Forgetting that the number count starts at 0 and not at 1.

TABLE 7.3 ONLINE SECURITY RESOURCES

Organization	Website
World Wide Web Consortium's CGI security page	http://www.w3.org/Security/Faq/www-security-faq.html
CERIAS at Purdue University	http://www.cerias.com
CCIPS of the U.S. Department of Justice	http://www.cybercrime.gov
Computer Emergency Response Team	http://www.cert.org
Computer Professionals for Social Responsibility(CPSR)	http://www.cpsr.org/
The Computer Security Institute	http://www.gocsi.com/
Defense Information Systems Agency's (DISA) Security and Privacy page	http://www.disa.mil/infosec/iaWeb/default.html
The Electronic Privacy Information Center	http://www.epic.org/
The IEEE Computer Society	http://www.computer.org/
NCSA's CGI security page	http://hoohoo.ncsa.uiuc.edu/cgi/security.html
The National Institute of Health's security page	http://www.cit.nih.gov/security.html
The National Security Institute's Internet security page	http://www.nsi.org/Computer/internet.html

TABLE 7.3 (CONTINUED)	
Organization	**Website**
NIST's Computer Security Resource Center	http://cs-www.ncsl.nist.gov/
SANS Institute	http://www.sans.org/newlook/home.php
Shake Communication's Security Search	http://www.securitysearch.net/
University of California, Berkley's ISAAC	http://www.isaac.cs.berkeley.edu/
The Princeton University's Secure Internet Programming Group	http://www.cs.princeton.edu/sip/index.php3
The World Wide Web Consortium's Security Resource page	http://www.w3.org/Security/Overview.html

Understanding Windows and Unix Compatibility

The Perl port documents that are a part of ActiveState's Perl help files (located in your C:\Perl\Docs directory) contain information on how to write portable Perl code, which can be confusing when you are dealing with multiple operating systems.

Perl actually has done a great job of being portable. The code valiantly braves multiple platforms on which most programming languages would choke. Most of the language's syntax is usable regardless of whether the program runs on a Windows, Macintosh, or UNIX platform. When you are designing with portability in mind, here are a few points to remember:

➤ Be careful with file permissions and utilizing `chmod`, which I discussed in the Saturday Evening session.

➤ The new line symbol (\n) does not always work to designate the end of a line on all platforms, which can also cause portability issues with Perl's chop command.

➤ The seek and tell commands might not port well between platforms.

➤ When you are navigating through file systems, you will encounter difficulties with porting. For instance, some file systems use \ to designate a switch from a file or directory, and others use / to accomplish the same task. This means a coded path on Windows would be \Documents\file, and the same path in Unix would be /Documents/file, and either operating system may reject the opposing path.

Also, some file systems might not contain the directories to which you are trying to navigate. For instance Windows usually has Program Files folders, and Unix does not. Likewise, almost all Unix platforms have several sbin folders, and Windows does not.

The File::Spec module is a downloadable extension that can help you use the correct techniques to navigate a file system regardless of where it resides. File::Basename is another module worth noting when you are dealing with file systems from different platforms. For more information on this issue, look through the Perlport documents from ActiveState.

➤ The ENV variables change from platform to platform. This is especially true when you are determining how a particular system keeps track of time.

➤ Portable socket programming can be difficult because of the way different platforms utilize the new line (\n) character. Perl's normal socket commands automatically translate data into a binary form (called *packing*) for portability. However, different operating systems deal with the end of line, or new line symbols, differently, which can cause communication to become garbled unless the socket connection is designed for the specific platform.

Keep in mind that if you are having difficulty porting a Perl application, there is probably already a solution. Don't panic. Leaf through the

ActiveState documentation or go online and look through the existing Perl resources, and you will likely find an answer.

Working with Databases

A database is an organized collection of data. There are different strategies for using databases, and there is a wide range of technologies for creating and utilizing them. Common database software includes SQL (*Structured Query Language*), Sybase, DB2, Oracle, and MySQL.

Programs connect to a database using an interface. Perl's popular interface is the Perl DBI (*Database Interface*). Perl's DBI is a database-independent interface that enables Perl to interact with the most common databases.

For Perl to use a particular database, a *software driver* is necessary. A software driver is simply a small program that helps provide links into and out of a database. Each database requires its own driver, and each driver can have its own syntax in a program.

The Perl DBI acts as a standard driver interface, which exists for Perl to interact with it. DBI isn't the only database interface available in Perl—there is always more than one way to do it—but it probably is the most common. The `DBI.pm` module can be found through the Perl Package Manager or online at CPAN. The `DBI.pm` module functions like a regular object-oriented module.

Beyond this Book

The most important concept you should take from this chapter is that you are not alone. Perl might very well be the most supported language on the planet. The programmers who make up the Perl community are perhaps the most active, vocal, and loyal of all programmers. Currently, the Perl language is actually being rewritten by the Perl community in a colossal effort spearheaded by the original language designer, Larry Wall.

Perhaps even more impressive than the large, supportive community of loyal users is the extremely organized and dedicated online resources that somehow manage to provide support, advice, and assistance to thousands of programmers on an hourly basis.

CPAN

The beginning of this session focused on ActiveState's PPM, which accesses the Comprehensive Perl Archive Network. This archive contains almost every Perl port ever developed and also maintains and organizes all of the Perl packages and modules, which is no small feat.

An extremely powerful resource of CPAN is the mailing lists. At http://www.cpan.org/authors/00whois.html, there are e-mail subscription instructions for getting on support lists for each and every distribution or module that has one. For instance, if you need help or want to join a community of people that use Perl's LWP.pm module, you can simply send an e-mail to libwww-subscribe@perl.org and you will be added to the subscription list.

Perl Mongers

The Perl community gathers at the Perl Mongers site (http://www.perl.org) to discuss the future of the language and also to answer questions and provide support (see Figure 7.7). Here you will find answers to common questions, scripts, and the musings of Larry Wall and other writers who have documented the Perl language.

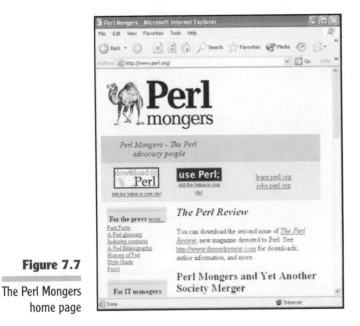

Figure 7.7

The Perl Mongers home page

Perl Mongers provides contact information and job listings for Perl programmers. The site also hosts some interesting articles on the history of Perl. One resource on Perl Mongers that you will want to consider is the information available on the latest version of Perl in development—Perl 6.

The Perl Journal

Located at http://www.tpj.com, the Perl Journal and Perl magazine contains article archives and source code and has a popular feature called the TPJ One-Liners, which is a collection of short Perl scripts (each approximately one line long) that do everything from draw fractals to act as alarm clocks. Although they have moved from their own site to under the wing of Sys Admin, they still are an excellent resource. You can catch a preview of the TPJ in Figure 7.8.

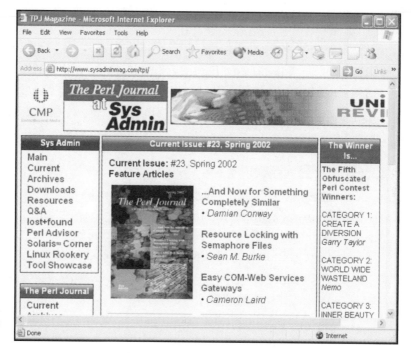

Figure 7.8

The Perl Journal.

ActiveState

Without ActiveState, there wouldn't be ActivePerl. ActivePerl (see Figure 7.9) is by far the most popular Perl port for the Win32, and ActiveState has been making Perl available for free to Windows users since the release of Windows 95, and is one of the largest contributors to the open-source model of development in the world.

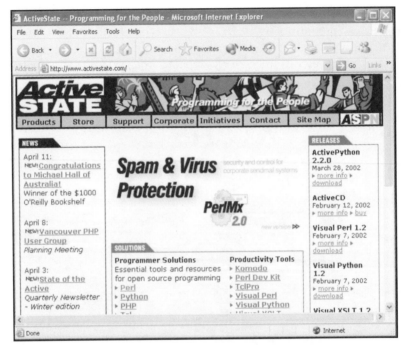

Figure 7.9

The ActiveState home page.

Other Online Resources

I have said it before: Perl is the child of the Internet. Being the child of millions of computers and their owners has its advantages, the primary advantage in Perl's case being the multitude of internet resources available for programmers. These sources are too extensive and are constantly changing, so providing a comprehensive list is nearly impossible. Table 7.4, however, is a good place to start.

This table is available on the companion Web site on the Perllinks.html page.

Perl 6

Currently, Perl 6 is in the later stages of development. This immense project is a complete rewrite of the language; the goal of this rewrite is to create a more powerful version of Perl with an even simpler syntax. Some other design objectives for the next Perl release are to make the language faster

TABLE 7.4   PERL RESOURCES FOUND ONLINE

Web site	Summary
http://docs.rinet.ru:8080/P7/	Teach Yourself Perl in 21 days online by Till
http://docs.rinet.ru:8080/Using_Perl5_in_Web/	Using Perl for Web programming
http://genome-www.stanford.edu/perlOOP/	OOP Perl hosted by Stanford
http://home.bluemarble.net/~scotty/Perl/index.html	An guide to learning Perl on a Unix system.
http://jmarshall.com/easy/	HTML and CGI lessons by Marshall
http://larc.ee.nthu.edu.tw/~cthuang/perl/	Online Perl programming Perl tutorial by Huang
http://virtual.park.uga.edu/humcomp/perl/	University of Georgia, Athens, site includes SED, CGI, and Perl lessons
http://wdvl.internet.com/Authoring/	Web Developers' site on Internet development (includes CGI)
http://www.cclabs.missouri.edu/things/instruction/perl/	Perl short courses from University of Missouri
http://www.cgi101.com/	Book promoter with sample chapters and lessons on CGI
http://www.devdaily.com/perl/	Devdaily's Perl
http://www.effectiveperl.com/toc.html	An online Perl book
sitehttp://www.geeksalad.org/business/training/perl/	An online Perl tutorial and book

TABLE 7.4	**(CONTINUED)**
Web site	**Summary**
http://media.njit.edu/~asim/perl_tutorial/	Online Perl Tutorial
http://www.networkcomputing.com/netdesign/perl1.html	TechWeb's intro to Perl
http://www.perlarchive.com/	The Perl Archive supplies Perl and CGI scripts for download
http://www.perl.com	O'Reilly's corporate Perl resource
http://www.pm.org/	Official home of the Perl Mongers
http://www.speakeasy.org/~cgires/	Speakeasy's CGI resources
http://www.troubleshooters.com/codecorn/littperl/index.htm	Considered "quick and dirty" Perl, the fast way to script
http://www.w3.org/CGI/	W3C's site on CGI

and more robust and to incorporate some of the features that have been brought to the world by modern languages.

Larry Wall is, of course, spearheading this effort; he wants Perl to be redesigned by the Perl community at a large. In fact, the Perl 6 specification is being written and released to the community for feedback. A small team of community programmers will write each new section of Perl 6.

One problem the Perl community will need to address is backward compatibility. Perl 6 will not be compatible with earlier versions of Perl, including Perl 5. Wall feels that the vast majority of Perl 5 will be transferable, however, and the current plan is to build an engine that is capable of translating Perl 5 into Perl 6.

Perl 6 has been in development since late 2000, and an alpha version of the Perl 6 run-time environment (dubbed "Parrot") is now available at the Perl Monger's Web site. Initial brainstorming for changes to the language ended in late 2000, with a total of 361 requests for change (RFCs). Larry Wall is addressing these RFCs, and then they will be turned over to the Perl community for development.

For information on Perl 6, visit the Perl Mongers Web site at http://www.perl.org/perl6. Several other online Perl 6 resources are outlined in Table 7.5.

This table is also available in HTML form on the companion Web site as Perl6.html.

TABLE 7.5 ONLINE PERL 6 RESOURCES	
Web site	**Summary**
http://dev.perl.org/perl6/lists	Numerous Perl 6 mailing lists
http://dev.perl.org/perl6/code	Latest code developments
http://www.cpan.org/src.	Parrot available for download at CPAN
http://www.infoworld.com/articles/ec/xml/00/03/24/000324ecperl.xml	Article on the advent of Perl 6 by David Legard
http://theoryx5.uwinnipeg.ca/CPAN/perl/pod/perlfaq1/What_is_perl6_.html	Perl 6 overview from the University of Winnipeg
http://topaz.sourceforge.net/	The official Topaz Web site
http://dev.perl.org/rfc/	The RFC index

Summary

You have just finished learning Perl in a weekend! Stop. Breathe. Relax.

Obviously, there is more to Perl than I can cover in just a weekend. After all, the language has been in development for more than a decade, and thousands of people have added to its flexibility and power during that time. The truth is, if you are heading down the path to becoming a programmer, you have just scratched the surface.

Still, what you have accomplished and now understand is no small feat. You have given yourself a great gift. You have taken your first step into the Perl world and glimpsed the shining sun that is the Perl community. More important, you have written your own Perl scripts using both structured programming techniques and object-oriented programming.

The most exciting and wonderful truth to technology is that is there is constant change and growth. Perl itself is a wonderful example of this. One programmer's lone project evolved into one of the most widely used languages on the Internet and is now experiencing a zenith of growth and support sponsored by an entire planet of programmers. Welcome to the wonderful world of programming Perl! I hope you enjoy your stay.

Using the Companion Web Site

P remier Press offers a Web site featuring downloadable source code files used in this book. The files are listed according to chapter and contain a list of files and instructions on downloading the files. The Web site, shown in Figure A.1 is located at http://www. premierpressbooks.com/downloads.asp.

The downloads for this book are listed under Learn Perl In a Weekend, along with the other Premier Press downloads. The site will ask you for your name, e-mail address, age, and gender before allowing you access to the download sections, which contain the following chapter files.

Figure A.1

Premier Press
Web site.

Chapter 1: Friday Evening

➤ blockl.pl

➤ getperl.html

➤ test.html

Chapter 2: Saturday Morning

➤ Action.pl

➤ album.pl

➤ block2.pl

➤ Chapter.pl

➤ Environment.pl

➤ format.pl

➤ joinem.pl

➤ List.pl

- Luccaarray.pl
- Luca.pl
- Math.pl
- mapping.pl
- mergeme.pl
- namel.pl
- Print.pl
- Profile.pl
- pushpop.pl
- round.pl
- sizearray.pl
- slicing.pl
- sorter.pl
- splicing.pl
- splitting.pl

Chapter 3: Saturday Afternoon

- block3.pl
- block3final.pl
- Crazymath.pl
- error.pl
- getcexample.pl
- increase.pl
- multiply.pl
- stdin.pl
- untilstdin.pl

Chapter 4: Saturday Evening

- ➤ Number.pl
- ➤ Guess.pl
- ➤ Scope.pl
- ➤ foreach1.pl
- ➤ foreach2.pl
- ➤ foreach3.pl
- ➤ block4.pl

Chapter 5: Sunday Morning

- ➤ block5.pl
- ➤ gameloop.pl
- ➤ GAMEVARS.pm
- ➤ MAP.pm
- ➤ NEWPACKAGE.pl
- ➤ NPtest.pl
- ➤ Pi.pl
- ➤ Tire.pl
- ➤ Tirepart2.pl

Chapter 6: Sunday Afternoon

- ➤ 8ball.pl
- ➤ calc.pl
- ➤ gameloop.pl
- ➤ gamelooptwo.pl
- ➤ GAMEVARS.pm

- guessme.pl
- MAP.pm
- notes.txt
- RDOM.pm
- rdomcall.pl
- truereand.pl
- words.pl

Chapter 7: Sunday Evening

- cexampl.pl
- cgi.html
- examplecgi.pl
- CGIsafe.pl
- COUNT.txt
- counter.pl
- counterhtml.pl
- Perl6.html
- Perlinks.html
- security.html
- shortxml.pl
- shortxml.xml

A Quick Perl Language Reference

This appendix covers some of the more common Perl commands and provides a quick summary of a specific command's syntax in case you need to look it up while reading. This appendix is by no means comprehensive, and most commands are described in an abbreviated form. For the purposes of this appendix:

➤ A **function** is a named section of the Perl language that performs a specific task.

➤ An **expression** is a combination of symbols that represent a value.

➤ A **statement** or **command** is a basic computer instruction.

➤ A **keyword** is a word reserved by Perl because it has special meaning.

➤ A **call** invokes or starts a routine in a programming language.

➤ An **operator** is a symbol that represents a certain action.

Often a function will take in an expression and give you a result. For instance, in the following example, the function `rand` takes in the expression 10 to create a random number:

```
rand ( 10 );
```

In this appendix, the code could be symbolized by

```
command ( expression );
```

The basic reference convention used in this appendix is:

Command (in bold text).

Brief description of the command (in normal text).

```
Example of command in proper syntax (in source code text).
```

Perl is an extremely deep and complex language, and whole works have been written, documenting the syntax of the language and particular commands. (Thumb through Sunday Evening's session for some ideas on where to look for online references.)

Perl is also flexible in its syntax, making the code easy to read, but, unfortunately, somewhat difficult to read. For instance, the `die` command is outlined as a statement in this appendix. However, Perl may consider the `die` command a function, statement, or a call depending on the syntax. In this book, I looked only at using `die` as a statement, which is how it is listed here. In this reference, I use only the most common form of the command, or I use the form of the command as it is used within the text.

A-C

Array: A collection of scalars organized by numerical value, assigned using the @ metacharacter, and referenced using brackets [] and the $ prefix dereferencer.

```
@array = (contents);
```

@ARGV: Perl's default array, @ARGV, is automatically used for array commands such as push or pop if no other array is specified.

binmode: The binmode function affects the file handle to ensure manipulation only through binary disciplines (:raw for binary mode and :crlf for carriage return line-feed pairs).

```
binmode FILEHANDLE, DISCIPLINE
```

bless: A function used to build a connection between a reference and a class, which creates an object. Bless is normally used within a new constructor and is returned as an object reference.

```
bless (class)
```

chdir: A function that changes the current directory to the expression. The chdir will return a 1 upon success and a 0 upon failure. By default, chdir will change the current directory to the home directory.

```
chdir( expression )
```

chmod: A Perl command that takes in a list and then changes permissions of the given list of files to mode (which is normally an octal number). The first entry in the list must be the mode. Chmod returns the number of files successfully changed.

```
chmod( mode, list )
```

chop: A Perl function that removes the last character from a string and returns that character. By default, chop operates on Perl's default variable: $_.

```
chop ( string )
```

close: A Perl function that will close a given file. Close returns a 1 if successful; otherwise, it returns the undefined value.

```
close file
close(FILEHANDLE)
```

cos: A Perl function that returns the cosine of an expression. By default cos will evaluate the cosine of Perl's default variable: $_.

```
cos (expression)
```

D

delete: A Perl function and operator normally used to remove an entry with the given key from an associative array.

```
delete $array(key)
```

die: A Perl statement that prints a list to Perl's standard error output: <STDERR>.

```
die(list)
```

do: A Perl statement that executes given input, but may also be used as a keyword or method. Do returns the value of the last command. Do can also execute a subroutine with a given list as a variable sent into a subroutine.

```
do fileName
do {program block}
do (expression)
do subroutine (list)
```

E

each: A Perl function that runs through an associative array. Every time each is executed, it returns another element of the associative array. When the array is totally read, a null is returned.

```
each( associative array )
```

exec: A command that executes a system call. The full path name of the command to be executed can be given by a scalar variable. (The first element of @ARGV is used by default.) The elements of the list form the command line.

```
exec [pathname] list
exec( list )
```

exit: A Perl function (can also be used as a statement) that exits the current program loop immediately.

```
exit ( expression )
```

exp: A Perl function that returns *e* to the power of expression. Exp uses Perl's default variable: $_ if no other variable is specified.

```
exp ( expression )
```

F-I

flock: A Perl function that calls a "file lock" on a file. Flock returns a true for success and a false for failure. Other operations are available depending on system and distribution.

```
flock ( file, operation )
```

getc: A Perl function that returns the next character from the file referenced (or through standard in, <STDIN>, by default).

```
getc( file )
```

goto: Halts execution. Goto moves immediately to a label and begins execution again at that point.

```
goto label
```

if: A simple statement that evaluates an expression.

```
if expression
```

int: A Perl function that returns the value of an expression as a decimal integer. Int uses Perl's default variable $_ if no other variable is specified.

```
int ( expression )
```

J-K

join: A Perl function that returns a string formed by joining the elements of a list or an array, separated by the string expression.

```
join( expression, list )
join( expression, array )
```

kill: A command that sends a signal to each of the processes in a list. Kill returns the number of processes that have been successfully signaled.

```
kill signal, list
```

L

last: A command that immediately leaves the innermost loop or the loop that is labeled. Any code block associated with the loop is not executed.

```
last [label]
```

local: A Perl keyword that creates the values in a list. Local possesses a scope ranging only within the innermost enclosing block, subroutine, eval, or do command. These values are destroyed when program flow leaves the block.

```
local ( list )
```

log: A Perl function that returns the logarithm (base e) of an expression. Log uses Perl's default variable $_ if no other variable is specified.

```
log ( expression )
```

M-O

mkdir: A Perl function that creates a directory called by a given name with the permissions set by mode (normally an octal number). If mkdir is unsuccessful, it returns a 0.

```
mkdir ( name, mode )
```

next: A Perl statement that executes the innermost block of the loop label by label and begins a new iteration.

```
next [label]
```

open: A command that opens a file whose name is given and associates it with a File Handle. By default, the file is $fileHandle. Open returns a 1 upon success. It can use <, >, >>, or +> to designate read-only, write-only, append, or read/write access, respectively. Open uses < by default. The open command also has numerous options depending on the shell and distribution.

```
open ( filehandle, file )
```

opendir: A Perl function that opens a directory named dir and associates it with a directory handle. Opendir returns a non-zero if it is successful or the undefined value if it is not.

```
opendir (directoryhandle, dir)
```

P

pop: A Perl function that returns the last value of an array after removing the value.

```
pop array
```

print: A command that prints the list of strings to the file referenced by a file handle. (The default is the selected output channel.) The print command prints $_ to standard out, <STDOUT>, by default. Print returns a 0 if it is unsuccessful.

```
print( filehandle list)
```

push: A Perl function that places a list at the end of an array, increasing the length of array by the length of list.

```
push ( array, list )
```

R-S

rand: A Perl function that returns a random number between 0 and the value of expression. The default expression is 1.

```
rand ( expression )
```

return: A Perl function that returns a list from the current subroutine.

```
return list
```

scalar: A Perl function that causes a given expression to be interpreted in a scalar context.

```
scalar ( expression )
```

shift: A Perl function that removes the first element from an array and returns it, shortening the array by 1.

```
shift ( array )
```

sin: A Perl function that returns the sine of an expression in radians. Sin uses Perl's default variable $_ unless another variable is specified.

```
sin ( expression )
```

sqrt: A Perl function that returns the square root of expression. Sqrt uses Perl's default variable $_ unless another variable is specified.

```
sqrt ( expression )
```

srand: A Perl function that sets the seed for rand to a given expression.

```
srand ( expression )
```

sub: A Perl keyword that declares the subroutine name for a program block.

```
sub name {programblock}
```

`system:` A Perl function that executes a system call. The full path name of the command to be executed can be given by a scalar variable. (The first element of `argv` is used by default.) The elements of the list form the command line.

```
system [pathname] list
system( list )
```

U

`unless:` A simple Perl statement (may also be used as a modifier) that evaluates an expression. The expression is evaluated before `unless` is executed.

```
unless expression
```

`until:` A simple statement that evaluates an expression. The expression is evaluated after `until` is executed.

```
until expression
```

W

`while:` A simple statement that evaluates an expression. The expression is evaluated before `while` is executed.

```
while expression
```

`write:` A Perl function (can also be a statement) that writes to the specified file using the format associated with that file. By default, the format for a file is the one that has the same name as the file handle.

```
write( filehandle )
write( expression )
```

GLOSSARY

A

abstraction. In programming, the act of hiding data or complex features from an implementation.

array. A collection of data organized and indexed within a programming structure.

associative array. An array that is referenced by a programmer-defined index instead of a standard numerical index. Also known as a *hash*.

attributes. See *data*.

B

base class. See *parent class*.

behavior. See *function*.

binary. A counting system that uses only the numbers 0 and 1. On a base mechanical level, all computers count and communicate in binary.

Boolean. Having only a true or false value.

branch. See *conditional statements*.

byte. A small amount of memory that varies depending on computer hardware and architecture, but which usually translates into a single character.

C

CGI. Common Gateway Interface. The common protocol with which Web servers and programs interact and communicate.

child class. A class that has been derived from a parent class. Also referred to as a *derived class, specific class,* or *subclass.*

class. A programming structure that encapsulates data and functions. Used primarily in object-oriented programming.

command line prompt. A prompt where you can enter commands to a shell or an operating system.

comments. Statements added to the source code of programs or scripts that act as notes or dialogues for programmers and are ignored by the program itself.

compile time. The time during which a compiler is in the act of compiling a program or script.

compiling. In programming, the act of bringing together and assembling the pieces of a program or script into one chunk of data that makes up an executable program.

complex statements. See *compound statements.*

compound statements. Code statements that take up more than one line and use many expressions. Compound statements in Perl are usually separated by braces ({}) and hold multiple simple statements. Also referred to as *complex statements* or *program blocks.*

conditional statements. Statements or blocks of code that may or may not run, depending on the flow of a program. Sometimes referred to as *branches.*

cookies. Small text files that a Web server can send to a browser to hold information about the client side of a transaction.

D

data. Information held by a programming construct. In object-oriented programming, data is also called *attributes.*

debugging. Testing programs or scripts.

derived class. See *child class.*

deriving. The act of inheritance in object-oriented programming.

directory handlers. Programming constructs that allow a program to manipulate or access a directory.

distributions. Different versions or releases of the same program.

DOS. Disk Operating System. A text-based operating system.

E

encapsulation. In programming, the art of separating functionality into small, manageable pieces.

escape sequence. Simple code you can add to text strings or other areas to represent and carry common commands (commands you would normally type, such as carriage returns, tabs, or indents) or to allow prefix dereferencers and other important metacharacters to be used in print-like statements.

executable. The product of a program or a script converted into runable data or a runable program.

extensibility. In object-oriented programming, the act of adding functionality to a derived class.

F-G

file handlers. Programming constructs that allow a program to manipulate or access a file.

function. A collection of statements that perform a specific action. In object-oriented programming, a function may also be called a *behavior*.

generic class. See *parent class.*

global variables. Variables that are generally accessible by the entire script or program. Also called *public variables.*

H

hash. An algorithm that turns messages or text into a fixed string of digits or characters. In Perl, a hash is also called an *associative array.*

hexadecimal. A counting system that utilizes a base-16 numbering system, using the digits 0–9 and the letters A–F. Perl uses hexadecimal numbering to keep track of file permissions.

HTML. Hypertext Markup Language. A programming language specifically designed to develop, encode, and display documents.

I-L

inheritance. In object-oriented programming, the ability of an object or class to know where it comes from or what construct created it.

Internet. See *WWW.*

instance methods. See *object methods.*

instance of a class. See *object.*

interface. In object-oriented programming, a means of interacting with an object.

interpreted language. A language that is interpreted into machine code by the computer while the program runs.

local variable. A variable whose scope has been restricted (normally to one program or program block).

M

machine code. A language that is easily read by a computer; machine code is usually an intermediary between a modern programming language and assembly or actual machine instructions. Most modern programming languages, such as C, C++, Java, and C#, are compiled into a type of machine code.

metacharacters. Special key characters, such as $, @, {, and }, used by a programming language to recognize specific command and program structures.

method. A subroutine built-in to a class or object that allows an abstracted interaction into a class.

mode. The state or setting of a program or device.

module. In Perl, a package or a group of packages.

N-O

namespace. See *package.*

object. In object-oriented programming, structures that encapsulate data or functions and come from classes. Also called an *instance of a class.*

object methods. Methods that are called upon an object. Can be called *instance methods.*

object-oriented programming. A type of programming where data types, data structures, and functionality are all defined by the programmer.

octal. A base-8 numbering system that uses only the digits 0–7.

operator precedence. The order in which a program executes operations or operators when given control of the order.

operators. Symbols used by a programming language to represent actions or functions. Most commonly refers to mathematical operators such as +, -, /, and *.

P

package. In Perl, a section of code that exists in its own physical space. Also called a *namespace*.

parent class. A class that has derived child classes. Sometimes called a *base class*, *generic class*, or *super class*.

Perl. Practical Extraction and Report Language. A programming language originally developed by Larry Wall that is specifically designed to process text.

polymorphism. The state of one interface being capable of interaction with many objects.

pragma. An argument set to engage compile-time options.

prefix dereferencer. A symbol that tells the program what type of data follows it.

private variables. Variables that have been restricted in accessibility or scope.

program. A list of instructions carried out by a computer.

program blocks. See *compound statements*.

protocol. An established method of doing something. In programming, this is normally an established format for two devices to communicate with each other.

public variables. See *global variables*.

R

relational operators. Operators that perform comparisons, such as less than, equal to, or greater than.

routines. Features or collections of related features that are saved as reusable scripts.

run time. The state that occurs when a program is running and operating properly.

S

scalars. A special type of variable in Perl; defined as any data that is composed of either a numerical value or a string of text.

scope. The range of influence of certain variables or commands.

script. A list of computer instructions.

socket. One end of a commutation between two programs running on a network.

software driver. A small program that helps control a device, such as a database, printer, or keyboard.

specific class. See *child class.*

statement. An instruction written in a computer language.

string. In Perl, a group of text characters. Sometimes called a *text string.*

string operators. Operators that are equivalent to mathematical operators but are designed to work on strings.

structured programming. A method of programming designed to help make large programs easier to read.

subclass. See *child class.*

subroutines. Sections of a program designed to perform specific tasks.

super class. See *parent class.*

T-Z

tags. Programming commands that normally define how text should be formatted.

text string. See *string.*

TIMTOWTDI. There Is More Than One Way To Do It. The Perl mantra, which refers to Perl's ability to solve a given problem with multiple different methods.

URL. Universal Resource Locator. An address used to identify a physical location on the World Wide Web.

variable. A program construct that contains a value and can be accessed by its assigned name.

WWW. World Wide Web. A global system of Internet servers that supports specifically formatted documents. Also called the *Internet* or simply the *Net*.

XML. Extensible Markup Language. A scripting language that was developed by the World Wide Web consortium in 1996.

INDEX

GAME DEVELOPMENT.
IT'S SERIOUS BUSINESS.

"Game programming is without a doubt the most intellectually challenging field of Computer Science in the world. However, we would be fooling ourselves if we said that we are 'serious' people! Writing (and reading) a game programming book should be an exciting adventure for both the author and the reader."

—André LaMothe,
Series Editor